Managing Expatriates

Managing Expatriates

A Return on Investment Approach

Yvonne McNulty, PhD
Kerr Inkson, PhD

businessexpert
Press

Managing Expatriates: A Return on Investment Approach
Copyright © Business Expert Press, 2013.

First published in 2013 by
Business Expert Press, LLC
222 East 46th Street, New York, NY 10017
www.businessexpertpress.com

ISBN-13: 978-1-60649-482-0 (paperback)
ISBN-13: 978-1-60649-483-7 (e-book)

Business Expert Press Human Resource Management and Organizational Behavior Collection

Collection ISSN: 1946-5637 (print)
Collection ISSN: 1946-5645 (electronic)

Cover and interior design by Exeter Premedia Services Private Ltd.
Chennai, India

First edition: 2013

10 9 8 7 6 5 4 3 2 1

Printed in the United States of America.

To Lauren and Cate,
the best return on investment of all
—YM

To Nan, Gordon, and Eileen,
for making our lifelong expatriation work brilliantly
—KI

Abstract

Expatriation is a big topic and is getting bigger. Over 200 million people worldwide now live and work in a country other than their country of origin. Tens of billions of dollars are spent annually by organizations that move expatriates around the world. Yet, despite the substantial costs involved, expatriation frequently results in an unsatisfactory return on investment (ROI), with little or no knowledge as to how to improve it. Why is this so? The problem overwhelmingly lies in the poor delivery of effective expatriate management which is frequently handicapped by a lack of understanding of international careers and the forces that drive competition in the "global war for talent," an increasingly short-term profit-driven focus and a failure to adopt the rational strategic approach that organizations automatically apply to other areas of their business.

Drawing on more than a decade of expertise, research, and publications in top journals, we contend that the key to getting a satisfactory ROI from expatriates is in understanding expatriates themselves, about whose experiences we have extensive information. We provide a practical "insider's" guide which reveals why expatriates seek and accept international assignments, how they feel impacted by new forms of remuneration and other working conditions, how international assignments fit in with their longer-term career aspirations, and what complications arise in terms of their families. These are considered in a context that includes the understanding of the drivers for mobility in organizations, emerging trends in global staffing, the global war for talent, and alternative strategies to expatriation. We outline for managers and consultants what modern-day global mobility is like (based on our decade-long study with nearly four hundred expatriates and their managers, over a hundred of whom we interviewed personally), how it is changing, and why now, more than ever, a hard-nosed ROI approach is necessary. By drawing on our extensive experience and research, observations of key trends, and "crystal ball" predictions, we define new practices for managing global mobility and consider forecasted trends in expatriation over the next decade.

Our aim is to explain what expatriate ROI is, why it matters, and how organizations can improve expatriate management to secure a higher ROI. This has not been addressed in any book to date. Our audience is executives responsible for strategy development across a range of functions including those who manage global staff such as expatriates. Our secondary audiences includes consultants and recruiters who may be enabled to provide more effective support to their clients; as a supplementary text for MBA courses in international HRM and international business; as a supplementary text or required reading for executive MBA programs; expatriates themselves who may gain potentially new insights into their career paths and how best to negotiate better employment contracts; and other professionals and managers who think they may be asked at some stage to expatriate or who wish to do so.

Keywords

expatriate, expatriation, expatriate assignment, expatriate compensation, expatriate family, expatriate management, expatriate return on investment, expatriate trends, global career, global mobility, global staffing, global war for talent, host country nationals (HCNs), human capital, international assignment, international business, international human resource management, international management, parent country nationals (PCNs), psychological contract, repatriation, return on investment, ROI, strategic planning, talent management.

Contents

Foreword

Global mobility has become more complex in the last 10 years and this book is a great example of how the dynamics of a rapidly changing international labor market can be understood and used by international organizations to cultivate, mobilize and manage their talent for competitive advantage.

I first met Dr. Yvonne McNulty several years ago when she was researching the global mobility practices of major corporations. At that time, the concept of expatriate return on investment was often talked about but rarely if ever attempted. Finally, after years of research including interviews with hundreds of organizations and their expatriates, expatriates' partners, and managers, Yvonne McNulty and Kerr Inkson have cracked the code on expatriate return on investment.

This book, the first of its kind, explains the balance needed between the individual return on investment that expatriates now seek and the corporate return on investment that companies expect. It shifts our thinking about how we classify expatriates from an outdated, almost colonialist, view and replaces it with a new vision of treating expatriates as global careerists. It gives us a fresh and thoughtful philosophy for a new era of employee mobility, and a practical roadmap for overcoming the challenges of quantifying and utilizing expatriate return on investment.

But the book does more than that. It also creates a new opportunity and framework for the human resources and mobility functions to effectively articulate the important strategic and financial value a well-integrated workforce mobility program can deliver to the business. It helps to align mobility practices and policies with the needs of the business *and* its employees, and therefore advances the discussion from the operational to the strategic, while also providing an analysis of the essential financial and non-financial costs and benefits that need to be considered in the return on investment value calculation.

Companies are different, and the approach to return on investment is not meant to be a one-size-fits-all mandate. Instead the research, solutions and case studies presented in this book, dealing with issues close to every expatriate's heart, such as compensation, families, and career, are intended to provide each organization with options to consider and to customize. Any organization, regardless of size, will find value in the content.

In this book we have at long last a clear and immediately practicable approach to defining, developing and measuring expatriate return on investment. Thank you Yvonne and Kerr!

Scott Sullivan
Executive Vice President
Brookfield Global Relocation Services

Preface

The extraordinary growth in corporate globalization and the corresponding rise in global mobility provide the basic leitmotif of this highly accessible, reflective book. Employing a science-practice approach, and drawing upon multiple sources of evidence, not least the "lived experience" itself, for which of course there are few substitutes, McNulty and Inkson present a rich and compelling narrative around the requirement for a fundamental paradigm shift in how we understand global mobility and how we evaluate it. This shift, directed at jettisoning the all-too-common piecemeal, transactional approach, in favor of a more strategic, integrated one, is occasioned because the expatriate management model characteristic of the theoretical literature is at variance with what often happens in practice. In McNulty and Inkson's view, global mobility needs to be more squarely focused on adding value and in order to achieve this focus, an expatriate return on investment lens, which is a composite blend of corporate and individual costs and benefits, offers the best prospect.

Their arguments, set out in nine chapters, arise from combining macro, meso and micro insights. At the outset, they call attention to altered patterns of foreign direct investment among multinational corporations (MNCs) and the contemporary and likely future consequences of these changes for patterns of mobility. Beyond this, definitional aspects are set down and the challenges that MNCs face in linking organizational and individual objectives in global mobility are illustrated. Here, core tenets of the international assignment, namely psychological contract, compensation, career and family issues, are treated in detail.

Against the backdrop of this extant knowledge, and the manifest shortcomings of seemingly preferred approaches, McNulty and Inkson make the case for an alternative focus centering on a return on investment approach. A model of expatriate return on investment is introduced, approaches to measuring return on investment are illustrated, and a framework to guide the choice of return on investment metrics is offered. The text culminates in the presenting of five core principles for executing and sustaining an effective expatriate return on investment program. Here, the authors demonstrate the importance of recognizing global mobility as an elemental building block of career capital, of ensuring resolute organizational support for the process, of combining short and longer-term horizons, of embracing the global careerist, of developing and safeguarding global talent pools and, above all, of appreciating the expatriate process as an heroic act, not in the name of self-aggrandizement, but in giving of one's very best to achieve corporate, career and personal goals.

Through insights from the established literature, from illustrative vignettes derived from corporate approaches, and from individual executive and trailing spouse descriptions of their professional and personal experiences, both positive and negative, this book provides a contemporary window into multiple-domain aspects of corporate expatriates' lives, the diverse contexts in which they operate, and the consequences of their choices for themselves, their families, their careers and their organizations.

It is in combining insights from these multiple sources that the book is, in my view, at its strongest and most insightful. The individual expatriate accounts, the organizational case studies, and the judicious quotes from key informants serve to really augment, and on occasion supplant, the more academic aspects of the book itself. The results, in combination, demonstrate the requirement for a renewed effort to bridge the academic-practice divide in charting the contemporary nature of global mobility.

Professor Michael J. Morley
University of Limerick, Ireland
Co-editor of *Global Industrial Relations*

Acknowledgments

The idea for this book first came to Yvonne in 2007 when she was presenting her still-in-progress doctoral research on "expatriate ROI" at the invitation of Deloitte Touche Tohmatsu at their global mobility conference in Barcelona, Spain. A standing ovation and over a hundred post-conference emails from participants wanting to know more about the topic planted the initial seed that a post-PhD book might be a worthwhile endeavor. Fast forward 3 years to the Australian and New Zealand Academy of Management conference in 2010 in Adelaide, where Yvonne, her PhD now complete, met Kerr Inkson and boldly asked him to consider helping a junior scholar turn her now-completed doctoral thesis into a book: the rest, as they say, is history.

While the writing journey for both of us has been a massive undertaking, taking place during Yvonne's international moves to China and then Singapore, and throughout Kerr's transition into "emeritus" retirement, it has thankfully been sustained by our families—Nan in New Zealand, and Stephen, Lauren, and Cate in Shanghai and now Singapore. Each has encouraged and supported us in a million little ways and through many long days and nights that took us away from them. We are grateful for the space and time they gave so that we could undertake this book project, across continents and in various time zones, amidst boxes, moving trucks and house sales, and sometimes even on vacation.

Yvonne is indebted to Phyllis Tharenou (Flinders) and Helen De Cieri (Monash) for their years of dedicated support, mentoring, and guidance during her PhD and since graduation. This book is in many ways the fruit of their labor as it is hers. Her thanks extend to other academic colleagues, including Kate Hutchings (Griffith), Charlie Vance (Loyola Marymount), Nina Cole (Ryerson), Leanda Lee (Monash), Margaret Carter (James Cook), Peter Dowling (La Trobe), Michael Harvey (Mississippi and Bond), and Michael Morley (Limerick). Yvonne is also grateful for the support of many practitioner colleagues, including Scott Sullivan, Jill Taylor, and Gill Aldred at Brookfield Global Relocation Services;

Kim Vierra at Mercer; Andrew Walker at WorleyParsons; and Rob Hodkinson and Siobhan Cummins at Deloitte Touche Tohmatsu.

Kerr extends his heartfelt thanks to Dave Thomas (New South Wales) for giving him the confidence to co-author this book.

We have others to thank. We are indebted to our publisher, David Parker, for his patience, support, and vision for this book; Aron Dobrowolski at Point Design Solutions for assistance with graphics and illustrations; Stan Gully and Jean Phillips at Rutgers University in New Jersey, the editors of this series, who provided valuable feedback on initial drafts; and various reviewers who endorsed the book after its completion.

Last, but by no means least, we extend our deep gratitude to the companies, mobility managers, expatriates, and families that participated in the studies reported in this book, without whom the research on which this book is based would not have been possible. All gave freely and generously of their time, patiently waited for the analysis and results, and made an outstanding—and perhaps unprecedented—contribution to the field of global mobility through the sheer scale, insight, and honesty of their comments. This book is written for them.

Testimonials

A book about expatriate ROI has been needed for a long time. At last, McNulty and Inkson—experts with a genuinely global background and extensive experience—tackle this important topic with an impressive array of research and practical insight not just to measure the return on investment, but to also manage expatriates in new and innovative ways. This is a groundbreaking book, essential for anyone researching expatriates or looking to improve their global mobility practice.

—Duncan Micallef, Vice President Compensation & Benefits, Asia, Middle East & Africa at PepsiCo

Drawing on a decade of research, this book is likely to quickly establish itself as the authoritative guide on expatriate return on investment and is a must for the bookshelf of any global mobility professional.

—David Collings, Professor at Dublin City University Business School, Ireland, and author of *Global Talent Management*

McNulty and Inkson have written the ideal guide in *Managing Expatriates: A Return on Investment Approach*—a practical 'how to' handbook for getting mobility exactly right. This book needs to be in every multinational organization's global mobility resource library, and be required reading for people managers that propose international assignments and HR managers that help to plan them.

—Kimberly Vierra, Principal, Mercer, and author of *Vietnam Business Guide: Getting Started in Tomorrow's Market Today*

Daring to tackle an issue that has long challenged global business leaders, McNulty and Inkson provide a compulsive argument for a fresh approach to expatriate ROI. With valuable evidence-based insights and a holistic, collaborative approach in managing these often highly undervalued employees, this book is mandatory reading for global business heads and mobility functions in all global companies.

—Jenny Castelino, Director Asia Pacific,
Cartus Intercultural & Language Solutions

Managing Expatriates: A Return on Investment Approach provides rare insights, extensive research, and highly relevant best practices to demonstrate how to measure the productivity of expatriates. I highly recommend this insightful book to both academics as well as practitioners.

—Michael G. Harvey, Distinguished Chair of Global Business
and Professor of Management at Mississippi University,
and Professor of International Business at Bond University

The authors offer readers—global mobility managers, international staffing consultants, and expatriates—a variety of new insights enabling them to take another look at international careers, employment contracts, and existing global staffing practices to modify them in accordance with their organization's strategic needs. I strongly recommend this interesting and highly informative book as an essential read to every international mobility expert.

—Vlad Vaiman, Professor of International Management
at Reykjavik University, and editor of *Talent Management
of Self-Initiated Expatriates*

Based on solid research, but written in an easy to access style, this book is highly recommended for those who need state of the art knowledge as well as practical solutions to one of international management's most difficult problems.

—David C. Thomas, Professor of International Business
at University of New South Wales,
and author of *Essentials of International HRM:
Managing People Globally*

This groundbreaking book by Yvonne McNulty and Kerr Inkson tackles the issue of expatriate ROI head on. Their detailed research and practical insights into measuring not only corporate ROI, but the individual ROI expectations of expatriates themselves, are an essential read for anyone involved in global mobility.

—Siobhan Cummins, Director,
Global Mobility Transformation at Deloitte

This is a timely and much-needed book, comprising an in-depth analysis and discourse of the contemporary landscape of expatriation. This is a worthy and significant addition to the bookshelves of scholars and managers alike.

—Yehuda Baruch, Professor of Management
at Rouen Business School, France,
and author of *Global Careers*

The authors have managed to synthesize a very complicated topic into an easy to read tome and provide a very conceptually clear and strategic roadmap for the successful management of expatriates now and of the future. This is a must-read for the seasoned and the novice practitioner.

—Rita Chye, Global Lead for Policy & Administration,
Global Mobility at General Motors

With this book, McNulty and Inkson have made an outstanding contribution. By following its well-researched recommended practices, organizations can be assured of a huge return on investment for competing abroad, while individuals can rest assured of building successful careers within the global marketplace.

—Charles M. Vance, Professor of Management
at Loyola Marymount University, USA,
and author of *Managing a Global Workforce*

With an extensive use of research and practical insight, Yvonne McNulty and Kerr Inkson examine this much-needed topic with equal parts rigor and candor. This is a 'must have' book, a very valuable contribution to the IHRM literature, and essential reading for global mobility professionals.

—Peter J. Dowling, Professor of International Management & Strategy at La Trobe University, Melbourne, and author of *International Human Resource Management*

This book is a must read for any executive or manager who, whether working in the global mobility field or not, wants to transform their company's employee mobility program into a strategic and value-adding enabler of broader corporate objectives.

—Andrew Walker, Group Director, Mobility at WorleyParsons

Introduction

Expatriation is a big topic and is getting bigger.

Over 200 million people worldwide now live and work in a country other than their country of origin. More and more companies operate internationally, and people seek to be internationally mobile in order to have a rich and fulfilling work-life and advance their careers.

The solution to both organizational and individual needs is often company-sponsored expatriation, a practice which is reported by more than half of the companies participating in global consulting surveys to be growing exponentially.[1] Millions of those who live away from their home countries are not permanent migrants but professional and managerial staff who have been expatriated by their multi-national companies. Tens of billions of dollars are spent annually by organizations to move such expatriates around the world. Expatriates originate in all parts of the world, travel *to* all parts of the world, and are vital to international business. Expatriation, in short, has become a critical organizational practice.

But does this practice *work* for expatriates? For their companies? The surprising answer is *We don't know, but probably not.* Year-on-year, companies continue to struggle to manage and improve the return from these expensive employees. Yet recent consulting reports show that fewer than 10% of companies attempt to even assess the return from their expatriates.[2] In addition, they often have a short-term profit-driven focus, ignore such forces as international careers and the "global war for talent," and fail to adopt rational strategic practices.

Let's compare, for example, existing expatriate management practices with those in the manufacturing industry. If a CEO said to a Vice President of manufacturing "How are we doing? Are we meeting our targets?" and the VP replied, "We're not entirely sure how we've done or where we need to improve because I don't track the data ... And what targets? Do we have targets?" she'd be fired. Yet based on a decade of our intensive research, we know that in the area of expatriation, conversations such as this occur all too frequently. They indicate the inability to clearly define why expatriates are favored over less expensive local employees, what value expatriates ultimately bring, and whether and how expatriation supports a company's strategic objectives.

If expatriates are among an organization's most expensive employees, surely we ought to be able to justify the money spent, and manage them effectively. There is much in the detail of expatriate management, its corporate purpose, its links to company strategy and human resource management, specific issues about the selection, compensation, careers, and families of expatriates that calls for a distinctive, well-informed practice of expatriate management. Also, expatriation is changing, with the familiar "there-and-back" models of the past being supplanted by a great diversity of new and complex patterns of mobility which create new challenges and opportunities for expatriates and their organizations. Yet state of the art in expatriate management is either buried and lost in abstract scholarly texts, or trivialized in "how-to-live-abroad" guides. We must do better.

Who This Book Is For

This book is written primarily for (1) global mobility managers who manage global staffing and expatriation; (2) managers who manage expatriates; (3) other executives with international operations responsibilities; (4) international staffing consultants; (5) graduate students considering expatriate careers; and (6) expatriates themselves. The functions from which readers will come include global mobility, human resource management, compensation and benefits, expatriate policy, talent management, and succession planning. We offer these managers new insights enabling them to challenge existing practices and to then move toward a more strategic approach to international staffing. Expatriates and potential expatriates too may benefit from this book by gaining new insights about their organizations' strategies and practices, their career paths and employment contracts. Finally, this book may be a good supplementary text for MBA courses in international management and HRM, and for graduate students researching expatriate careers for class work.

What This Book Is About

In this book, we focus the concept of *return on investment* (ROI)—both corporate ROI and the individual ROI expectations of expatriates themselves—and explain how to manage expatriates with an ROI approach in mind. We replace the traditional model of expatriation with a new model. We define what "expatriate ROI" (eROI) is, why it matters, and how organizations can improve expatriate management to secure a higher eROI. We focus particularly on expatriates themselves and the "mobility managers" who manage them, and on the expatriation processes and practices of their organizations.

We also provide a practical "insider's" guide which reveals why expatriates seek and accept international assignments, how they feel impacted by new forms of remuneration and other working conditions, how international assignments fit in with their career aspirations, and what complications arise for their families. We consider the effects of organizations' need for global mobility, emerging trends in global staffing, the global war for talent, and alternative strategies to expatriation. By drawing on our extensive experience and research, our observations of key trends, and some "crystal ball" predictions, we define new practices for managing global mobility.

Where We Gained Our Knowledge for This Book

To achieve the goals of this book, we anchor our opinions, concepts, and recommended practices in three major types of information: our *own research,* our *informal interviews,* and *the research of others.*

Our *own research* comprises three recently completed major studies with nearly 400 expatriates and their managers, over a hundred of whom were interviewed personally. The first author of this book, Dr. Yvonne McNulty, completed these studies for her graduate research, including doctoral research at Monash University (Australia). The *Mobility Manager Study* ("MM Study" for short) involved interviews with 51 executives, all from different firms, across 18 industries who work directly with expatriates or manage mobility programs. The *Expatriate Study* ("Expat Study" for short) involved interviews with 71 "company-assigned" expatriates, drawn from five global firms with headquarters in the United States, UK, and Europe, representing four industries: financial services/banking, pharmaceuticals, transportation services, and media/communications. Both these studies were completed by means of one-to-one telephone dialogues initiated and conducted by Yvonne McNulty personally following a detailed semi-structured interview methodology, the interviewees being based all around the world. The *Trailing Spouse Study* ("TS Study" for short) involved surveying 264 "trailing spouses"—partners of company expatriates—on assignment in 54 host countries. Full details of all these studies are in Appendices.[3]

In addition to the above three *formal* studies, our book benefits from the "personal touch" obtained from many hundreds of hours of *informal* interviews and conversations that Yvonne McNulty, an Australian, has had with mobility managers, senior executives, consultants, expatriates, and globally mobile families over the course of her 14 years as an expatriate "insider", having lived (at times as a "trailing spouse") and worked as a global mobility researcher and consultant in the United States, China, and Singapore. These conversations—conducted in informal settings as varied as expatriates' own backyards, international social events, intimate dinner parties, and even shared taxi rides—together with Dr. McNulty's personal understanding, draw on "lived experience" to provide a unique authenticity. The material in our formal and informal research thereby enables us to provide illustrative case material throughout the book.

In addition to our own research, some of the ideas in this book are informed by the *research of others*. The thousands of documents we have read and analyzed include academic studies in journals, books, and research theses; the reports of consulting firms such as PricewaterhouseCoopers, Brookfield Global Relocation Services, ORC Worldwide, Cartus, Ernst & Young, AIR Inc., Mercer HR, The Conference Board, and McKinsey & Co; government documents and white papers; and the international press. For those who seek it, we have included some of this material as a guide to further reading in *Notes* and *References*. A further resource is an extensive *Glossary* that defines and explains over one hundred global mobility terms.

What You Can Expect Chapter-by-Chapter

In Part 1 of the book, **Expatriation and Return on Investment**, we introduce the key concepts on which this book is based.

Chapter 1 Basics of Expatriation sets the scene by establishing the basic features of expatriation—the typical challenges faced by expatriate employees, the growing dominance of multi-national corporations (MNCs), the business purposes of expatriation, the changing international labor market, the need for strategic management of expatriation, the changing meanings and types of expatriation, and new patterns of mobility. The stage is set to consider more specifically the management of expatriates.

In *Chapter 2 Expatriation and ROI* we outline the current state of knowledge about expatriate ROI (eROI) and discuss how international organizations are avidly in favor of it as a means of directing their expatriation programs but have failed to achieve much in practice. We note some of the corporate and individual issues that get in the way and focus particularly on the growing divergence of objectives between expatriates and their organizations, and the concept of iROI (individual ROI) as a complement to eROI.

In Part 2 of the book, **Understanding Expatriates,** we use our research studies to provide an in-depth understanding of today's corporate expatriates, the lives they lead and the issues they face. We focus specifically on four key issues for expatriates along with emerging trends that indicate how eROI is likely to change and develop in the future.

In *Chapter 3 Expatriate Compensation* we move from the macro- to the micro-level by focusing on compensation: its change over the past two decades, the rapid increase in local-plus and hybrid packages, and the effects on expatriate loyalty. Through an insiders' "warts-and-all" commentary, we show that it really isn't about the money at all. We also outline how managers can deal with expatriates' compensation concerns and develop packages that motivate and reward for optimum return.

In *Chapter 4 Expatriate Families* we explore why families are often a major consideration and a common cause of poor eROI. Our in-depth exposé of the expatriate family shows how families (wrongly) suffer when assignments don't go according to plan (and sometimes even when they do). We look specifically at the "dual-career," the challenges for expatriates' partners ("trailing spouses"), what organizations can do to help, the remedial "best practice" strategies of successful Fortune 100 companies, and the benefits of a "family first" policy.

In *Chapter 5 Global Careers* we explore why people pursue international careers, explaining that although expatriation is an opportunity for career development, it also involves challenges and setbacks. We illustrate new forms of careers such as self-initiated expatriation and boundaryless global careers showing how they unfold and what people do with them in a changing international labor market. We then offer guidelines for the effective career support of "global careerists," a new type of international employee whose free agent mentality can have significant implications for global staffing.

In *Chapter 6 Expatriate Psychological Contracts* we introduce the concept of the "psychological contract" between expatriates and their organizations, and explain what a psychological contract is, what it means to expatriates, and how its utilization can assist effective expatriation. We illustrate through case examples that there is frequently a mismatch between the career expectations of expatriates and the objectives of employers leading to problems for the organizations that employ them. We then show how psychological contract-based "new deals" between expatriates and their managers can facilitate discussions about employment relationships, and greater expatriate and assignment success.

In Part 3, **Managing Expatriation Using ROI,** we return to ROI and show how the concept can be applied to expatriation to provide new strategically based practices for the management of expatriates, applicable in international organizations worldwide.

In *Chapter 7 A New Model of Expatriate ROI* we build a model of eROI and demonstrate how we believe its management should be approached. In adopting a cost-benefit perspective, we outline the financial and non-financial costs and outcomes arising from global mobility activities, before moving on to the core of our methodology—the *expatriate management system*. We advocate a proper strategic base for expatriation and an integrated set of policies and practices by illustrating how expatriation is a strategic choice and eROI a directing goal.

In *Chapter 8 Evaluating Expatriate ROI* we illustrate how, specifically, to measure eROI taking into account how eROI has been assessed in the past, the pros and cons of the particular measures, and new metrics that are being developed. On the basis that it is important to find the best available metrics to assess eROI, but what matters is less the method than the *philosophy*, we present an evaluation framework to guide both the choice of eROI metrics (vertical fit/strategic alignment) and how eROI measurement should be approached (horizontal fit/operationalization).

In *Chapter 9 Five Core Principles for Effective eROI* we translate the points raised in prior chapters into five "core principles" that offer a roadmap for executing and sustaining an effective eROI program. Using case studies of good organizational practice we outline a series of practical implications, expatriation trends for the next 10 years, and on the mushrooming significance of global careers.

PART 1

Expatriation and Return on Investment

CHAPTER 1

Basics of Expatriation

CASE: Craig Phillips, Fly-In Commando

Craig Phillips is English. He is in his early forties. And he describes himself as a "fly-in commando." What does he mean?

For the past 15 months, Craig has been in Vietnam with his wife and three children, working for a large multinational company, Praxis, in a service industry. Craig's job title is "country manager": he manages all his company's operations in Vietnam. His main task is to set up and expand a joint venture between his parent company and local business interests. He has been with Praxis for 12 years, and in that time Vietnam has become the fifth country he has resided and worked in.

Craig's suitability for the role in Vietnam are his understanding of the company's business, structure and culture, his ability to get things done fast, and his skill at functioning well in emerging markets. He is a combination of tried-and-trusted corporate grunt and socially skilled action-man. "I've always been a fly-in commando," he says. "We'll have a problem, I go in. I fix it. I leave." For Vietnam, he wants to "fly in, develop the culture ... and then hopefully have enough managers at local level that they can continue to get the rest of the organization to follow." "The goal," he says, "is to make myself redundant from the Vietnam business."

Craig faces an enormous change management responsibility: to turn a joint venture with a former communist bureaucracy in an Eastern culture into a Western-style business unit with high standards. Craig is proud of his success so far, but it hasn't been easy: as an expatriate he finds that he is more ruthlessly judged than others. Also, expatriate work is much tougher than working in one's home base: there are government restrictions, human resource inefficiencies, language, and logistics difficulties—all problems he faces on a daily basis but which his home-country office doesn't seem to quite understand.

For example, the company's relationship with local Vietnamese officials is so important that Craig feels obligated to take them out to dinners and their favored Karaoke. Another Praxis expatriate, a religious man, found this so intolerable that he quit the company: he was unable to be multi-culturally flexible enough for the job.

Craig says changes are taking place in the expatriate way of life. Expatriate compensation has changed: the fat packages loaded with benefits and premiums and allowances have become "local-plus" versions with fewer benefits than ever before. Salaries and savings in fluctuating currencies are hard to maintain. Competitors "poach" Praxis staff. Craig's job is temporary and his future uncertain. And there are family considerations, such as the constant moving that disrupts the education of Craig's children.

Although Praxis has been supportive—Craig has often been told, "Don't worry. We'll look after you. You don't need to find another job."—there are times when he feels he is little more than a commodity, used for the company's benefit without much consultation as to where it might ultimately take him in his career. And being constantly mobile has become a company *expectation* of Craig, without which he cannot acquire career development or promotion. Fortunately, Craig loves travel: "I can't think of any more fun I could have than travelling and experiencing different cultures and learning their languages and meeting different people."

Yet long-term, Craig hankers after a post-expatriate life either in his native England or in an equally desirable and acceptable location such as Singapore. His children are already booked into London schools in 4 years' time, with applications also going into international schools in Singapore, just in case. His expatriate experience has given him highly marketable skills in general management that he can use "back home" or regionally if he chooses to remain in Asia. In that respect, expatriation has served Craig well.

We have chosen Craig as our opening case study because his experience, both as an expatriate and as a manager of expatriates, illustrates the issues associated with expatriates' work, and the managerial problems that expatriates present.

What are the characteristics of Craig's current situation? *Temporariness, a project focus, cross-cultural reach, uncertainty, national versus global identity, ambiguity in remuneration, alienation from the corporate culture, above-normal expectations of performance, "nomadic" family issues,* and *career issues.* While some of these might occur in any managerial role, all of them are increased and made more complex by Craig's expatriate identity. All of them are problems not just for Craig but for expatriates in general. All of them also raise challenges for Praxis's more senior managers, at corporate HQ and elsewhere, and for the HRM people, consultants and others who manage expatriates such as Craig and determine the company's international staffing policies: managers who we term "mobility managers."

Craig is a walking demonstration that the management of expatriates is a specialized field that deserves its own book such as this one. In the pages that follow, we will combine our knowledge of the best research, the best principles, and the best practice concerning the management of expatriates.

In this chapter, we will first look at the contexts within which expatriation takes place: the dominating multi-national corporation (MNC), the complex international labor market in which expatriates seek opportunities, and the wide range of contrasting cultures in which they find themselves. We will re-examine the traditional idea that has driven much managerial practice and business research about expatriation, the notion of the *international assignment*: the project or temporary role in another country to which the expatriate is dispatched by his or her employing organization in service of corporate goals. We will also consider the breathtaking speed with which the internationalization of business and of life in general is growing and changing expatriation.

What will arise from this consideration will be the realization that wisdom and practice concerning the traditional international assignment have become not just unproductive, but counterproductive. In particular, expatriation has changed far beyond the traditional assignment management model of the 1980s and 1990s. In its multiple new forms and its dynamic new environments, expatriation becomes the expression not of management, but of strategic choice in pursuit of a return on investment, and expatriates are not just human resources to be managed from a distance, but global career actors with ambitions and changing attributes that the organization must increasingly integrate. We argue, in short, for a major revolution in international human resource practice. Let us start, however, from the beginning—the traditional view.

The Context of Expatriation: Multinational Corporations

Wherever we live, wherever we go, MNCs—for example, Sony, BMW, McDonald's, and Hewlett Packard—are part of the scene: the signs that we see, the products and services that we buy, and the television programs that we view. From New York to Nagasaki, Berlin to Beijing, the world's great cities look similar and flash the same names at us. In these cities, ethnic and national culture are infused increasingly with global culture. We feel engagement, but sometimes conflict, between the precious, historical, and ethnic cultures ingrained in each society and the spectacular, mass-consumer, and organizational cultures developed during the twentieth and twenty-first centuries. It is these same unique, historical cultures that take expatriates out of their comfort zone and provide some of the very special challenges they face, contradicted by the global culture they experience—represented, for example, by a Starbuck's on the corner—that feels at once familiar and safe.

These contrasts are important for expatriation because they embody what it is that expatriates *do*: not only do they transition between countries and between cultures, they also live and work simultaneously in two different types of society—the foreign country and the business organization. Expatriates are typically agents of the MNC charged with bringing its philosophies, goals, and practices into worlds whose core philosophies and rhythms of life may be very different: Craig Phillips' competitively driven mission in the ancient delicate society of Vietnam and its recent communist overlay is a case in point. Yet MNCs also move less developed societies toward the kinds of infrastructure, technology, employment, and consumer goods and services they desire and that Westerners are used to. MNCs provide developed societies with new markets, but arguably they also assist political and economic stability in emerging nations. Corporate expatriates often play a major role in providing this stability.

Simultaneously with this activity, MNCs also pursue competitive advantage: they look abroad for essential raw materials, new markets, and lower-cost resources. But they are different from mere traders. They invest directly in other countries, buy majority shareholdings in their overseas assets, and actively manage these assets. They integrate their foreign operations structurally and try to integrate them psychologically, attempting to help foreign employees to feel they "belong." They share resources and responsibilities that may be geographically scattered, and develop central strategies as a basis to link decisions in different countries. Such organizations are *global*—a vast change in both scale and character. And they are—or strive to be—integrated and cohesive.

Organizations of this type have existed for less than 100 years, but in the past 50 years, they have mushroomed and spread across the globe. In doing so, they present management challenges that are not only enormous but novel. They manage across diverse cultures. They motivate faraway people to identify with a "faceless" MNC. They deal with foreign regulations and customs. They move responsibilities from their "home-country" HQs to subsidiaries in countries such as India and China. And in doing all this, they must observe the sovereignty of nations that may have grossly inefficient bureaucracies, major religious prohibitions, or rampant corruption.

MNCs are big and dominant. Between 1970 and 2005 the number of MNCs grew from 7,000 to 70,000, with the same rate of growth expected to continue for the next 30 years.[1] In 2008 MNCs were estimated to employ 90 million people or 20% of the non-agricultural global workforce. KPMG predicts that the number of global MNCs and the number of people employed in global MNCs will continue to expand.[2] But headquarters in Western countries will decrease, with more non-Western HQs emerging, requiring different management skills.

Consider the current growth in world economies. A recent PricewaterhouseCoopers report shows that over the 7-year period 2002–2009 using GDP as a measure BRIC economies (Brazil, Russia, India, China) grew by 83%, with Central and Eastern Europe (47%) and Asia (62%) not far behind.[3] At the current rate, economists predict that within 20 years the mature economies will be overtaken by resource-rich countries like Brazil, Australia, Canada, and Russia, and some Middle East States, and people-rich countries like China and India. The likely city locations in which expatriates will be deployed by 2025 will also change, with three cities not yet ranked on the "30 most highly populated cities" index—Lahore, Shenzhen, and Chennai—emerging as major destinations.[4]

Where there are MNCs, there are expatriates, so more and bigger MNCs means more and more expatriates. From this perspective, expatriation represents not just a unique management challenge, but one that is also growing rapidly *as a cost of doing business*. In 2012, for example, 64% of companies surveyed by Brookfield reported an increase in international assignee population growth, representing a 43% increase over the 2011 rate.[5] Similarly, PricewaterhouseCoopers reports that over the period 2001–2010 assignee levels have increased by 25%, with a further 50% growth in assignments expected by 2020. Assignee host locations also continue to rise, from 13 locations per organization in 1998, to 22 per organization in 2009, to a predicted 33 per organization in 2020.[6] Clearly, expatriation continues to grow exponentially as a practice, but why has there been so much growth? And does the growth in MNCs *have* to mean the growth of expatriation?

Traditional Expatriation

In thinking about expatriation and its role in global operations, MNCs and the researchers who study them have focused mainly on a particular form of expatriation, known as the *international assignment*. Such assignments typically involve a manager or technical specialist, usually from the MNC's home-country base, who is assigned temporarily to fill a specific role or complete a specific project in an overseas subsidiary, usually over a predetermined period, perhaps 2 or 3 years. After that time, the expatriate returns home through a process of *repatriation* and is then re-integrated within the organization.

The notion of an "international assignment" creates a challenge, and an opportunity, for any sponsoring organization to ensure it uses "best practice" in managing the situation. The assignment is typically finite, with clear objectives, and raises, in microcosm, all the classic issues and functions of "human resource management" (HRM). That is, the assignment must be *planned*, and the expatriate must be *recruited, selected, prepared, trained, transported, housed, compensated, mentored, supported, performance-managed*, and eventually *repatriated*. In other words, the whole gamut of rational HRM processes can be deployed to ensure international assignments run like clockwork. Moreover, if the expatriate has an immediate family (as the majority do), then the family's needs in the foreign setting (e.g. for education) must also be dealt with.

Since the 1980s, business-school HRM scholars have had a field-day in championing best practices for managing international assignments and assessing their effects in terms of the adjustment and performance of assignees. This thinking has led to much good practice for MNCs to take on board, and the evidence that some of them do is growing. However, there is a continuing preoccupation with single "there-and-back" assignments. Such assignments, popular in the 1980s and 1990s, were easier to manage than today's more diverse and complex ones. But even back then companies struggled to get it right: selection and repatriation, for example, caused major difficulties. More importantly, the notion of an assignment focused attention on the management of the immediate project rather than on the arguably more important ongoing international staffing of the organization or ongoing career of the assignee. In fact, today's focus on "global staffing" did not achieve momentum until the early 2000s.[7]

Interviewing expatriates and mobility managers in our studies, we have found them on the whole to be disappointed with the global mobility and global staffing practices they have experienced. Their organizations, they say, have had a low uptake of recommended best practices, have continued to conceptualize expatriation as a "one-off" event rather than as part of an organizational process to be integrated into its overall global staffing and strategic plans, and have failed to measure their investment in expatriation and the returns on that investment. Thus, although their companies have managed expatriation reasonably efficiently, few have been particularly effective or strategic about it.

These same companies have asked, "How can we make an assignment work well? How should we select, prepare, train, and support an expatriate through it?" We suggest that instead they might have asked, "Why are expatriates sent? What are they supposed to accomplish? What lies beyond international assignments, both for the subsidiary and for the expatriate?" This lack of enquiry in asking only "how" questions, but not "what" and "why" questions is problematic.

To be sure, traditional expatriation *is* changing. Today we see an increasing trend toward short-term and rotational assignments, and to work on specific projects that may last only a few months, but which do not necessarily require full-scale relocation, involving the selling of a home or transfer of a whole family. These alternatives to expensive long-term assignments are certainly more manageable for organizations in terms of cost and convenience. Such assignments enable more and more employees to get a "taste" of expatriate life without the heavy burden of physically relocating, and there is evidence that these briefer projects are often used for employee development.[8] Other types of alternative assignments handle "international business" through short-term business travel and international commuting, which do not count as expatriation at all.

But is this the extent of the change we are seeing in expatriation? We contend that recent changes go far beyond this, and in this book, we'll explain why these "types" of assignment are only the tip of the iceberg when it comes to understanding modern expatriation.

First, however, let us consider some of the features of the wider context in which Craig and other expatriates work, particularly the MNCs in which they are employed, and the new international labor market of which they are members. It is in these contexts that modern expatriation is emerging and rapidly changing.

The Purposes of Expatriation

What is expatriation *for?* Why not staff foreign subsidiaries entirely with local people? After all, Vietnamese people surely understand the Vietnamese business environment better than any Australian or American could and are likely to be more acceptable to locals. Could an MNC survive without expatriates?

Expatriation in its historic form arose because of things that expatriates could do that locals might not be able to. Local employees' knowledge of things like local conventions in business practice, language, organizational culture, and social networks might be very important to an MNC. But other vital knowledge—for example, specialist expertise, technical qualifications, the parent MNC's vision and culture—might only be available to staff who had been employed for some time in the headquarters of the MNC. Corporate expatriates, through their elsewhere-in-the-company experience, also make it possible for the MNC to become more integrated.

According to a 2007 study of German, Japanese, UK, and US organizations,[9] the most important reasons for filling a managerial position with an expatriate are to set up a new operation, to fill a skills gap, to develop international management skills, to train and orient local staff, to control the operation, to ensure the same company standards worldwide, to co-ordinate with headquarters, and to provide career development opportunities. Expatriation may also provide new feedback loops to head office or improve relationships, or enable knowledge sharing. Thus, some international assignments are demand-driven (e.g. a particular job needs to be done), while others have long-term objectives of increasing expertise both for the organization and for the expatriate (e.g. building a succession or leadership pipeline).

There will often, therefore, be compelling reasons for the MNC to staff some roles using expatriates. Expatriation can become part of an MNC's "international human resource management" (IHRM). Globalizing organizations can use expatriation not just to solve immediate problems, but also as part of a longer-term resource-building strategy.

But considering expatriation only from the perspective of organizational needs turns the expatriate into something of a pool-ball, being directed skillfully by the all-powerful cue of the MNC. Companies frequently forget, to their detriment, that expatriates themselves are stakeholders in the process, and they have their own needs—for example, related to personal adventure, their career, or their family, and a degree of control over their own activities. Expatriates have to be willing, indeed enthusiastic, to travel to a foreign country and spend years working there. But their objectives in doing so may be very different from the company's objectives in sending them. Although MNCs want, and expect, expatriates to achieve success and remain loyal to the company, they need to ask the question: What do expatriates want? Exploring the congruence between organizational and expatriate needs, and the consequences arising from the similarities and differences between each, will be a key feature of this book.

The Meanings of "Expatriate"

What *is* an expatriate, anyway? Does expatriation have definable characteristics? Since the 1960s, and through the 1970s and 1980s, expatriates have been largely viewed as *parent-country nationals*—labeled "PCNs" for short. In the early days of expatriation, these employees were from Western countries and were typically senior male staff in their late forties or early fifties sent by a corporate headquarters to a subsidiary office in another country. They generally had a generous remuneration package with substantial benefits and premiums—home leave, cost-of-living allowance, housing subsidies, country club membership, tax equalization if required, annual bonus, hardship premium, and school fees—and each was almost always accompanied by his wife and children.

During the late 1990s different types of expatriates began to emerge: more women, married couples with no children or single and unaccompanied people, same-sex partnerships, and younger expatriates (e.g. in the Expat Study we found that nearly 45% of the expatriates in our sample were under the age of 40), assigned for career development purposes, and on less generous remuneration packages without many of the perks and benefits of their predecessors.[10] There are also increasing numbers of non-Western, particularly Asian, expatriates.[11]

Today, new meanings of "expatriate" are emerging. To help meet changing and broadening demands for talent in key markets, *third-country nationals*—"TCNs"—are increasingly employed. TCNs (or "foreign local hires" as they are sometimes called) originate from neither the home-country where corporate headquarters is located, nor the host-country where they are employed, but instead are sourced from a third country where they have lived either temporarily or permanently before agreeing to be moved to the host country. Foreign executives in local organizations (FELOs) represent another type of expatriate.[12] TCNs tend to receive little organizational support, largely because they are generally recruited externally and are perceived to have received cross-cultural training and language support during a prior assignment, or to be already "globally minded" as a result of prior international experience. Being recruited externally, TCNs tend to suffer from being "out of sight, out of mind" to HR support people.

Both PCNs and TCNs are likely to compete on the labor market against *host-country nationals*—"HCNs"—to help meet local skill demands and to work with them as colleagues. These HCNs are mostly non-expatriate employees who provide organizations with alternative staffing options and who generally cost less to employ, require less cross-cultural training and no relocation assistance, and by default generally receive less, if any, head office support. Sometimes HCNs are selected for "inpatriation," a short-term assignment that requires sending them to the headquarters location to acquire valuable exposure to organizational practices and customs that then enables them to compete back in their home country for promotion opportunities on par with PCNs and TCNs.[13] Other HCNs may be disguised as host-country origin expatriates (HCOEs)—people from the host country who have lived and worked overseas as expatriates themselves, who then relocate home under special "returnee" compensation arrangements that situates them slightly above HCN status, but not quite at the same level as PCNs and TCNs.[14]

The trend over time, as MNCs become more complex and cosmopolitan, as the importance of "regional" experience becomes increasingly recognized, and as organizations seek to reduce costs, is for PCNs to be supplemented or even supplanted by HCNs and TCNs.[15] For TCNs, in particular, this is largely because expatriation has become a less risky undertaking today than in previous years when PCNs' company packages and "apron string ties" have been seen as a more secure way to reduce the risks of living and working overseas. Because being a TCN is a riskier way of life—with far less job security than the repatriation models of the past have afforded typical PCNs—these types of expatriates are more common today than they were 20 years ago.

Nowadays, TCNs are on the rise, mostly because the next generation of employees is increasingly exposed to what globalization has to offer and are conditioned to take more risks in order to avail themselves of its advantages. In the next 7 years to 2020, the number of assignees drawn from headquarters MNCs (i.e. PCNs) is predicted to drop from 80 to 40%, with no more than 10% drawn from senior (executive) management (down from 50% currently).[16] This says a lot about the type of employee that will make up the majority of the global talent pool.

Another significant trend is that expatriates no longer tend to do just a single assignment and then repatriate. Craig Phillips, the PCN in our opening case, is on his fourth consecutive expatriate assignment in 12 years, with the same company. Craig is a "career expatriate," building specialist expertise in getting things done in foreign environments. More and more, expatriates are rejecting the "one assignment" concept of expatriation and instead adopting a "career" concept, stringing together re-assignments into meaningful sequences that meet their long-term personal aspirations.[17] And when Craig decides to finally repatriate, he already knows it may not be to his native England, but instead to a location that is equally desirable, and perhaps more in keeping with whom and what he and his family have become: citizens of the world, capable of living anywhere.

One consequence of this is that many expatriates offered the opportunity to go abroad no longer look at just the "next" assignment: instead, in an attempt to piece together how expatriation, as a career choice, furthers their career and personal aspirations, they look far beyond the next assignment, sometimes 7 or 10 years down the track, through subsequent re-assignments. Their focus nowadays is frequently much longer-term than that of the organizations they work for. This can be highly problematic because in the absence of a clearly defined and openly communicated organizational life, expatriates recognize that some of the skills they are acquiring (e.g. cultural flexibility) are generic rather than organization-specific and that they can often pursue their careers across organizational boundaries, in *inter-organizational careers*. As in Craig Phillips' case, the situation may be further complicated by family considerations, for example, a spouse's career, or the desire for stable and high-quality education for one's children in alternative suitable locations.

There is also a growing phenomenon of *self-initiated expatriates* (SIEs), a little like migrants but more temporary, qualified people who move to new countries of their own volition, without company support, and seek to "see the world" or develop their careers there. They may have no intention of settling permanently in the country they choose, but would like to "try it out" or use it as a base for further travel, before deciding whether to settle there, return to their home country, or move on to somewhere else. The concept of a "gap year" between secondary and tertiary education provides a "junior" version of such opportunities and many teenagers go abroad at this time for personal exploration and self-development, much like many SIEs also tend to do.[18]

Self-initiated expatriates are not sponsored by MNCs, but they *are* expatriates, and there are a significant number in the international labor market. SIEs act more like entrepreneurial "free agents" than traditional *company-assigned expatriates* (CAEs) whose moves are directed and controlled by the MNC. Instead, SIEs are subject to "market forces" whereby those with in-demand skills can cultivate their own "boundaryless careers" in and across organizations, projects, and countries of their choosing.[19] We predict that SIEs who morph into "global citizens"—cosmopolitan people to whom "at home" might be anywhere in the world, and who will travel to, and live in, whatever location suits their purpose at the moment—will come to dominate the international labor market.

So what exactly is any given expatriate? A PCN or a TCN? An assignee on a project or a long-term careerist? A company-assigned loyal organizational servant or a "global nomad" disguised as an SIE? How do these different types of expatriates merge into one another, and what would it mean to an organization if they started out as one type and became another? While the focus of this book is "expatriates," particularly PCNs and TCNs, we need to be aware that the term covers an ever-widening and ever-diversifying set of individuals, as outlined in Table 1.1.

Furthermore, it is clear that these types of expatriates constitute the building blocks of much wider groups and movements, terms coined by practitioners and scholars in recent years to include *global staffing, international itinerants, brain drain, global managers, talent flow,* and *the war for talent.* Many of these terms capture the collective nature, the value, and the dynamic movement of these new types of international employees much better than the neutral term "expatriate." And as we will show in this book, the types of employees who become expatriates are as varied as the locations they are sent to, with significant implications for how they are managed from an eROI standpoint.

Table 1.1. The Meanings of Expatriate

Type of assignee	Definition	Where to find
PCNs: parent country nationals	Citizens of the headquarters country location of a company, from which they are then sent abroad	Home-country
TCNs: third country nationals, foreign local hires	Originate from neither the home country where corporate "headquarters" is located, nor the host country where they are employed, but a third country where they have lived either temporarily or permanently before agreeing to move to the host country	Host-country region
EHCOs: expatriates of host country origin/returnees	Permanent residents of the parent country but belong to ethnicity of the host country and are hired and/or transferred by the parent-country organization to the host location on a temporary assignment or permanent transfer	Host-country
FELOs: foreign executives in local organizations	Foreign individuals at the executive level who hold local managerial positions supervising HCNs in local organizations where these organizations have their headquarters	Host-country
HCNs: host country nationals	Mostly non-expatriate employees residing in the host-location as citizens of that country	Host country
Inpatriates: reverse expatriates	HCNs (local managers) and TCNs of a subsidiary sent to the parent-country headquarters on an international assignment to provide them with an international perspective, exposure to corporate culture and a network of contacts	Host-country
Millennials	Members of "Generation Y," those born in 1982–2000	Home-country

The International Labor Market

A key factor that causes MNCs to utilize expatriates is the increasingly international market for skilled labor, and the ease with which skilled workers are able to work around the world, wherever they choose, on the *international labor market*. For professionals and managers worldwide, distance has been defeated and barriers abolished by such developments as the growth of great new trading blocs such as the European Economic Community (EEC); the fall of the Berlin Wall and the demise of European communism; developed countries' access to cheap land in, and labor from, emerging economies like China and India; the adoption of English as a common business language; and the growth of rapid technological innovation enabling instantaneous intercontinental communication.

Another important factor is the so-called global war for talent, as organizations seek competitive advantage over each other through their utilization of knowledgeable people and vie with each other to recruit the best and the brightest. "Free migrants" from impoverished nations with scarce technical and professional skills—IT specialists, engineers, financial analysts, and doctors—leave the economic poverty, unemployment, and political oppression of their home countries for the supposed affluence and democracy of the West. Corporate expatriates travel in the opposite direction, seeking personal and organizational challenges by bringing their expertise to new and often under-developed settings.

And so, as travel becomes more efficient, and education and mass media publicize the exciting world beyond each country's borders, men and women with scarce skills travel around the world—many as global nomads—and settle in different locations, at least for a time. Attracted by political or economic conditions, career challenges, and lifestyle options, or merely by a thirst for novelty, they create intercountry and intercontinental flows popularly labeled "brain drain" and "brain gain," creating oversupplies and shortages of talent.

Increasingly, the international labor market is attracting more and more under-represented employees and as such becoming a more diverse labor pool, particularly of women. Indeed, female expatriates have been historically under-represented in disproportion to the size of the qualified female labor pool,[20] despite the growing acceptance that gender diversity can be a corporate performance driver.[21] Estimates of the percentage of expatriates that are female have increased over the last two decades—from 3% in the early 1990s to 20% in 2012.[22]

Many expatriates are now also members of "Generation Y"—those born 1982–2000. Often called the "me" generation or "millennials," compared with their parents they tend to show less loyalty to employers.[23] Unwilling to spend their lives as gray, secure organizational servants with linear careers, they instead seek work–life balance, access to the latest technology, and constant novelty.[24] Even when they are still children, many have experienced international tourism, educational exchanges, study or work abroad, foreign language learning, interaction with immigrants from different and diverse cultures, cosmopolitan television programs, internet experiences of foreign lands, and even childhood stints abroad.[25]

Many of these people seem to believe that international travel is neither a luxury nor a corporate necessity but part of their birthright. Their goal is not to secure lifetime employment but *lifetime employability*, through the building of career skills that are not organization or location specific. They welcome the stimulation and challenge of expatriation and may engineer it themselves without corporate help, but if they find better opportunities elsewhere, they will be quite prepared, even during an international assignment, to move from one company to another. They seek glamorous lives in multiple exotic settings. They cease to identify as American, French, Chinese, or whatever, and see themselves instead as global citizens in a borderless world. With such expectations and flexibility, which have recently been further increased by the impact of the 2008–09 global financial crisis and consequent historically high unemployment among young people of this generation, young expatriates create major problems for employers trying to figure out how they can turn the "me" generation into the "we" generation.

In this book, we will extend the concept of expatriation beyond the traditional international assignment to cover the new forms of expatriation and the new trends in the international labor market. We will consider both organizations' *management of expatriates* and their *strategies for expatriation*. We will seek to demonstrate a cohesive, systematic, and future-oriented approach.

Summary

In this chapter, we've set the scene by establishing the basic features of expatriation. We have explained the context of expatriation and the growing dominance of MNCs, along with the business purposes of expatriation, the various meanings and definitions of the term "expatriate" from its origin to the present day, and the changing characteristics of the international labor market. We concluded the chapter by showing new patterns of mobility and highlighting how expatriation and expatriates have changed, and why.

What has been especially important, particularly within the context of globalization today and in the future, is to debunk the myth of one type of assignee: the "there-and-back" expatriate. Instead, there are many alternatives as well as new forms of mobility that are likely to dominate global staffing strategies for the coming decade. The stage is set to consider more specifically the management of expatriates across a broad range of contexts.

CHAPTER 2

Expatriation and ROI

> Recognizing that successful assignments play a vital role in an organization's ability to compete effectively in the global marketplace, one would think that ROI-based management techniques—or some equally objective method for evaluating and managing assignment success—would be a key strategic tool wielded by most managers of international assignment programs. It is mystifying that this basic management concept is observed primarily in its breach.
>
> —GMAC 2003–2004, Global Relocation Trends Report

For decades, nearly every significant advance in the field of management has required replacing an existing model with a fundamentally different way of thinking: a paradigm shift that completely challenges existing "truths." Business examples include Porter's *Competitive Strategy*, Perlmutter's *Staffing Typology*, and Bartlett and Ghoshal's Transnational Solution.[1] These models emerged to challenge—and forever change—existing thinking. For global staffing, we believe the time for such a change, in terms of expatriation becoming a strategic choice, and the concept of "expatriate return on investment" (eROI) a directing goal, is now. In this chapter, we will show that today's expatriation model is at best piecemeal and at worst lacking a proper strategic base and an integrated set of policies and practices. Without a fundamental paradigm shift, it is unlikely to ever reach its full potential. Here's why.

Think of today's expatriation model as a house with many rooms. Each room is designed to perform a different global mobility function: planning, selection and recruitment, relocation, training, compensation, performance management, and repatriation. Each function is assumed to be perfectly aligned with the one before, or the one after, in a systematic follow-on of tasks. When we look at expatriation in this way, the model works very well. The house should function because each room does what it is supposed to do.

The problem is that this expatriation model, though it exists in theory, seldom does so in practice. Yet international assignments are still managed as though it does. It was, after all, developed over 30 years ago when expatriation emerged in MNCs as a new activity. Back then, HR departments ran expatriate programs with the short-term goal of getting employees into new locations and ticking all the functional boxes to ensure that it was done properly. They gave little thought to what happens when some rooms in the house did not function properly, or not at all, or to the impact of one function on another, or to the expected long-term value from international assignments.

Was this model successful 30 years ago? Absolutely. Is it appropriate in today's conditions? Absolutely not.

Expatriation needs to undergo a dramatic sea change from how it began: from piecemeal and operational to integrated and strategic. Some recent change is apparent, at least in terminology: there is less talk of "expatriation" and instead a renewed focus on *global mobility*. Many "HR managers" have become "human capital executives," and the "personnel function" has been rapidly supplanted by "talent management."

Yet, in spite of the changes in terminology, the expatriation function has remained largely unchanged: it is still functional and transactional, providing administrative services and offering advice, but not adding value. Mobility managers tend to act as advisors rather than as providers of solutions. They pursue activities rather than results. They work with piecemeal practices rather than developing integrated systems to manage global mobility. Because they are not accountable for the millions of dollars invested annually in expatriation (with these costs resting squarely on line managers), there is a frequent performance gap between expectations and results. To address this performance gap, global mobility practice needs to shift to a new operational paradigm.

Expatriate ROI: The Current Situation

For more than a decade, eROI has been the "holy grail" of the mobility industry. Countless magazines and industry articles have been devoted to the topic, with titles such as "What are your international assignments worth?" and "Darned expensive to take for granted." The quote we started with suggests that every company that utilizes expatriates has a clear goal in doing so: to ensure assignment success. But what does that mean?

Knowing what we want to achieve and having a strategy to get there are fundamental to business success. Yet few companies run their mobility programs like they often do other areas of their business: with a clear strategy and focus to ensure an acceptable level of "success." We know this because in our interviews with companies and their expatriates, we encountered again and again—and again—statements like "We don't have anything written down but we kind of know what we're supposed to get out of these assignments," and "The return? It's all perception."

In our introduction, we positioned eROI as a basic yardstick and starting point for every organization serious about getting better results from its mobility program. But the reality is that many still struggle to define what international assignment success really means and have made little to no progress on eROI in practice. More alarmingly, few have a clear strategy on how to achieve assignment success or to measure eROI in a meaningful way.

For example, the annual report quoted above, now in its 17th edition as *The Brookfield 2012 Global Relocation Trends Report*, shows that there has been very little improvement in eROI-based management techniques: of the 123 companies surveyed, only 9% formally measure eROI. The main barriers include not knowing how to achieve eROI (39%), not having time (18%), and it not being important to their organization (11%). None of the companies rated their ROI from expatriation as "excellent." While 42% *estimated* their ROI as "very good" or "good," 58% said it was "fair" or "poor." In our view, these figures indicate a massive waste of time, money, and resources to secure a return on investment that is considered marginal at best. As Brookfield noted in its commentary, "These are the lowest ROI self-ratings in the history of the report, and they continue a downward trend."

What is going on here? How can global organizations *talk* about eROI for so long and still make so little progress? And why, to assess eROI, do we have to rely on self-ratings rather than more formal and reliable measures?

From our research, we find that overcoming the barriers to measuring eROI really comes down to managers' ability to create change around existing internal processes in spite of many obstacles. Creating such change is, according to one involved commentator,[2] "a very process-driven, rational, and frequently politically charged process." We know from our MM study that few mobility managers are equipped, in terms of available time, resources, or inclination, to handle such a change.

We also know that when organizations think about eROI, many don't know what they are looking for: they just know they are not getting the results they want. Other organizations might have troubled mobility programs that they haven't been able to manage effectively, or their program might be functional, but they want to get from "good" to "great." Still others are clear that they want to look at their strategy for the future and they want some help to diagnose unforeseen problems and gain new ideas. Whatever their situation is, one of the most important "take-aways" from this book is not to wait until your company has got it all figured out to begin implementing an eROI approach.

To consider the kinds of stifling tangles that organizations get into when they *don't* manage their global mobility program strategically and wait too long to start considering eROI, let us examine the case of NexCorp (a fictitiously named MNC).

CASE: Expatriation Gone Wild!

In early 2009, as the financial markets were constricting after the global financial crisis, NexCorp—a financial services company with approximately 5% of its total workforce on an international assignment at any one time—decided to reduce assignee headcount, upgrade equipment and facilities, and just be smarter across the board about how it operated. This was partly in response to client pressure to deliver a more cost-effective service and partly because of operating costs. But it was also because NexCorp recognized that, despite a very significant annual investment in global mobility, the program itself was being managed purely as an administrative function without a strategic focus or influence. As a result, there was no cohesive strategy for the use of international assignments, nor had the company leveraged these assignments to implement its broader human capital agenda.

Immediately, in an effort to trim overall mobility costs, the company's senior management decided to reduce the number of international assignments over the ensuing 3 years and improve the ROI of those assignments it retained. But despite that decision, by early 2012 assignment usage actually *grew* by 36%. How, despite senior management's agenda, had this happened?

The first problem was that it was too easy to effect and approve an international assignment. In NexCorp's decentralized operation, business unit managers had complete discretion to approve international assignments, and there was no vetting process to ensure that assignments were reviewed and approved at the right levels. "For a while," says NexCorp's Senior Vice President (SVP) of mobility, "it was harder to buy a laptop here than to go on an international assignment."

The second problem was that mobility decisions were driven more by individual compensation than by business needs. Specific assignment objectives or deliverables were seldom defined. In fact, money was the overwhelming driver for expatriating and the main reason why more than 50% of NexCorp's expatriate population accepted an international assignment. Business unit managers were using assignments as a way to compensate employees they couldn't otherwise reward via conventional remuneration vehicles.

There were also few budgetary controls. There was no checking system to ensure that managers didn't agree to include things in expatriate packages post-approval just because the employee was putting pressure on them. If an employee balked at the assignment's terms and conditions, the manager would often increase the package to include a significant position premium, resulting in a package significantly more expensive than even NexCorp's own policies suggested it should be. Because there was also no system in place to ensure that business units tracked and captured mobility costs, managers were less likely to accept responsibility and ownership for the costs associated with using expatriates, and less likely to try to control those costs. In many instances, costs would significantly exceed budgets, but headquarters wouldn't know about it and wouldn't discover it until the assignment was over.

Further compounding the situation were a plethora of inconsistent policies arising from individual negotiations with each assignee. This not only created a burdensome administrative task for the global mobility department, but also led to widespread inconsistencies in expatriate benefits across the organization and across all levels of assignees.

There were two major challenges, however, creating the biggest problems. One was that it was too hard to end an assignment. An exit strategy—a plan to repatriate or re-assign the individual—was rarely specified before an assignment commenced, so the company had no idea what to do with expatriates when their assignments were over. Although it had a comprehensive repatriation program to ease the transition for those returning to their home country after assignment, managers were often reluctant to utilize it. In many instances, reassignment to another location, usually employee-initiated, became the preferred exit strategy, thus extending assignee status beyond the period originally approved, as well as escalating costs.

The other challenge was that global mobility was not linked to talent management. Analysis showed that less than a quarter of expatriates were in the firm's top 10% of performers worldwide, which suggested that the company was not necessarily sending its strongest talent on these important high-cost assignments, and that assignment decisions had no apparent tie to talent management.

It was clear that the existing mobility program and practices were out of alignment with the pressing business need to reduce costs, and with other compelling business and organizational needs such as talent development. Nor was there any way of assuring that the best skills were being deployed to the right places.

Faced with these realities, the SVP of mobility and his team were charged with overhauling policies and processes to resolve the situation. But how could they achieve this when the fundamental problem was not just the administrative overhaul of the relevant systems and processes, but the much larger problem of an organizational culture problem that needed to be changed—and fast?

NexCorp was certainly in a mess when it began diagnosing its eROI problems in earnest. The reality is that no company has its global mobility program "nailed"—perfectly aligned with other business units, free from bumps in the road, cost-cutting woes, and other challenges. International assignments do not always operate under conditions of rationality, logic, and efficiency, as NexCorp came to realize.

In our consulting work, we've met enough mobility managers like the one at NexCorp to know that their departments are under-staffed, and they often lack the expertise to take on a large-scale, long-term change-management project such as introducing eROI. And no matter how well-intentioned they may be, it's not enough to charge one department with a new eROI project because that is beyond what one single department does. This represents a common critique not only of mobility departments but of HR departments, not to mention operations, manufacturing, services, and a whole host of other business functions with a stake in, and an effect on, eROI. The whole business reaps rewards from an effective eROI program.

The mess at NexCorp is not an isolated case. Many companies face similar barriers when building their eROI program and evaluating the value to be gained from global mobility but, like NexCorp, are hard pressed to know how to overcome them. Although, as we will show in Chapter 9, NexCorp solved some of the problems described here by applying a number of the principles advocated in this book, it's still important to understand the barriers many MNCs are facing.

From our MM study, we found that there are *cultural, operational,* and *conceptual* barriers common to many organizations when attempting to measure eROI. In terms of organization *culture*, there is often no buy-in or support because expatriates are seen as the cost of doing business and will still be used even if eROI is minimal: evaluating eROI is therefore considered pointless. For others, international assignments are a necessary step for career development, so evaluating eROI is not seen as an important activity that adds value.

Operational barriers are typically due to inefficiencies in day-to-day activities and processes. This includes inadequate HR information systems, poor assignment planning, and a lack of ownership of mobility programs leading to little or no accountability for developing appropriate measures to gauge the successful achievement of an assignment's intended objectives.

There are also *conceptual* challenges that can impede operational progress on eROI. Managers have a tendency to view costs, benefits, and the purpose of the assignment separately and as mutually exclusive factors, thus failing to "connect the dots." Although managers see the value in embracing a cost-benefit approach, many, due to their poor planning, lack of time, and/or lack of technological or senior management support, are unable to articulate it formally.

In their book on *Global Staffing*, Hugh Scullion and David Collings point to the measurement of eROI as being able to:

> …help managers effectively evaluate the utility of expatriate assignments through illuminating the contribution of expatriates to firm performance … beyond only traditional historical cost analyses and measurements of failure and turnover on repatriation.[3]

Clearly they are right: it's time to be more *strategic*. In the remainder of this chapter, we (1) define eROI; (2) outline the various expatriation objectives at the heart of eROI; and (3) consider expatriates' views about international assignments that must be taken into account to determine effective eROI approaches. Later in the book, in Chapters 7–9, we will look at how eROI principles can be used to transform expatriation practices and achievement.

Defining Expatriate ROI

International management needs to better understand eROI, but how is it defined? The most common definition we could find is that of Brookfield:[4] *"achievement of the assignment objectives at the expected cost."* We know this definition is inadequate because expatriation is more than simply a financial "cost"—there is also a non-financial cost and value that needs to be included. This shortcoming led us to develop an alternative definition that has come to be the most widely accepted and cited, both in academia and among practitioners.[5]

> ### eROI
> 'expatriate return on investment'
> A calculation in which the financial and non-financial benefits to the firm are compared with the financial and non-financial costs of the international assignment, as appropriate to the assignment's purpose

Here, we explicitly recognize that while the concept of eROI should include and acknowledge a financial cost and benefit component, it must also include a non-financial component, which represents what many managers believe is the primary reason for using expatriates, particularly those on long-term assignments. Our focus is therefore not on the financial cost alone, but on the *value* as well. A senior executive at a US finance company told us:

> If you're talking about return on investment, you've got to build in the longer-term learning, the longer-term benefits of an assignment into the definition ... the actual contribution of that experience in some way to the organization, either immediately ... (or) more long-term ... it could be as broad as that the organization has now extended its cadre of experienced people from five percent to ten percent.

Sometimes objectives may be too nebulous to identify, making eROI clearer for some organizations than for others: objectives such as "professional development," "succession planning," and "building leadership capabilities" are too "woolly" to articulate in a meaningful way. That's why in our definition we avoid being overly prescriptive. Instead, eROI can be customized to consider a wide range of financial and non-financial costs and benefits appropriate to different assignment purposes and company expatriation strategies. This is necessary because there are multiple reasons for using international assignments, which makes it impossible to determine a "one best" definition of eROI that will fit every company or every assignment.

Essentially then, the value derived from investments in expatriation is likely to be defined differently across various assignment types within different business units, industries, and regions. This thinking is summed up well by a UK-based mobility manager:

> [It] depends on the organization ... if you look at BP, by and large, their expatriate policy is driven by the fact they need people to work in Nigeria and all sorts of other diabolical parts of the world. Ours is designed by and large to develop our talent within the organization ... so what you're looking at is companies who have

got different end points that they wish to achieve ... it's fatally flawed to think that one answer suits everyone because it doesn't.

A US bank Vice President adds a further perspective:

> The investment banking business, the retail business, the credit card business, the home mortgage business, the cash management business, those are all viewed very differently. They have different goals and different revenue streams. So I don't know that there would be necessarily one program or definition to manage expatriate effectiveness across the board.

It is apparent from the above that the starting point for an eROI approach is that of *strategic intent.* How is the international assignment intended to contribute to the organization's strategic goals and the elaboration of these goals in tactical and operational terms? If an international assignment does not have a clear purpose from which expected assignment outcomes and value can be determined, then how can it be evaluated and how can the MNC ever know whether the investment was justified? Just as MNCs differ greatly across industries, they will have different reasons for using expatriates. However, the motives for expatriation are not always mutually exclusive: there may be more than one reason for using expatriates and there may be more than one benefit to be gained or multiple potential failures and lost opportunities to be suffered.

Strategy should then be a key *determinant* of assignment purpose. Although this seems obvious, we found in our MM study that some companies still use expatriates for reasons that make little strategic sense: for example, for employee convenience or to serve the interests of an "old boy's club." These, and other, purposes for which international assignments are used can be found in Table 2.1, which also indicates the percentages of mobility managers in our MM study giving each item as a reason.

But there are other reasons that knowing the assignment purpose matters. Differences in assignment purpose will lead to different choices in the HR practices used to support expatriates. For example, if the purpose

Table 2.1. Reasons Given by Mobility Managers for Using Expatriates

Reason	%	Sample quotes
1. Development purposes for career planning and rewarding high-potential employees	86	We're looking at key talent within the organization and giving them an opportunity to gain experience in a different environment ... ultimately they acquire a lot of leadership skill having worked in different sets of circumstances in different countries.
2. Filling a skills gap/providing technical experts	70	We send employees on assignment when skills are lacking in that location.
3. Corporate control and governance particularly for start-up operations	39	In some cases, it is a key position of confidence, like the Chief Financial Officer of India or China. These are very fast, emerging countries for us, and very critical ... it helps us manage the risk a lot better.
4. Strategic planning for succession, leadership, and talent management	33	The reason is leadership development, building a succession plan with high potential employees that are going to grow and broaden their careers.
5. Cultural reasons, such as an old boys network, or continuing to use expatriates because they have always been used	26	There's still a bit of the old boys network going on where the manager feels it's a good thing to move someone because of personal reasons, compensation reasons, or because he's got family there ... not every assignment is skill or developmental reasons.
6. Functional requirements	25	Ninety percent is project-based mobility; the client needs our people there on site.
7. Financial reasons, such as bottom-line driven objectives or the cost advantages associated with using expatriates from a certain location (e.g. India)	10	There's a cost advantage in India ... there's a liberty of economical skill compared to the United States ... in India it's cheaper. Even if we pay the minimum US salary, when we send expats to the United States they are very happy to get their overseas experience ... [but] you can't always pay the minimum in the United States because people there won't work for that if they're experienced.
8. Convenience reasons, for employees requesting self-initiated transfers for their personal benefit	4	Probably a third of all our moves fall into this mystery "other" category: employee convenience. Employees are holding their managers hostage. They say, "I'm a good employee and my spouse is moving to another country. I think the firm should not pay for me to go and be with my spouse." According to our executives we should not pay for that, we have no strategy around it, and we have no desire to invest in that kind of relocation, but it's about 25–30% of our moves ... we don't have any dollars we want to invest in it, yet it goes on every day.

Note:
1. Managers provided multiple responses so percentages do not add up to 100.
2. % = the number of participants expressed as a percentage.

of an assignment is to control, co-ordinate, and assist in the transfer of a company's culture, then expatriates will be selected, trained, and compensated differently than if the purpose of the assignment is mostly knowledge transfer or to fill a technical position. The purpose of an assignment also moderates the costs and benefits arising from international assignments. For instance, more eROI may be gained by pre-departure training of an expatriate who will be a chief executive abroad than of an expatriate who will provide the technical skill for a company project.

On the other hand, the purpose of an assignment will also dictate *who* is selected to go. Here we are concerned with individual factors relating to expatriates themselves and the ways in which these may ultimately impact on eROI. A good example is developmental assignments: these typically take place over a 3- to 5-year period (and perhaps beyond, in subsequent re-assignments) and require stronger support, non-work and family life support, and higher levels of expatriate adaptability than would be required for shorter technical/skills transfer assignments of limited duration. Ideally, the choice of candidate for a developmental assignment should be dictated by what the assignment is intended to achieve. For instance, if repatriation is a major goal, then selecting a company-assigned expatriate (rather than an SIE), or a PCN over a TCN, would be a better strategic fit for that particular assignment.

The Expatriate's View

Although this book is focused predominantly on corporate ROI ("cROI" for short)—improving expatriate ROI for companies—we want, for a moment, to take our focus off returns to the company and put it on to returns for the individual expatriate, his or her response to eROI, and indeed his or her personal return on investment, or *individual* ROI (iROI). After all, expatriates are the very people that companies rely on to deliver the value they seek—the *e* in eROI—and they too are making their own investments of time, energy, and skill into an international assignment.

So, what do expatriates think about expatriate ROI and how it should be measured? How do their views inform our approach to evaluating and managing eROI? And how do they evaluate their own ROI?

One surprising finding from our Expat Study is that expatriates do not really care if their company measures ROI, and if so, whether it is measured formally or informally. But when ROI *is* measured, expatriates are adamant that it must be done fairly across both the financial and non-financial contributions they make to the global business they are sent to support. We found that a major complaint by many expatriates is that they are told they are going on an international assignment for non-financial reasons (e.g. career development), but then they find that their performance is assessed almost exclusively in financial terms. As a transportation company executive explained, there is frequently a disconnect between why expatriates are sent and how their performance is evaluated, wherein "the measurement is a very shallow scratching of the surface approach. It is 'he cost x dollars and in his time there we've seen the profit increase x dollars, so he's paying for himself.'"

Expatriates are right in asking, if an eROI measure assesses only a financial contribution, what other important contributions are excluded? These could include when an expatriate achieves assignment success and proves his or her worth as the critical competitive advantage in a key location where only international and cultural expertise could deliver the desired value. A telecommunications executive summed up this concern when he said,

> the degree of difficulty is something that is not really assessed; the degree of complexity in dealing in a foreign environment, dealing with a set up of a joint venture, multiple government restrictions, multiple human resource inefficiencies because the local population is not yet attuned to a capital market situation, language, logistics—instead it's all simplified to a revenue-based assessment

One area where expatriates feel immediate improvement is necessary is in the use of the *annual performance review*. Seen by most as the predominant tool that companies use to assess eROI, we were nonetheless taken aback during our Expat Study by the amount of criticism, apathy, debate, resentment, anxiety, and anger sparked by discussion of the annual performance review. Many feel that the review is a flawed and pointless process in which getting it done ("ticking the box") tends to override much of the real value that could be gained from it. While some view it as nothing more than an annoying nuisance, others consider it to be a "toilet paper exercise." A key concern for expatriates is that the annual performance review process for international assignees lacks *context*, in that assessments of performance fail to acknowledge and take into account the unique stress factors expatriates face (in terms of host-location challenges and opportunities) relative to their domestic counterparts against whom they are being compared and assessed.

The strong desire by expatriates for companies to develop a better performance review process for assessing eROI (as well as for other purposes) is understandable when we consider that most expatriates in our study (more than 90%) view their eROI to the company as one that is predominantly non-financial and value-based; only 6% said that eROI would also include a financial benefit in terms of organizational profitability (i.e. revenue gains), but none felt that their eROI would solely be based on these financial gains. Expatriates believe that the non-financial benefits they provide to companies include capability development in terms of improving internationalization efforts, improvements in global networks, cultural understanding, and knowledge transfer, as well as career enhancement leading to improved global staffing capabilities.

There is more to eROI, however, than simply determining corporate benefits—or cROI. A large part of the overall eROI equation is also tied up in the costs and benefits that accrue to individual expatriates—iROI. We explain what we mean by this in the next section.

Individual ROI

In simple terms, eROI is an amalgamation of corporate and individual costs and benefits that combine to impact on the overall return on investment from expatriates (eROI) that companies expect. Thus, we have the following equation:

Corporate ROI (cROI) is defined as the benefits that accrue to companies arising from expatriation, whereas *individual ROI* (iROI) is a construct that draws on individuals' motives for undertaking and accepting international assignments and the benefits they expect to gain by doing so. We know from others',[6] as well as our own research,[7] that expatriates are driven by intrinsic career aspirations as much as by extrinsic personal desires. On this basis, we define cROI and iROI as follows:

> ## cROI
> 'corporate return on investment'
> The return on investment to companies from expatriation

> ## iROI
> 'individual return on investment'
> The perceived benefits that accrue to expatriates arising from international assignment experience in relation to professional and personal gains

Our definition of iROI both draws on, and extends, what is commonly referred to as expatriates' "career capital," that is their energy, values, skills, and networks built up over their working lives, enabling each to acquire competencies that can be used within, as well as across, companies.[8]

What are some of the beneficial iROI outcomes that expatriates receive through their international assignments? In our Expat Study, more than 95% identified personal *career enhancement* as a major benefit, followed by *family and personal opportunities* (43%). This confirms data from Cartus showing that employees are highly motivated to accept assignments: 90% of companies say that *career development* is a major reason for their employees to engage in global mobility.[9] But there are individual costs that expatriates also incur, in areas such as family difficulties and decreased compensation arising from local-plus and localization strategies deployed by their companies. In Part 2 of this book, we will explore specific "pinch points" that impact on iROI directly. For now, let us examine why iROI plays such a critical role in overall eROI.

A Dual-Dependency Perspective

As a starting point, the employer–employee relationship during expatriation is no longer one that is largely dominated only by the interests of the company. Gone are the traditional days when expatriation was a solely company-controlled activity, used by firms as a somewhat ruthless tool to reward, incentivize, and direct employees as faceless commodities and resources for MNCs' overall gain. As countless studies and reports now attest,[10] the increasing internationalization of work, the changing nature of employment (e.g. where individuals are now expected to have upwards of seven or more career changes during their lifetime), and the routine acceptance of global mobility as an inevitable part of one's working life have compelled many employees to seek out long-term international assignments as a way to ensure continued employment. Thus, employees, and expatriates in particular, are nowadays increasingly focused on how best to negotiate the opportunities that international work presents, and how personal investments in global mobility can ensure "lifetime employability."[11]

This balancing of the playing field between expatriates and their companies points to a change in perspective—from single-dependency to dual-dependency[12]—wherein a company's stance as the dominant stakeholder in the expatriate employment relationship is weakening. Today's companies need expatriates more than ever, and expatriates know it. This affects eROI because finding expatriates is one of the biggest challenges companies face. The "global war for talent" is not a fallacy, and the shortage of talent is very real.

As companies scramble to fill their international subsidiaries with qualified staff, the fallout from this talent shortage has given rise to alternative forms of global staffing that enable firms to build a dynamic pool of candidates and render themselves no longer reliant on only PCNs. Assignees today are increasingly being drawn from different candidate pools, including HCNs, foreign local hires, inpatriates, FELOs, and expatriates of host-country origin (returnees). But at what cost to eROI? While it is true that many of these alternative assignee types cost less to employ, and deploy, many also receive less support in their international roles in comparison to PCNs, in areas such as reduced compensation, benefits, and career support, causing additional unforeseen problems. As we explain in Part 2 of this book, these are precisely the areas in which eROI—and cROI in particular—can be most effected.

eROI and Expatriate Loyalty

The second point to consider is that, with the emergence of a dual-dependency perspective that is heavily focused on iROI outcomes, many expatriates—and especially those that are company-assigned—are no longer as loyal to their employers as they once were. For expatriation, this represents a dramatic shift in the expatriate employment relationship, not least because the traditional view of expatriates' commitment to their firm has rested on the assumption that there are significant "ties that bind" them to their organizations as a result of the compensation package they receive that minimizes financial and other risks they face in being abroad.

Unfortunately, the introduction of local-plus compensation as a cost-saving measure for MNCs (explained in Chapter 3) has resulted in diminished loyalty among many expatriates. Indeed, today's expatriates are increasingly more inclined to reject the traditional safety net afforded by company-assigned expatriation in favor of having more control over their international careers and their family life. This is seen in our Expat Study with over 40% of expatriates moving away from long-term loyalty-based international assignment contracts (i.e. many assignments with the same firm) toward more short-term transactional contracts (i.e. many assignments with many firms). Indeed, we found that "vertical mobility" (i.e. promotion) to enhance career growth in only one firm was less important than "lateral mobility" across a range of jobs, functions, borders, *and employers*.

What we are witnessing here is a change in expatriates' career orientation, from company-controlled "servant" to free-agent "entrepreneur." In simple terms, expatriates are increasingly pursuing "boundaryless careers," a term that signifies the progression of career moves across multiple employment settings and multiple borders.[13] What matters for eROI is whether, and how, this change in career orientation occurs—are expatriates *pulled* by a deeply held desire to "work and travel abroad" over which companies have no control, or *pushed* inadvertently by employers who are unresponsive to their personal and career needs?[14] And what are the implications for the long-term eROI of the company, if its expatriates leave and take their newly developed expertise to other companies, even competitors?

While we discuss the pull–push dilemma in more detail in Chapter 5, what matters for eROI is that boundaryless careerists cause new retention problems for companies that have thus far not been anticipated, nor addressed. These problems include (1) that "external marketability" to other employers has emerged as a new and valuable iROI commodity on the international labor market; (2) that the personal goals of expatriates seem often to be in conflict with the strategic goals of the companies they work for; and (3) that the values, types of work, careers, and lifestyles that expatriates now wish to pursue appear to be changing.

Why do these problems exist? Mostly because companies do not reward and support today's modern expatriates in a way that matters. As subsequent chapters in this book will show, there exists a very wide gap between the value that companies perceive their expatriates' hold and the feeling by expatriates' that they are even valued by the companies that employ them.

Summary

In this chapter, we introduced eROI as a means of conceptualizing and evaluating not only individual expatriate assignments but the overall global mobility of the company. We noted that eROI has become a kind of "holy grail" that many organizations aspire to utilize, but few have made progress toward it. We used the case of NexCorp to illustrate how progress toward a strategic and eROI-based approach to expatriation can be impeded by "status quo" forces within the organization. Noting that eROI requires clarity in terms of the objectives of expatriation against which returns are measured, we detailed some of the key objectives that organizations have when deciding to use expatriates as part of their global staffing mix.

In the second half of the chapter, we considered *expatriates'* views of eROI and the frustration that many feel because of their organizations inadequacies in practice. We introduced the concept of iROI—individual return on investment—and began to note the divergences of objectives likely to exist between expatriates and their employing organizations, which we expand upon in subsequent chapters. We considered the potential effects on eROI of the sea change brought about by new forms of expatriation and a new generation of expatriates with different goals from their predecessors, motivated largely by a drive for mobility that requires less loyalty to their organizations.

Our focus in Part 1 makes it clear that the effective management of expatriates, with or without the adoption of an eROI approach, involves resolving a number of issues that are unique to this group, including compensation, family life, careers, and psychological contracts. Therefore, in Part 2 of this book (Chapters 3–6), we will explore each of these in depth, as background to the development (in Part 3) of an approach to expatriate management that takes full account of them, within an overall management framework based on ROI.

PART 2

Understanding Expatriates

CHAPTER 3

Expatriate Compensation

The fundamental thing that has changed is the attitude to the international assignee. In the old days you were needed, you were wanted and desired—and you were paid accordingly. Now, you are much more of a number. I see this in the discernable effort to whittle away at my package because somebody is sitting in the ivory tower in headquarters and sees an opportunity to reduce costs. Little things get reduced on a regular basis and it's always justified because it's 'only a small thing'. But there's lots and lots of small things that add up ... unfortunately, employees have it beaten into them that you're lucky to be there and the company expects you to be flexible.

—Senior Vice President, 47 years, Asia Pacific

Expatriate compensation is complex: it is complicated by fluctuating exchange rates, inflation, challenging locations, and the recruitment of expatriates *in*, *to*, and *from* new emerging markets. Talent retention is a key issue for most companies, and an increasing concern, particularly in Asia where many expatriates are now located.[1] Some commentators even suggest that retaining talent may be more difficult than retaining clients.[2] This fierce competition causes issues in executive compensation not because it is driving salaries up as one would logically expect, but because it is driving salaries *down*. So, how should top expatriate talent be remunerated?

A 2010 survey by Ernst & Young found that 67% of mobility managers report "compensation packages" as the biggest area where assignee expectations are not met.[3] Yet expatriates do not seek or accept international assignments purely for financial reasons: other important considerations—often the most important—are intercultural experience, career enhancement, and personal adventure.[4] Why then is compensation such a big source of dissatisfaction?

In this chapter, we'll get to bottom of this conundrum. We'll explore how expatriate compensation has changed over the past two decades and why the rapid increase in "local-plus" and other "hybrid" host-based packages, which have increased rapidly in frequency and importance, can be both a useful tool and, if not properly understood, a disaster. Drawing on extensive data from our MM and Expat Studies, we provide an insiders' "warts-and-all" perspective about the aspects of compensation and benefits that matter to expatriates—and why it really isn't about the money after all.

Table 3.1 provides an overview of compensation strategies, some of which are well established (see page 47).[5] Of special importance is the third category of package, "local-plus." Local-plus is a relatively new approach in which expatriate employees are paid according to the salary levels, structure, and administration guidelines of the host location, as well as being provided, in recognition of the employee's foreign status, with special expatriate benefits such as transportation, housing, and the costs of dependents' education.[6] It is worth noting that not all expatriates on local-plus receive the full range of additional benefits, these being at the discretion of the employing organization and largely determined by the location of the assignment (e.g. hardship versus non-hardship), among other factors.[7]

In this chapter, we will focus a lot of attention on local-plus and other "new" forms of compensation because, according to our research, these are some of the main drivers of the sea change in global mobility we are currently witnessing. To begin, though, let's first take a look at Eduardo's story.

CASE: Eduardo Rodriguez, Reluctant Expatriate

Eduardo is Spanish, 46 years old, and has worked for 16 years for his Dutch-based transport industry company, MOVER Inc. Nearly 7 years ago Eduardo took his first international position, heading up the company's operations in India, and then two and a half years ago he moved laterally to a position in Singapore to "round out" his experience by taking a regional, rather than just a country-manager, responsibility. Six months ago he was promoted, still in Singapore, to Asia Vice President of a major division of the company, responsible for operations in 11 Asian countries. Eduardo likes being an expatriate: "I think there's an element of excitement in the whole process in terms of the type of work I do and the fact that I do live overseas where I have the opportunity to travel and learn and develop."

Eduardo's move to Singapore was, he thinks, more about "activities that (the company) needed to be done" than about his own career objectives: "I'm not sure that I wanted to accept it … I had my doubts … but as an international assignee you go where you're told, even if that means having to go on local-plus."

Being "flexible" includes large disparities in remuneration even for employees in the same or similar roles: "If I was sitting next to an American doing exactly the same job, that person would net 70% more income than I would, doing exactly the same role," he says, "and that's because he's an American and I'm Spanish."

Eduardo's problems do not end there. Only 6 months into his new contract in Singapore, he was unilaterally told that his COLA (cost-of-living allowance) was to drop by 50% and his schooling allowance by $5,000 per child: loss of the allowances was immediate, representing a 12% drop in his take-home salary.

Eduardo says he has learned to roll with the punches, that "basically in a company of this size you take it or you leave it, and you have to make a conscious decision each time you sign an international contract that you're enjoying it and happy to take what you're given."

"People used to call HR 'human remains' and now I call them the 'human finance department' because it's all about numbers," says Eduardo. "To be a successful HR manager they've got to pay you as little as they possibly can without losing you … this whole process of change has alienated the expat from the company, so we're almost like a contractor. But I know that (my boss) wouldn't see it that way; we're in a job that's assumed to be high cost and in some of our markets it's now cheaper to put an international assignee into some jobs and some countries than employ locals."

Eduardo feels the resentment he has about his compensation may affect his long-term attitude to, and long-term future at, MOVER Inc. In the medium-term, he is considering leaving the organization earlier than planned. Eighteen months ago, after a series of disappointments including poor company support for his move to Singapore, Eduardo interviewed for a position in Beijing with another company, but finally decided instead to stay on at MOVER Inc. But for how long? "You have to have a mindset that says there's a point at which you'll say 'that's it' and you go and do something else, somewhere else. I haven't reached that point quite yet, but I'm close."

By "close" Eduardo means he has not yet reached "the tipping point." Currently, he's about 5% ahead of where he might have been had he stayed in his native Spain. What keeps him in the company now is "little things," such as being able to rent out his Barcelona house and being able to employ a maid in Singapore to assist his family.

Eventually, Eduardo is certain he will leave MOVER Inc., because, as expatriation has grown, he says, the typical expat package has been "reduced to resemble probably half of what it used to be say, 15 or 20 years ago."

Notwithstanding his gripes about the company, Eduardo retains a commitment to it: "Once you've invested so much into a company you want to get something out of it rather than jumping to another." But what does he feel the company gets for its investment in him? "Tangible results that I deliver in the business." Eduardo gives chapter and verse in eROI terms of some of his accomplishments at MOVER Inc.: "At the end of the day I would be comfortable in saying I can deliver ten times the cost of employing me and that's without counting the intangible aspects, the fact that we've got a thousand people in my group that have got to be managed and developed. You can't really put a monetary value around that."

His advice to new expatriates is to look more closely at their initial contracts and to negotiate harder on compensation than he has tended to do. "Looking back, I should have been tougher from the outset."

Table 3.1. Compensation Strategies for International Assignments

Policy name	Strategy	Description of policy	Purpose used for
Balance sheet (full package home-based)	Development	• Full "bells and whistles", i.e. generous remuneration (including bonus and incentives) and benefits (including tax equalization, look-see trip, cost-of-living allowance, housing, education, spousal allowance, car, home leave, and club memberships) • Designed to ensure employee lifestyle in comparison to "home" not disadvantaged by relocating • Based on notion that there is a "home-country" from where the expatriate originates	• Targeted at executives for career development who possess universal skills and considered high potential • Used for "cadre" approach to develop careers of elite group of high performers whose permanent mobility is long-term strategic goal • Used for retention purposes where goal is to repatriate to corporate headquarters or business group headquarters • Used sparingly as a reward for key individuals • Complex to administer with many home–host country combinations
Balance sheet (light package home-based)	Skills/ secondment	• Reduced version of full package, i.e. generous remuneration with/ without bonus and incentives, and inclusion of some benefits but not others (e.g. housing, education, car, and home leave) but not others (e.g. club memberships, spousal allowance, and cost of living)	• Expatriates with deep technical skills or competencies • Specific goal is to transfer skills and knowledge for duration of assignment only (no more than 2 years) • Expatriate relocates for a fixed period and repatriates with no intention to relocate again unless a specific skill need arises • Used to service clients in location where local skills not available
Local-plus (host-based)	Cost savings	• Provides some benefits of developmental strategy but on greatly reduced basis • Expatriates often localized with some additional benefits provided to sustain retention • No ongoing allowances (e.g. cost of living) • Initial allowances typically phased out over period of assignment (50% benefit Y2, 20% benefit Y3)	• Combination of developmental and skills/secondment expatriates, but generally targeted at middle management executives who are specialized, functional people, or broad business managers and/or generalists who move between variety of different positions (and locations) throughout their career • Typically offered to managers initiating relocation or indicating willingness to relocate
Localization (host-based)	Cost savings, functional retention	• Initial allowances from any of above phased out over period of assignment (50% benefit Y2, 20% benefit Y3) to achieve full "local" remuneration	• Offered to managers initiating relocation and long-term assignees exceeding term of contract (i.e. beyond initial assignment) but who wish to remain in location or firm does not wish to repatriate
Permanent trans-fer (host-based)	Self-initiated transfers	• One-way relocation package to host-destination • Salary, incentives, and benefits from local payroll	• Self-initiated/employee-initiated relocation

Is Eduardo an isolated case? Unfortunately, no. Today's expatriate is not only expected to be mobile, often over multiple assignments, and at the whim and demands of the MNC, but also to do the job for a lower salary, and yet still over-deliver on required performance, all the while supposedly feeling "lucky" about the opportunity.

Is Eduardo an ungrateful expatriate, a "world champion whiner," who by comparison with the average home-country employee leads a glamorous life that affords him more benefits than others can dream of? Or does Eduardo's story highlight that modern expatriation is a less-than-perfect evolution of traditional expatriation, with many negative elements?

First, Eduardo's situation shows that global mobility bears considerable costs that are prohibitive for many companies, the response to which is to engage in cost-cutting. While the traditional reasons for needing expatriates (e.g. knowledge and skills transfer, global control and culture, and career development) remain valid, more localized and local-plus expatriates now have a level of managerial talent that they can often compete for jobs with "full package" expatriates.

Second, although Eduardo was not happy with his change in status from "full package" in India to "local-plus" in Singapore, he nonetheless understood that it is becoming an increasingly popular compensation strategy. This is often because, in addition to meeting cost-cutting directives, it helps to bridge the gap in perceived unfairness in compensation between locals and expatriates, where the former have been traditionally paid according to local salary rates, and the latter according to their home-country labor market. This has frequently led to negative outcomes among local employees, including low morale, uncooperativeness, withdrawal, and reduced commitment.[8] But, as we see in Eduardo's story, those same negative outcomes can also emerge from those expatriates who are willing, or forced, to accept local-plus rather than a traditional full package. What we clearly see is that the dynamics of two different bases of compensation for the same work is a complex and delicate matter, with significant implications.

Is Money Important to Expatriates?

For decades, many have believed that the fundamental driver for expatriates to accept international assignments has been financial gain, mostly as a result of the substantial benefits and allowances they receive over and above base salary, including COLA, hardship premiums, relocation bonuses, lifestyle allowances (housing, schooling, and car), and other perquisites (country club memberships, home leave, home-country storage costs, and home sale reimbursement). For many years (as we saw in the NexCorp case, Chapter 2), this was a major reason why expatriates agreed to go: few people are willing to uproot their lives, families, established networks, and familiarity of home to simply "break even" in terms of home-country salary.

The latest research shows, however, that the five top criteria for expatriates when making the decision to accept an international assignment go beyond only financial reasons.[9] While base salary (71%) and a location bonus (to incentivize the move) (32%) are important, so too is accompanying partner support to assist in adjustment and the dual-career issue (finding employment) (60%), re-integration guarantees for an expatriate's career (58%), and the quality of schooling for children (whether fully or partially funded by the company) (41%). How do these compare with Eduardo's story?

Clearly, money *does* matter to some extent: expatriates, like everyone else, need to earn their keep, pay their bills, and support their families. Expatriation—and global mobility in general—is often a fast-track way to earn more money more quickly to meet this need, and sometimes to save money as well, making mobility attractive to many employees, at least in the short term.

Employees close to retirement may be especially focused on money: one 59-year-old South African expatriate on assignment in Canada was brutally honest in admitting,

> I don't have a big part of my career ahead of me, so I want to maximize my earnings until I retire. Money first for me and, frankly, if a competitor walked in the door and said, "Come and work for us and we'll give you maybe as little as 10% more," I'd probably move because I've got to be loyal to me first.

One reason retirement matters is that maintaining home-country retirement plans is one of the most challenging aspects of compensation, particularly for career expatriates; indeed, only 12% of companies in a Mercer survey had established international pension plans to ensure long-term expatriates their continuity of benefits.[10]

The HSBC Expat Explorer series of reports shows that finances among expatriates remain very positive, with the majority saving more since moving abroad, accumulating less debt, and having higher levels of spending. Most wealthy expatriates reside in the Middle East and Asia, with the highest net-worth expatriate individuals in Russia and Singapore.[11] This might explain why Eduardo—despite having a poor employer–employee relationship—will remain on the international circuit as an expatriate. All things considered, he's financially better off, even if marginally so.

But, as we found, money may not be everything. As noted above "job guarantees" upon returning to the home country, "partner support," and "children's schooling" are also ranked as important criteria. In fact, many in our Expat Study were clear that they would not compromise on things such as family support, security and safety (especially after 9/11), quality of life, and work/life balance. On these issues, expatriates expect MNCs to overcome their unbending view of money as a "means to an end," to instead help them maintain some semblance of home-country (or equivalent) standards in areas such as housing for their family, medical care, and education for their children. One informant, a China-based expatriate from New Zealand, made this point clear when he explained a planned move to South Korea:

> I talked about the move with my wife and daughter and we agreed it's a good job and it pays more money. However, the American school there doesn't have a good reputation. So I went to see the CEO and I said, "I'll think about that job. However, in order for me to make a decision you need to break the rules a bit and I need you to agree to provide my wife and daughter with accommodation in China for one more year so she can finish her last year in high school there. I need you to agree to keep my daughter in the American school in China, and I will need a two-bedroom flat in Seoul as well so that when they visit there's somewhere for them to stay." Effectively I asked for two apartments. And the answer was "yes." I know that's breaking the rules, but that's how I think things should be done—it should be based on circumstances.

Our research, and that of others, provides compelling evidence that expatriates have many non-financial reasons to engage in global mobility, with career enhancement and progression, seeking a personal or family adventure, and fulfilling a lifelong dream among them. This tells us a lot about modern expatriation—that we are witnessing a change in the drivers that motivate expatriates to go abroad, with corresponding changes in MNCs strategies to attract the right people into global employment. Whereas in years gone by MNCs used fat compensation packages to create a "home away from home" as an incentive to relocate, the availability of more expatriates (like Eduardo) willing to accept local-plus compensation and live more like locals has caused a decline in the need for these full packages.

Why Local-Plus Is Here to Stay

One reason for the trend to local-plus in expatriate compensation is the fact that the traditional full expatriate compensation package—often called the "balance sheet" because it is balanced back to home-country conditions—is fast becoming an outdated and overly expensive approach. How can we say this about a compensation package that has been around for over two decades?

Simply put, the balance-sheet approach is ineffective for moving MNCs' global competitive advantage to where it should be because it is based on a repatriation model that insists on maintaining a link to expatriates' home country or headquarters, despite that many expatriates may never return there. Furthermore, if compensation is strategically geared toward an expatriate who will one day return to their home country, it is not then capable of effectively supporting the high demand for "career expatriates" whose continual movement across borders—often over decades—helps to facilitate true global staffing, nor will it enable expatriates to culturally integrate to local norms and customs.

A good example of the problems caused by the balance-sheet approach is the disparity between PCNs and TCNs in terms of how they are compensated for often doing the same job: both are expatriates, neither are locals, yet the former are nearly always paid on the basis of the balance-sheet approach and the latter frequently on a local-plus package, predominantly because TCNs have few, if any, home-country links.[12] If TCNs can do the same job for half the cost, then a radical shake-up in PCN compensation is overdue. Expatriate compensation—and PCN compensation in particular—needs a major overhaul to ensure that a small link to the HQ or home-country standard of living is maintained, while a larger emphasis is placed on the local market context which expatriates are sent to support.

There is considerable evidence, then, that local-plus is not only on the rise, but that it will soon eclipse the balance sheet/full package as the dominant, and preferred, type of compensation among MNCs and expatriates alike. This is particularly the case in Asia, where reports by ORC and AIRINC,[13] as well as our own research,[14] show that local-plus compensation is a popular alternative to the balance sheet. Mercer found among 37 MNCs operating in China, Hong Kong, and Singapore that local plus is the second most popular compensation approach, only slightly behind the balance sheet. Indeed, among TCNs, permanent transferees, and intra-regional hires (those moving between Asian countries) in China, local-plus is the most common approach.[15]

In relation to eROI, there are many advantages to local-plus compensation, one important benefit for firms being the inherent flexibility to tailor each "plus" component (i.e. add or remove a benefit) according to a variety of corporate objectives. In doing so, a local-plus approach can better address, at the individual level, what is most needed to attract and retain expatriates, as well as maintaining observable equity with locals, without over-paying expatriates whose performance does not warrant excessive compensation. A senior executive in our MM study confirmed this view, when he said:

> We switched all staff onto host-based packages [because] we have a very large performance-reward culture. By switching and having people directly rewarded based on their performance in the context of the location where they work, that I think has got to increase [and] impact on the performance of the individuals relative to cost, to output. So in terms of ROI that's going to be a big thing … it's got to impact ROI.

From this perspective, local-plus compensation is clearly a more cost-effective means by which MNCs can manage various types of expatriate staff, while simultaneously attempting to meet organizational objectives. But that's not where it ends. In fact, it is just the beginning, as we explain next.

Global Compensation, Not Expatriate Compensation

In our view, "expatriate" compensation needs to transition to "global" compensation. The shift in terminology reflects a shift in mindset, firstly, that while expatriates clearly perform in an international context, many are nonetheless employed in jobs similar to those of their local counterparts, or in jobs that locals can also do at some point in the future. Additionally, local employees often relocate domestically for much the same reasons as expatriates do internationally (e.g. for career development and promotion), yet even when locals' standard of living is impacted, they are not compensated for it like expatriates.

The distinction, then, is to focus less on "expatriate status" as the defining criterion and more on the international nature of the employee performing the job. Essentially, global employees require global compensation. This suggests that "global" compensation needs to move away from remunerating expatriates to instead remunerating *international employees*. How can this be done?

Our own research, and that of others,[16] tells us that expatriate compensation needs to avoid being based on assignee or home-country status, but instead on *the role that expatriates perform*. This is because it is the *worth of the position* that should be aligned to strategic objectives, not whether an employee has assignee status. Furthermore, it is the role that expatriates perform that ideally dictates whether they are compensated according to local, regional, or global wage and salary considerations. In this way, a global compensation approach enables MNCs to find the most appropriate candidate—PCN or TCN or some other alternative—and then compensate them not because of who they are, but according to what they are *expected to, and do, achieve*. Additionally, a global compensation approach is more equitable because it is performance based, thereby eliminating overpaying and perceived unfairness.

In reality, global compensation is much simpler to administer than a balance-sheet approach because it represents an extension of most organizations' existing domestic (home country) pay-for-performance model.[17]

The benefits of a global compensation approach are exemplified by a mining company executive in our MM study based in Singapore, explaining why his company has switched to such a model:

> Global compensation works for us because it doesn't reduce the expat to a 7-year-old mentality, where the decision about whether to have a third child or buy a property is somehow tied to their fat expat package and all the allowances that the balance-sheet policy typically brings. What I mean is that our expats are no longer beholden to the company via their compensation in making decisions about their life. We pay our expats based on what they do for us, and we make it very clear from before the contract is signed what and how they will be remunerated; if they then want to go and have another child or buy a Porsche, that is their decision based on what they earn and how they choose to spend it, not on whether a certain allowance will cover it and whether that allowance will still be in place 2 or 3 years from now … so that's performance-based salary in action, isn't it. We choose people to fill a need and we look at them on a case by case basis. We don't presume that every expat from the same home-country performs at the same level and should get the same salary. So what we have is clearer expectations. We have a global workforce, not an expat workforce. We have far less hassles and headaches because we do it that way.

Another company, in the consumer manufacturing industry, views their compensation approach as an important retention tool by,

> targeting different aspects of our pay to individuals; it might be salary, bonus, or shares in stock, but all of those are levers that we apply on an individual basis for our people, as a financial piece of our ROI focus.

While innovative methods such as the global compensation approach we suggest will, in some instances, also reduce expatriates' compensation, one advantage in using local-plus to facilitate a global compensation approach is that it allows organizations to expand their global talent pool by targeting candidates eager to pursue international and global careers, who are willing to expatriate not just because of the compensation being offered, but often *in spite of it*. This includes career and self-initiated expatriates for whom many have already acquired the intercultural competencies, cultural intelligence, and language abilities necessary to succeed in an international role, and who also have the necessary desire, skills, and attitudes. This resembles less the traditional and same-across-the-board PCN approach that has been the mainstay of expatriation for decades, and moves instead toward a more innovative and strategic TCN and local-plus approach that is customized according to regio-centric or geocentric concerns according to the demand, location, cost, and other strategic and operational concerns of the MNC.

A further advantage of a global compensation approach is that it is inherently more flexible than that of a PCN-focused balance sheet. Because a global compensation approach is based on pay-for-performance and local-plus terms and conditions, it can continue even after an expatriate repatriates or decides to relinquish their "expatriate" status. Unlike the balance-sheet approach that can only be used for employees deployed abroad, global compensation is not necessarily location- or status-specific, but can be leveraged over the long-term to facilitate the retention of employees—global or otherwise—as a means of ensuring eROI. For example, a global careerist who expatriates, relocates back to the home-country, and expatriates again as part of their overall career progression, need not change compensation status during each move, thereby alleviating a heavy transactional burden on the global mobility or compensation and benefits department in terms of administering pay and benefits for each subsequent change in host or home location. Furthermore, a global compensation approach contributes to, and fosters, a type of "dynamic global career" that we predict will become a normal part of global mobility over the next two decades (see Chapter 5).

In advocating for a global compensation approach, we are *not* suggesting, however, that expatriates should be treated like (local) HCNs or domestic employees: clearly PCNs and TCNs incur more substantial expenses and greater disruption to their lives than employees who choose not to relocate. As such, expatriates should be compensated accordingly and subjected to a different set of policies, but only insofar as the compensation approach remains appropriate to the jobs that expatriates actually do, rather than the status they hold or the home country they originate from. As we saw in the case of Eduardo when he compared himself to his American colleagues during his first international assignment to India, disparity in compensation among PCN expatriates from different home countries is a major problem which could be overcome by adopting a global compensation approach based on a local-plus and pay-for-performance strategy, as occurred in Eduardo's subsequent relocation to Singapore.

The Opportunity Cost of Local-Plus

Despite the growing prevalence and many advantages of a global compensation approach based on local-plus terms and conditions, it can also be a problematic compensation method that, from an eROI perspective, requires extremely careful management.

We say this because, in our Expat Study, expatriates held very negative views about having their compensation status altered to local-plus. The most significant issue they raised was that MNCs often tend to change compensation contracts during an assignment (e.g. by withdrawing or reducing a housing allowance, school allowance, or home leave, as was the case for Eduardo), leaving many feeling that they are backed into a corner because they are forced to accept changed conditions when an international assignment is already under way. Others resent that once they are established as career expatriates, MNCs "move the goal posts" by reducing compensation packages at the point of re-assignment or assignment extension. Doing so creates a heightened sense of unjustified loss for those expatriates forced onto local-plus compensation, not necessarily because they are unhappy with the package, but because they are unhappy with the *process*. As one informant said,

> I know it's easy to dwell on the negatives. I mean at the end of
> the day, it's a pretty damn good deal. We send our kids to the best

school, we get a company car. There are a lot of good things. What it boils down to really is "process untidiness." The tension would be much less if there was a closer dialogue between the company and me when changes in compensation are under way.

More transparency is clearly needed. We need to remember, too, that when expatriates perceive that an "unjustified loss" has occurred in their compensation, there are ramifications. Our Expat Study shows, for example, that when changes in expatriates' compensation are made during an assignment, there is likely to be a clear and direct psychological shift in their loyalty and commitment to the MNC. We found strong evidence among expatriates that local-plus compensation increases their willingness to change jobs *because money is no longer the defining factor that binds them to their employers.* Essentially, reduced compensation reduces loyalty thus leading to less job commitment:[18] money can be found anywhere, even—and perhaps especially—on the international labor market.

The take-away from this chapter is that whereas fat packages bind expatriates to their firm, local-plus puts expatriates on a level playing field akin to their domestic counterparts, meaning that job movement in and out of the organization can be facilitated with greater ease. The opportunity cost of local-plus, therefore, is that because it provides fewer ties that bind expatriates to their employers financially, it facilitates higher levels of risk taking on their part: because there are fewer allowances and benefits, and virtually no pension or retirement plans, local-plus affords easier job mobility *out* of the organization.

The opportunity cost of local-plus becomes crystal clear when turnover among expatriates increases as an unintended side-effect, particularly when an assignment is already underway, given that existing expatriate systems are not designed to cope with turnover other than during repatriation. While local-plus compensation brings very direct benefits to firms via cost savings, among expatriates it often leads to increased tension and frustration, and reduced job satisfaction and commitment. Firms may save money by adopting local-plus practices, but they also risk losing high-potential global staff to competitors; hence short-term financial eROI gains can be mitigated by long-term non-financial losses.

The real question for MNCs then is whether the compensation approach they adopt has sufficient fit to produce organizationally relevant outcomes, that is the desired behavior among expatriates, including their retention to the end of an assignment. If compensation fit is poor, has the organization thought through how it might respond to, and deal with, the fallout? Has it even considered that there may *be* fallout?

Summary

Our starting point in this chapter was that compensation is a big issue in terms of eROI because of the costs involved, the tendency for costs to balloon if not controlled, and the personal effect of compensation on expatriates themselves and their feelings about it. We outlined some of the most common types of packages and provided a case study of an employee who became de-motivated when changes were made to his package during an assignment: but we also noted that compensation issues were not the only, or even the most important, consideration for many expatriates, and that the process through which companies deal with compensation might be as important as the remuneration itself. Finally, we looked specifically at the "pros" and "cons" of the increasingly utilized "local plus" type of package. Local plus, we believe, is here to stay because it enhances global staffing options, facilitates greater mobility, and is far less costly to administer and sustain, but it also carries risks in terms of encouraging expatriates to move between organizations.

CHAPTER 4

Expatriate Families

I was a barrister in Australia who thought it might be fun to take a year to live with my husband in far north Finland. It wasn't, because I couldn't work. I was ignored and my whole identity disappeared. We now live apart for five days a week—he in far north Finland, me in Helsinki. I am working, but it is not the same senior job I had in Australia and this has caused intense bitterness.

—Belinda, 32 years, Expat Wife

Ask mobility managers their biggest challenge in overcoming some of the barriers to mobility or providing on-assignment support, and almost without exception they will say, "when things aren't working out it's primarily family issues."[1] "Family concerns," "partner dissatisfaction," and "spouse's career" are common areas of difficulty.[2] Clearly, spouses and families are a major consideration in most international assignments and family issues are often responsible for a poor eROI.

In this chapter, we provide an in-depth exposé of the problems expatriation creates for spouses, partners, and families. Specifically, we explain why the partner's career is commonly an intractable challenge, and what the expatriate's organization can do to help. We explain the causes and outcomes of marital stress, work–life "spillover," partners' identity crises, and third culture kid challenges, and we indicate remedial "best practice" strategies currently used by successful companies. We show what expatriate families need in order to thrive, and why anything other than a "family first" approach by both expatriates and the companies that employ them seldom succeeds. Throughout this chapter, we will frequently use the term "trailing spouse" to refer to the expatriate's partner, and "dual career" to refer the situation where both members of a couple seek to pursue careers in employment simultaneously. If you're not sure of the full connotations of these terms, check them out in our Glossary at the end of the book.

To begin, let's take a look at the Fletcher family.

CASE: The "Trailing Spouse" as Career—or Not

Julie Fletcher is a 38-year-old mother of two, has a master's degree in international relations, and is about to embark on her husband Jonathan's third consecutive international assignment. A month ago he signed a 3-year contract with his employer, a US-based technology company, to relocate their family to Beijing. In less than 4 weeks, Julie will be living in China.

Julie is excited about the move, yet hesitant. Moving to China means giving up her job as a consultant at a global relocation firm that she was able to obtain only after 7 years of (unemployed) expatriation. On the other hand, she and Jonathan have always wanted to "try out" China. So, the decision to go has not been easy, even though Julie and Jonathan are seasoned expatriates who have moved internationally twice before—first from their native Dublin to Seattle, and 4 years later to Amsterdam, their current home.

In many ways, the move to China seems good for them. Good for Jonathan's career, good for their two young sons, and potentially a wonderful, perhaps life-changing, cultural experience for the whole family. Yet in other ways this move is anything but simple: there are new issues now on the radar, and important decisions to be made that will likely affect the family for many years.

A constant worry is the children and particularly their ability to integrate in a new school: Does China have international schools of the caliber they've become accustomed to in the Netherlands? International schools in Asia are at or near capacity and the demand and strain are growing, with tuition fees increasing. Will Julie be able to find the school she wants in Beijing? This, she realizes, is an area where the trailing spouse always has to take major responsibility.

Schools aside, foremost in Julie's mind is whether she can find employment in Beijing. The thought of being a stay-at-home, unemployed accompanying spouse again—as she has been for most of their expatriate life—makes her heart sink. Although in Seattle she initially relished her trailing spouse status—sightseeing, setting up their new home, and entertaining business colleagues for her husband—it quickly became a tedious existence of "wives'" coffee mornings, tennis games, and charity work, compounded by her inability to obtain a US work permit. Many times Julie longed for the career she had given up in Dublin in order to move abroad—consulting at Accenture—and the independence it had provided. Without a business card and a job title, she felt invisible at the many functions she attended as "Jonathan's wife." Her decision to be a trailing spouse had resulted in a major loss of identity, much of which Julie painfully realized had been tied up in a career that was now impossible for her to continue.

The subsequent move to Amsterdam had proved little better: the Fletchers welcomed twin sons in the early years in America, necessitating that Julie stay home in Seattle and Amsterdam to raise them. It was only in the last year, when the children entered an international school full-time, that Julie returned to paid employment as a global relocation consultant. Although it did not pay as well as management consulting, they didn't need the money anyway; Jonathan's career was flourishing, each move a promotion. Julie told herself she needed a portable career, compatible with constant mobility, and what better job than working in relocation?

Now, she finds, her career prospects—or the lack of them—pre-occupy her. She knows her life in Beijing will be dull and boring if she is not employed. She must not allow herself to succumb to a life of resigned acceptance as "Mrs. Nobody" as so many of her expatriate girlfriends have done, resulting in all sorts of psychological problems and addictions as they tried to cope. She needs to retain her self-esteem and confidence in a continuing career.

Julie also feels a deep obligation to regain some balance and equality in her marriage, as in the years when she and Jonathan first married and were both working. The stress their marriage has endured during expatriation, particularly when the children were born, blindsided them both, being exacerbated by their lack of family support and Julie's uneasiness about her growing dependence on her husband (and his company) for even day-to-day necessities. Like many trailing spouses, Julie believes that the longer she remains a supportive non-working wife, the harder it will be for her to have a voice in major family decisions.

Will she be able to get a work permit in China? As a foreigner in Beijing speaking only basic Mandarin, how quickly can she establish a new network and find a job? What employment barriers will she face as an expatriate wife?

Julie Fletcher, driven by her desire to regain balance in her marriage and to obtain a measure of financial and career independence, exemplifies the modern trailing spouse. Her life is tied up in a myriad of roles and responsibilities—career, children, family networks, husband's job, and marriage. It is also subject to constant, and frequent, "identity disruptions."

As Julie's story shows, family expatriation is changing, and is becoming more challenging. Julie is typical of many expatriates' partners: college educated, career-focused, and independent. Like Julie, more and more trailing spouses are unwilling to give up their own careers to support someone else's, or to be relegated to the role of unpaid company skivvy. They are also increasingly "serial movers," relocating multiple times. But with each relocation, they face huge barriers to employment that spouses who remain in their own country do not: lack of access to a work permit, labor markets that do not recognize their qualifications, an inability to commit to long-term job tenure, language and cultural differences, local stereotyping, and prejudice.

What can organizations, and in particular mobility managers, do to help? Twenty years ago, when assignments were typically of the "there and back" type, simple solutions were available for trailing spouses to "pass the time" until repatriation: providing a spouse allowance of, for example, $5000 to pacify the wife for her loss of career; company coffee mornings; and buddying newly relocated spouses with the wives of senior expatriates in the same location. Today that's not enough: trailing spouses re-assign more often than they repatriate, and they increasingly desire continuation of their careers and employment opportunities. Expatriation therefore involves long-term issues that were previously unheard of, such as re-establishing and continuing partners' careers across many geographical locations, and children transitioning through new foreign locations and multiple schools.

There's also the inner life of the trailing spouse to consider: How does one retain purpose and meaning when each move positions one's life "back to zero," requiring months of downtime planning, packing and unpacking boxes, leaving old homes and finding new ones, and re-establishing social networks in every new city? As one spouse in our TS Study stated,

> It's a lonely way to live as we are left to reinvent ourselves and our children after every relocation. It's exhausting and unrewarding. I regret my life.

Clearly, the inner life of the trailing spouse also needs to be addressed, often over a long period of time.

Spouse Adjustment

The core of the inner life we refer to is trailing spouses' adjustment to both the host-location and their new (or continuing) expatriate life. Our TS Study found strong evidence that when the trailing spouse is "cut off from a process that affects my life deeply," it can have a devastating effect on their self-esteem and adjustment.

Findings from our and others' research show that trailing spouse adjustment involves the minimization of stressors plus the development of effective coping behaviors so that demands and capabilities can be constantly balanced.[3] The demands include *stressors* typically seen in one-off events such as the relocation itself; *strains* represented by ongoing unresolved tensions that manifest over time, such as that from giving up a job/career, changed family routines, children starting new schools, and/ or changes in financial status; and *daily hassles* such as dealing with locals in a foreign language.

Capabilities are those resources the trailing spouse draws on to cope with the new situation. These include *emotional* resources found in friendships, clubs, associations, and even online; *informational* resources such as company assistance with finding a job; and *instrumental* resources that include, for example, relocation allowances and residency permits.[4] Children may be an additional source of support, often playing a "socio-cultural brokerage" role in facilitating access to parental social networks.[5]

Spouse adjustment has been the subject of much recent research[6] because poor adjustment can have "crossover" effects on other members of the family, including their willingness to relocate and the work performance of the employed expatriate.[7] During expatriation, families invariably go through various stages of adjustment as they acclimatize to their new environment and their often changed family roles, which simultaneously affects the psychological state of all family members;[8] although families try to maintain a sense of equilibrium, it is often unachievable. For the trailing spouse, we suggest that dealing with demands and building capabilities to enhance positive crossover are likely to be helped by organizational support, as we explain in more detail later in this chapter.

We know from our TS Study that trailing spouse adjustment is frequently exacerbated by losses: of employment, of a career, of financial independence, of social networks, and of extended family support. It also tends to result in new and unexpected family roles and responsibilities, along with shifts in relationship dynamics within the family. A further challenge is that the trailing spouse has no official employment status with his/her partners' company but is nevertheless greatly affected by its expatriate policies and practices. Being "dumped in to sink or swim" and being "treated by the company as totally invisible" are frequent complaints, and appropriate organizational support is generally felt to be poor.[9]

Identity Re-Construction

Trailing spouse adjustment is about the reconstruction of one's identity in a new environment, whether career-focused or not. While Julie had returned to full-time employment in Amsterdam for practical reasons—to alleviate her boredom—she had also done so in order to address her intrinsic adjustment by way of developing a *meaningful portable identity*.

Why is identity so important? One participant in our TS Study compared her trailing spouse life to "being a woman in a third world country; I'm not permitted to work and everything is at the discretion of my husband." Another said, "I'm not living my life. I'm living his." Others felt that identity issues were caused by "dreams being destroyed in a minute," and resentment at being stereotyped as a trailing spouse who wanted only to "drink coffee, do charity work, gossip, and watch day-time TV every day." More intense feelings led some spouses to "feel like a second-class citizen," where "my self-esteem has taken a beating" and "I have given up my real self and become less of a person."

In a recent study,[10] three aspects of identity reformulation were found to be important to trailing spouses' adjustment: their personal identity in such things as language fluency, employment status, and self-efficacy; their social identity tied up in relationships with family, friends, and acquaintances; and their situational identity arising from the cultural novelty of the host-location, living conditions, and the expected duration of the assignment. What mattered most to them, however, was not the retention of a past identity, but the establishment of a *new* identity, predominantly through the building of interpersonal relationships in the host country.

In our TS Study, we found that social and professional support were important facilitators of spouses' identity reconstruction, as a way "to belong" and "to be able to create a life of my own." For example, fluency in the host-country language provides power and independence; hence, language training helps to build self-esteem. Access to internet and email early in a move, socialization with expatriates, and spending time with a spouse and children can also help (see Table 4.1 for a full list).

Table 4.1. Adjustment Coping Mechanisms for the Trailing Spouse

Activity	%	n
Using internet or email	91	260
Socializing with expatriates	90	263
Spending time with spouse/children	81	264
Keeping in touch with family back home	79	264
Socializing with locals	74	259
Learning host-country language	71	262
Sporting clubs and associations	57	263
Massage, yoga, meditation, journal writing	47	262
Voluntary or unpaid work	41	264

Unfortunately, not spending enough time with an (employed) partner often proves to be a tremendous challenge for the trailing spouse and is a major source of marital tension and frustration. The least important activity appears to be voluntary or unpaid work (see Table 4.1), which is resented by some spouses as "supporting the local citizens for free," without being "good enough to be employed, pay my taxes, and be given my independence."

A "Family First" Approach

Our goal in this chapter is to consider the expatriate family as a critical part of the eROI mix. Although family issues can, and do, impact on eROI and for decades have been blamed as the leading cause of failed assignments, we don't believe this trend needs to continue. With a better understanding of the issues, and thoughtful application of "best practice" solutions, we are hopeful that expatriate families will learn not only to survive, but also thrive, on the global mobility circuit.

While the list of trailing spouse stressors, strains, and daily hassles referred to earlier is potentially long, in our TS Study we found that two of the most common ongoing unresolved family tensions are the trailing spouse's career and the couple's marital stress. Let's explore each, along with how they might be addressed. But first, let's see what's happening with the Fletchers in Beijing.

CASE: Who Is To Blame When Assignments Fail?

Two years have passed since the Fletchers' move from Amsterdam to Beijing. Now we find Julie and her children—but not Jonathan— boarding BA188 in Beijing, en route to Dublin. Tears stream down Julie's face. She has just said good-bye to her husband, knowing it will be 12 months until he can hopefully be reunited and living with their family again in Dublin. After everything their family has endured in the previous 2 years in Beijing, nothing has prepared her for splitting up their family while Jonathan completes his international assignment, and she and the children return to their original home.

Although technically theirs is not considered an unsuccessful assignment by company standards, Julie knows deep in her heart that the China relocation has been a massive failure. What's more, there had been nothing to suggest that moving to Beijing would be any different from moving to Seattle, or Amsterdam. The first 6 months in China had passed by with relatively minor hiccups, or so they thought. There were a few typical culture shocks and stresses: for example, setting up a new home in an "expat compound" and acclimatizing to the ever-present pollution. Jonathan settled into his new role as Regional Vice President; the children into theirs at Dulwich College; and Julie in her part-time job at the subsidiary office of The MI Group, the global relocation firm she had worked for in Holland. Although her position was not full-time, she was hopeful that in time it would become a more permanent role.

Although they did not initially see the signs, the first appearance of trouble arose during the initial weeks of the relocation itself. Moves to China relied almost exclusively on local HR support, and the problems were immense: local HR's poor English; a US-centric company relocation policy incapable of meeting their unique China needs (e.g. the non-provision of a car and driver, given that for safety reasons the company did not permit employees to own a car or to drive in China); and no resources to help the family secure necessary vaccinations to guard against rabies and Japanese encephalitis, serious local threats to their health and safety. There was also the matter of Jonathan being denied company reimbursement for the customs duty on their household goods shipment, an unexpected local levy amounting to US$8200.

As the months progressed, daily life for the Fletchers became increasingly difficult. Sourcing local healthy food that had not been contaminated or tampered with became a major challenge, and Julie spent a lot of time searching out groceries from expensive stores. Spitting and sanitation problems were very common, particularly in public places. Wherever they went, the children were stared at and photographed by the locals, which was unsettling and made them reluctant to leave their compound. While the compound itself was an expatriate "bubble" that afforded a higher standard of living relative to the local population, it also meant the families living there were cut off from the rest of society.

Unexpectedly, Jonathan's new role required extensive regional travel. Unlike the situation in Seattle and Amsterdam, where Jonathan had had local roles, in Beijing he had an Asia Pacific role covering 14 countries. Travel within Asia kept him away from home for most of the week. Business trips to US headquarters took place quarterly, meaning more missed weekends and jet lag. The extent of his travel forced Julie into a "solo parenting" situation, making her lonely and resentful, and giving her an overwhelming "home versus work" juggling act, all the while in a foreign country. Although the family had hired a part-time Chinese "ayi" (maid) to help combat the lack of family support, language remained a significant barrier, and the care of their children fell exclusively to Julie.

Nothing, however, prepared the Fletchers, 6 months after they arrived in Beijing, for two medical emergencies. First, with Jonathan away, one of their sons suffered an allergic reaction to a prescribed antibiotic which turned out to have been from a "fake" batch sourced locally, with unknown side effects, including a type of asthma attack. Julie's late-night dash to the emergency room through chaotic traffic in a dirty Chinese taxi, cradling her son while the other watched in horror, followed by the language difficulties upon arrival at the hospital, was a nightmare. She realized that although Beijing boasted a well-staffed "international medical center" for the exclusive use of expatriate clientele, the system was relatively inept.

In the second emergency, the Fletchers' other son was bitten by a neighbor's dog adopted from a local animal shelter, but Julie was skeptical that the rabies vaccine they had obtained when they arrived was genuine. Knowing that her son might need a blood transfusion and that China's blood supply was not screened for major diseases such as HIV and hepatitis, she made the decision to forego local treatment and instead flew with her son to Hong Kong. The logistics of this situation were another nightmare: Jonathan was away, the healthy child at home needed care to attend school, and Julie might be in Hong Kong for weeks. Because there was no provision in the relocation policy for medical emergencies, local HR support was of little help. In the end, Julie's 71-year-old mother made a mercy dash to Beijing from her home in Ireland to care for the family during this time.

As the months went by, Julie felt emotionally, psychologically, and physically exhausted from her husband's continual absence, the constant juggling of children with job, and the lack of any "safety net" should things again go wrong. She hardly saw Jonathan anymore and her marriage had taken a real beating. She thought, "When did I sign up for this kind of life?" Although she knew it was not Jonathan's fault, her resentment toward him had deepened to anger that she felt ill-equipped—and too tired—to address. After 2 years in China, she felt sure she could not endure a third.

Sensing her despair, Jonathan urged her to take some time for herself and to re-energize with extended family by attending a week-long work conference in the UK. But whilst there, Julie was unexpectedly offered, through a former consulting contact, the job of her dreams: a fulltime job at a global consulting firm with an office and salary to match. And in *Dublin*, her hometown! It was too good an opportunity to turn down. But accepting it would require that the family repatriate. Would Jonathan go along with it?

After much discussion, Julie and Jonathan agreed that their lifestyle in China was no match for the one they could have back in Ireland. But Jonathan was contractually obligated to his Beijing job for another 12 months, and as the breadwinner, he earned many times Julie's prospective salary. Furthermore, he had been classed as a "high-potential" employee and earmarked for two subsequent international relocations, most likely to Sao Paulo for the next 3-year assignment, and then to a Global VP role at the new Silicon Valley headquarters. With a bit of luck, he was planning to be in the job of *his* dreams in 4 years time, and he needed Julie's support to make it a reality. There was no chance of him causing the assignment to fail or wrecking his reputation with the company and such a glittering future by leaving Beijing a year early.

Julie was fed up at having sacrificed her career for someone else's. As to the future, she had little more to go on than "maybe" Sao Paulo and "possibly" Silicon Valley: MNCs, she had found, often talked about likely career paths for expatriates, but equally often changed their plans at the last moment. After some thought, the Fletchers reluctantly made the very difficult decision for Julie to accept the Dublin job and to repatriate with the children, leaving Jonathan behind in China. "International assignments need to benefit everyone in our family," Julie told her husband, "not just one person." Because it was not a separation or divorce (which company policy provided for), but instead a reality check that Julie felt she and Jonathan both needed, his company would not pay for the repatriation nor support their commuting expenses. This added an additional financial burden to the emotional toll the split assignment had placed on them.

Further compounding Julie's distress was her guilt about separating the children from their father. She had had contingency plans for him losing his job, her parents dying, or the family needing to be evacuated, but had never thought she needed a plan for this. She was unsure whether her husband might one day re-join the family in Dublin, but also knew that it had to be his decision, not hers, to give up or suspend his global career, even temporarily, to allow her to pursue her own dreams.

For now, Jonathan will commute to Dublin twice a month. But the questions remain: Will he be as effective as he could be if his family was in Beijing? What will happen when his proposed move to Sao Paulo becomes imminent? Will the Fletchers ever have a family life again, or has expatriation shattered it forever?

The Dual-Career Dilemma

For more than 25 years, the dual-career issue has been the most common cause of assignment refusal, and a major factor hindering trailing spouses' adjustment.[11] It's easy to see why the dilemma exists. Expatriates represent an organization's most highly educated and intelligent employees. The majority of expatriates are males who typically marry partners with a similar background to themselves, with careers and strong notions of female independence. For example, in our TS Study more than 80% of trailing spouses had a tertiary or college education and 79% had a career prior to relocating. Yet only 36% were able to continue their career once relocated. Brookfield reported similar findings.[12] The problem then is how to incentivize employees and their partners to expatriate when only one of them is being recruited for their professional skills and the other will likely end up in a "hobby" career or job to pass the time.

As we saw earlier in the case of Julie Fletcher, a trailing spouse's abandonment of, or interruption to, her career can lead to a loss of power, identity, and self-worth.[13] Although research on the smaller population of male trailing spouses (tracking at between 10 and 15%) is limited,[14] there is every reason to believe that the dual-career issue for men is even more critical, not because they are necessarily uncomfortable with their role but because people around them find it difficult to understand their status.[15]

The participants in our TS Study reported some serious outcomes from dual-career problems, for example, a strong urge to return home, high stress levels, over-dependence on anti-depressants, addiction to alcohol, and even potential suicide cases. The positive effects of paid employment for trailing spouses are equally clear. The Permits Foundation reports that employed trailing spouses perceive that working during an assignment has a positive impact on their adjustment, family relationships, health and well-being, as well as willingness to complete and to extend their current assignment and to go on a new one.[16]

The Permits Foundation is an international non-profit corporate initiative to promote access of accompanying spouses and partners of international staff to employment through an improvement of work permit regulations. More than 40 major international organizations worldwide have joined the foundation to encourage governments to relax work permit regulations that currently make it difficult for spouses to work in many countries. As expatriate dual careers increase, work permit barriers inhibit not only trailing spouse adjustment, but also employee diversity and mobility.

The Permits Foundation has already contributed to change in France, the Netherlands, and the United States. It is currently promoting improvements in other countries in Europe, has started to develop networks in Asia, and is working to raise awareness of this issue world-wide. The foundation corresponds with government ministries and agencies directly and/or through local networks of interested bodies.

Governments increasingly recognize the importance of dual careers in making their countries attractive trade and investment destinations. These successes are based on the Permits Foundation's initiatives to:

- make representations to host governments to liberalize business-related work permit legislation to allow accompanying expatriate spouses to participate freely in local employment markets;
- seek and co-ordinate support from national governments and international organizations;
- share best practices and news of progress;
- raise awareness through conferences and seminars;
- encourage debate by preparing briefing materials for selected media.

In this way, the Permits Foundation continues to help spouses of all nationalities to maintain and develop skills during expatriation and facilitates re-integration to their home-country.

www.PermitsFoundation.com

Our own research shows that expatriates and their spouses highly value dual-career support in areas such as outplacement, career guidance and counseling, and education reimbursement, assistance to obtain a work permit, and professional contacts. They do not see cash allowances to be of much benefit.

Marital Stress

International assignments can take a toll on marriages. In our TS Study, 6% of trailing spouses indicated that they were considering separating or divorcing because of the stress of relocating. In comparison, 99% rated "a strong and stable relationship" as the most important adjustment factor during an international assignment. The "Family Matters" survey similarly found that "marital breakdown" was reported by nearly 70% of expatriates and their spouses as the most important reason why relocations fail.[17]

Stories abound about expatriate husbands whose wives discover a local mistress or rampant infidelity, and who then repatriate and divorce them. *The Telegraph* claimed that 445 foreign couples living in Dubai ended their marriages in 2011, a 30% rise on 2009.[18] Fact or fiction? While we may never know for sure because for a long time expatriate marriage has been a taboo subject, even among trailing spouses, Canadian Robin Pascoe in her book, *A Moveable Marriage: Relocate Your Relationship Without Breaking It*, is the first to bring it into the public domain and to delve deeper.[19] She found that trailing spouses are just as likely to be as unfaithful as their employed husbands, but for different reasons: whereas unfaithful men typically have the opportunity to stray "thrown at them" in the anonymity of business trips, unfaithful wives more often seek emotional support in new relationships because of their absent husbands.

In our own research,[20] we found that many female trailing spouses felt their marital needs were trivialized by their husbands because they were perceived to be on holiday, having "a cook, a maid, and a driver and you get to do whatever you want at any time of the day." One very candid participant revealed that,

> The breaking up of marriages is dealt with like an embarrassing individual failure and the more than 50 percent [of] separations and divorces are simply ignored. The rest of these marriages [are] having affairs or uncontrolled eating, shopping, drinking, suicidal attacks, depression, drug abuse, you name it. After two different spouse support groups, I have seen it all!

As we saw with the Fletchers, marital problems can result from a divergence of priorities among couples as the number of assignments increases and as high-level careers advance. Some expatriates learn by hard experience. For example:

> Having already lost one family basically because of expat work, I'm sure as hell not going to lose my next one. So lesson learnt if you will on that one.

Even though my first marriage didn't work out, I think as you get older family becomes a lot more important to you. Earlier in my career I would be a little bit more risky, I would accept more challenging assignments, to the consequence of the marriage unfortunately. I had to learn the hard way but unfortunately that's what I did ... quite a lot [of colleagues] have similar experiences, but having been able to hold onto their first marriage they have consequently become far more family central in what they're trying to do and what they're thinking about for the future. I didn't get that until it was too late.

One male participant in our Expat Study suggested that the stage of family life is a particularly delicate issue. His wife, having recently waved off their youngest child to university after relocating for 20 years with four children in tow, told him that she, too, was heading back to the UK to begin studying for her doctorate. Rather than divorce, he convinced her to agree to live apart—she in their home country, and he in Thailand—until they could figure out "what next." Such stories are not uncommon. A 2011 Brookfield report showed a steady rise in "split" assignments, where 39% of single-status assignees on long-term assignments were surmised to be married employees whose spouse was reluctant to sacrifice a second income and the family support network in order to relocate. While technically such assignments do not appear on the mobility manager's radar as "assignment refusal" or "assignment failure," it nonetheless implies that companies can be affected by marital issues.

Expatriate divorce is devastating to all concerned, with HR departments often being required to help assignees and their spouses obtain competent legal advice. The distraction of divorce is likely to have strong crossover effects on expatriates' work, thus impacting on eROI. Additionally, it can be difficult to determine which country will have jurisdiction, and divorce settlements, too, can vary considerably from one country to another,[21] thereby creating further stress. For example, an expatriate wife holding a UK passport in Singapore must be resident there for 3 continuous years or longer to allow Singapore jurisdiction to deal with the divorce. Similarly, an expatriate wife in Denmark can be awarded maintenance under Danish law for only 1 or 2 years. Custody battles also require great care, as recently seen in the Australian press.[22]

Organizational Support

Expatriates and their families typically face huge relocation challenges: spouse employment, new cultures, languages, locations, homes, schools, and networks. And there is no handbook for "how to do" expatriate marriage or dual careers. Families literally make it up as they go. As we saw with the Fletchers, family expatriation is one of the hardest things to build a skill set for, and because of this, expatriates and their families tend to suffer years of stress, strain, and unhealthy living before it possibly ends in divorce, separation, a split assignment, or failure. If professional intervention is offered before or during the process, perhaps the deterioration can be avoided or reversed. Employing organizations can play a part in this.

While company intervention in employees' marriages and spouses' careers is usually neither possible nor welcome, the most helpful way to increase eROI where family is concerned is to provide expatriates with appropriate organizational support. Had the Fletchers been offered the support they needed, perhaps their assignment would not have ended in them being a split family. Without knowing what Jonathan could have achieved had he had his family there, it is impossible to know how much more eROI he could have gained for the company had they remained in China to support him. Subsequent lost eROI when Jonathan moves to Sao Paulo or elsewhere without his family is also impossible to calculate but could be considerable.

ORC found that up to 80% of organizations provide extensive practical support to international assignees, yet only 50% provide support toward the professional integration of the trailing spouse, and fewer than 30% toward the social integration of their families.[23] Furthermore, Cartus and Primacy reported that firms' interest in improving spouse and family assistance is weak and waning.[24] This low prioritization sometimes results in unexpected outcomes, as one mobility manager explains:

> We had a senior manager, [sent] from Brazil to Indonesia, very different cultures, and the individual got very little cultural awareness support before going over there, the family didn't get anything ... [the wife] was very much into her local family and just didn't want to go, wasn't prepared, and it lasted two and a half months.

To counteract such problems, we advocate that organizations provide realistic overviews prior to an assignment to help trailing spouses accurately identify the challenges they might face and personal attributes they may bring to their situation to overcome these challenges. This could be facilitated through coaching, counseling, or the provision of reading material and access to appropriate online resources (for examples, see the "resources" section at the end of this chapter). What is critical is that expatriates are not lied to or misled, specifically about work permit availability for their spouse and living conditions, as these are areas of frequent complaint. Accuracy of information contributes to increased motivation, as well as providing a more solid day-to-day structure for trailing spouses, thus facilitating increased adjustment with respect to the care and maintenance of expatriate families.

In our TS Study we found that the following types of ongoing family support are essential:

Practical support: To assist in the logistics of a relocation, for example, pre-assignment visit to the host location, furniture storage, tax advice, interim accommodation, home-sale assistance, language courses, translation services, cross-cultural training, school orientation and assistance, and immigration paperwork and advice.

Professional support: For the trailing spouse to address the dual-career issue, for example, job search assistance, information about local job opportunities and vacancies, labor market information, career counseling, CV preparation and improvement, work permit assistance, (where appropriate) employment in the host company, advice on tax and pension implications, local interview training, self-employment and business start-up advice, vocational training, and retraining/tuition reimbursement.

Social support: To help alleviate marital stress, for example, introductions to other expatriates, information about and access to expatriate forums, sporting and social clubs, and spouse networking groups, babysitting and childcare resources, and referrals to confidential counseling and therapy.

Table 4.2 summarizes data drawn from our TS Study, ranking the perceived importance of various types of organizational support for the trailing spouse.

Table 4.2. Ranking of Organizational Support in Order of Perceived Importance

Item	Important	Neither important or unimportant	Unimportant	n
Access to technology (email and internet)	95%	4%	1%	261
Finding and/or subsidizing housing	94	5	1	262
Ongoing support after first 3 months	85	9	6	261
Sufficient time for family to adjust	82	14	4	257
Company funded home-country visits	82	13	5	260
Subsidization of family income to compensate decreases	80	15	5	260
Education assistance for trailing spouse	76	18	6	260
Outsourcing relocation program to external vendors	74	20	6	262
Pre-departure training	71	25	4	259
Expatriate employee's availability to assist with relocation	68	11	21	260
Access to a mentoring or coaching program	51	39	10	258
Assistance with finding paid work for the trailing spouse	44	29	27	259
Expatriate employee's work-related travel schedule	43	20	37	262

Like ORC and Cartus,[25] we found in our TS Study that many of these types of support are lacking. Furthermore, the support that was offered was frequently criticized for being inflexible, outdated, and poorly administered by local HR staff. A major improvement at the policy level would be to allow the trade-off of unnecessary allowances against items that are perceived to be more useful, for instance, where a pet-relocation allowance (made available to a family with no pets) could instead be used to ship a piano or to reimburse the cost of buying a pet in the host-location.[26]

In order for expatriate families to obtain the necessary levels of required support, it is essential that HR staff have the right attitude and that expatriates employed by the MNC are proactive in seeking assistance. Findings in our TS Study point to an urgent need for local HR staff, as a necessary prerequisite for working in this field, to have personal relocation experience. A direct communication link is also needed between the company and the trailing spouse. Funneling important documents about a relocation through the expatriate employee, or posting them on an "employee-only" intranet, is too risky as the information often does not make it home. Time free of work for newly arrived expatriates to settle in with their families is also important.

Participants in our Expat and TS Studies also suggested more vacation time for expatriate families, time off during the relocation for the expatriate to help with the move, a reduction in business-related travel during the first month of the assignment, flex-Fridays, accompanying spouses on business trips, company functions for the family, and not scheduling business meetings and conferences during leisure time and on weekends. Organizations need to come to terms with having moved a whole family and not just the employee, and to recognize that they have a responsibility to all the family members they have moved.

To alleviate marital stress, counseling sessions for couples during the selection process, and after relocation if required, can be helpful in terms of outlining possible areas of future conflicts, as well as providing advice on how to deal with them in a foreign location. Having in place an *Employee Assistance Program* (EAP),[27] an outsourced and confidential service that offers counselors to assist employees and their household members with personal issues, can be particularly useful in many locations.

The Global Family Skill Set

We want to end this chapter by discussing the "global family skill set." Many families have it, many do not want it, and some, like the Fletchers, attempt to develop it but often don't succeed. What is it, and why is it so crucial to eROI?

The Fletchers' ability to relocate for Jonathan's company over 10 years across developed and emerging markets—with children—is an endeavor few families are willing to undertake, and a skill set even fewer families can successfully master. When they do, the benefits that companies reap from these relatively well-adjusted and *willing* global nomads are enormous. So, although it has not yet worked out favorably for this particular family, it might have done if company support had been better, and the family—with better advice and assistance from Jonathan's employer—had put in place some key structures to support their mobile lifestyle, things like more family support at home (perhaps a live-in maid or two part-timers, or company-funded extended visits by Julie's mother), an improved medical plan for emergencies, a dedicated car and driver, and a more reasonable travel schedule for Jonathan.

What is absolutely clear is that family issues have implications for eROI, not just in terms of benefits but also on the cost side. The challenges associated with spouse's career, identity, and adjustment, along with issues related to children, health, and marital fidelity and happiness can break an expatriate and wreck his or her eROI. These costs are not just felt by the company, but also personally in individual ROI gains and losses. It goes without saying that MNCs have a moral as well as a business obligation to do what they can to support expatriates and their families.

The reality, however, is that many companies either do not sufficiently acknowledge expatriate family issues, or worse, do little about them even when the problems are evident and escalating. We suggest then, that when family problems are added to the ROI equation, it may sometimes be better for an organization to find another global staffing solution that does not involve traditional expatriation of the type we see with the Fletcher family. Alternatively, sourcing expatriates with the "global family skill set" is one way to reduce the risks associated with family expatriation, because the experience and stability that global careerists and their families bring to an organization is an extremely valuable commodity that can increase a firm's competitive advantage.

Summary

In this chapter we have shown that expatriation often brings unanticipated changes to living conditions that place special pressures on spouses and children that can be hard to adapt to. Decades of research, including our own, show that situational factors are important considerations for expatriate families, for example, dual-career status, prior expatriate experience, and the stage of family life-cycle. Trailing spouses often experience an acute loss of identity, particularly when expatriation interrupts their careers and they are forced to replace it with a "hobby" job or unpaid charity work resulting in being financially dependent on their partners. And although not openly talked about, depression, addiction, and marital break-up are not uncommon outcomes.

While the building of "portable careers" and other types of proactive adjustment can be used to counteract these challenges, the problems can nonetheless be immense and sometimes unsolvable in eROI terms, as we saw with the Fletchers. Organizations can play a critical role in supporting expatriate families by providing effective social, professional, and practical support, by demonstrating a "can-do" attitude, and by providing a direct communication link with family members as they transition across countries and cultures.

Resources

Bryson, D., & Hoge, C. (2005). *A portable identity: A woman's guide to maintaining a sense of self while moving overseas.* Glen Echo, MD: Transition Press International.

Heinzer, J. (2009). *Living your best life abroad: Resources, tips and tools for women accompanying their partners on an international move.* USA: Summertime Publishing.

Pollock, D., & Van Reken, R. (2009). *Third culture kids: Growing up among worlds.* Boston, MA: Nicholas Brealey Publishing.

Parfitt, J. (2013). *A career in your suitcase* (4th ed.). London, UK: Summertime Publishing.

Martins, A., & Hepworth, V. (2011). *Expat women confessions: 50 answers to your real-life questions about living abroad.* Cotton Tree, QLD: Expat Women Enterprises.

www.NetExpat.com

www.ExpatBookshop.com

www.ExpatWomen.com

www.PermitsFoundation.com

www.Primetime.org.sg

www.SpousesWithoutBorders.com

CHAPTER 5

Global Careers

Is somebody sitting down with me and doing career planning? There may be, but they 'ain't talking to me. I think it's part of the culture of the organization. You're as good as your last project. I don't think sending people on assignment is in some cases linked to career progression. It's more or less, well there's a hole and just put somebody in there.

—Senior Vice President, 45 years, Asia Pacific

Forget repatriation. The world is now a giant employment pool, where international experience acquired through continuous global mobility is a critical asset. Talent shortages are the norm, and those with talent willing to move across geographical borders are in demand. Expatriate careers may not be new, but how they unfold, what they represent, and what individuals do with them is rapidly changing. Gone is the notion of "organizational expatriates" directed by companies to work in emerging economies. In its place are "global careerists" who choose *where* to work as much as who to work *for*. "Talent flows" are the new normal, where the poaching ("buying") of high-potential staff *from* competitors is frequently balanced by the simultaneous loss of talent *to* them in a revolving door of entrances and departures. "Building talent" among existing employees may make sense too, but is also compromised by "brain drain" and "brain gain." What does it mean for eROI? It means plenty.

In this chapter, we explore why people pursue global careers, including new forms of careers, such as "self-initiated expatriation" and "boundaryless global careers." Drawing on data from our Expat Study, we will show that there is frequently a mismatch between the career expectations of expatriates and the objectives of employers, and the implications that arise from that mismatch. We offer organizations guidelines for effective career support.

Careers in Today's World

People's careers are very important to them. While "jobs" bring the potential for material gain, security, and social relationships, "careers" bring more, including esteem, status, and fulfillment. Careers involve not just the present, but the past and the future. Careers extend across our lives as a series of linked experiences, a developing story where each chapter sets the scene for the next. Into our careers we invest personal resources—our motivation, energy, qualifications, expertise, experience, and networks—and from our career experiences we expect to reap a return on investment of personal "capital."[1] While the organization values eROI, the individual values "iROI"—individual return on investment.

Global careerists, like other employees, are constantly thinking in career terms: "How does each experience, each crossing of an international boundary, each project, each new contact, build my resources and get me where I want to be? What is my career return on this investment? And not just the immediate return—but the *long-term* return?" They find international work intellectually and culturally interesting, work across multiple cultures simultaneously, have a "permanent commitment to working in an international context,"[2] and draw global competencies and marketability from the global economy as well as their current employer.[3]

Global careerists may be young or old, managerial or non-managerial, Western or Eastern, male or female, married or single, heterosexual or gay. There is no perfect stage of life or career to pursue a global career. Indeed, those who least expect a global career can find themselves drawn into one. In our Expat Study, the unlikeliest expatriates had global careers—a family man with five children, a bachelor in his sixties, a single-parent female breadwinner, a divorcee, a lesbian partnership, and many with step-families.

Global careers do not just "happen." Some expatriates find themselves in global careers at the behest of their companies; others actively plan and manage, often well in advance, their next international career move. To illustrate how global careers unfold, let's take a look at Simon's story.

CASE: Compulsive Globe-Trotter

Simon Haig, a 47-year-old Englishman, migrated to Montreal in his early twenties, a starting point, he hoped, for "seeing the world." An architect by profession and self-employed, Simon moved after a few years—and a marriage to Swedish gym instructor Anneke, and twin daughters—into IT with Oracle, a US-based MNC, partly because of its better opportunities for overseas work. Transfers followed, first to corporate HQ in San Francisco, then to India, and then a regional VP role in South-East Asia, from a Singapore base.

"My bosses knew, very early on, that I was willing and ready to move for the right opportunity. I was then much more aware of the opportunities when they did arise. In reality, Anneke and I first decide we will move, and then I work with the company to put the job in place to make it possible for me to live and work wherever it might be."

But having been a willing participant in building a 9-year "organizational career" with Oracle, Simon noted that his company had been calling all the shots and he "missed the freedom to direct and control where I might go and what I might do next." With tightening budgets and hiring-freezes, Simon also felt that it was getting harder and harder to secure promotions.

In Asia, his luck changed. With a newly acquired "Personal Employment Pass" issued by the Singapore authorities that did not tie Simon's residency to any one employer, he resigned from Oracle to take up a locally based Managing Director position with SAP, a role that he relished for the next 6 years. Then the old wanderlust got to him (and Anneke), and curious about China, he moved to a new employer—a Chinese-owned IT firm—where, as President Asia, he runs all of the company's operations from its Shanghai headquarters. Fluent in Mandarin, and with three bilingual daughters, Simon is nonetheless ready to move again, this time to Seoul, South Korea, to take up a position with yet another IT company.

Such a high level of mobility obviously has its drawbacks, not in the least the lack of permanency for his family and the constant change in environment every few years. But Simon loves new cultures. "I get bored easily, and moving around every few years makes life much more interesting."

The secret to his success, he says, is family support. Anneke shares his passion for travel and is willing to be flexible in her own career choices. Further, his large salary enables them to afford the expat life they desire, even, in this case, paying for their own housing and children's education.

Like many global careerists, Simon walks a fine line balancing career aspirations, personal relationships, and the desire for travel: his self-starter personality has brought him a level of global career success that few can equal, and in each company he works for, his status as a valued member of an organization provides security and structure.

Careers for Women Expatriates

Gender diversity has been shown as a corporate performance driver,[4] particularly during expatriation.[5] Yet in pursuit of global careers, women expatriates tend to face far more barriers than their male counterparts,[6] despite their increasing rate of overall employment.[7] While the pace of women sent on international assignments has increased over the last two decades, the proportion of the total has remained static at 17–20%,[8] suggesting that there may be a glass ceiling for women with global career ambitions. Many female candidates are denied global career opportunities because of personal and family issues.[9] Female expatriates with equal tenure and/ or prior expatriate experience tend to occupy lower positions and get less access to fast-track career programs, career counseling, and career planning.[10] Other problems can arise in creating options for the accompanying male trailing spouse or in finding countries that are appealing to females in terms of cultural mores and political risk.[11] Lesbians can find themselves in a "double minority," that is a gender *and* sexual orientation minority.[12]

Barriers aside, some researchers note that women represent up to half of those who self-initiate expatriation for work.[13] US researcher Charlie Vance found that female American expatriates in Europe were predominantly SIEs that worked in their own or local businesses, whereas men largely worked as traditional CAEs.[14] Thus, women who self-initiate global career opportunities and rely on self-managing the development of their own international careers are probably more likely to succeed as global careerists than those pursuing "organizational careers."

Why People Pursue Global Careers

What drives a global career? Professional and personal aspirations, supply of and demand for one's occupation, family and personal life, politics, personal finances, personality, and the global economy itself are all competing priorities. UK researchers Michael Dickmann and Noelene Doherty observe that a key factor in motivating international careers is "symbolic capital," wherein global mobility provides employees with a special kind of legitimacy regarding their contribution to a particular company, an industry, or the national or global economy itself.[15] Such symbolic capital includes authority, knowledge, prestige, and reputation that can be leveraged personally as iROI, as well as organizationally as cROI, giving the employee sought-after individual status as a self-styled member of the "jet set," or, more importantly, as a "high-potential" member of a talent management program.

What other capital do global careerists acquire? It includes global business understanding, cross-cultural sensitivity and competence, leadership development across diverse backgrounds, the ability to deal with global integration and co-ordination, foreign languages, and increased labor market value. Global careerists also acquire "social capital": network relationships that are international in scope thereby facilitating access to knowledge and opportunities helpful to their global careers.[16]

But global careers are not just determined by physical mobility. They also reflect *psychological* mobility,[17] involving "personal agency": such careerists expect high outcomes and are proactive in directing their career in order to achieve their goals. If they also work in organizations with an international focus and have few barriers to international experience (e.g. children with particular medical or educational needs, or partners with inflexible careers), then they are more likely to become serial expatriates and/or global careerists.[18]

Reviewing the careers reported by the expatriates in our Expat Study we find, however, that there is no one "type" of global careerist, no single "profile" of a person pursuing an international career. Some global career-ists are "born" (much like Simon in our earlier case), whereas others are "made";[19] some "pushed" (by negative experiences in their situation) and others "pulled" (by positive opportunities in a different environment) onto the international labor market.[20] Each has unique circumstances, attitudes, personality, and opportunities, creating a major challenge for companies in pursuit of eROI: to figure out each global careerist's motives and long-term objectives, and to collaborate with them in developing career opportunities to mutual advantage.

Global careerists are increasing in number: Like Simon, they are empowered at a young age and confident about their worth on the inter-national labor market. They take risks, and they are often driven by com-peting priorities of career, romance, travel, and personal opportunity. They can also be hard to find, hard to reach, and hard to engage, mostly because they do not advertise to all and sundry who they are and what they do; part of their success lies in their ability to "blend in" while simul-taneously seeking new opportunities their colleagues are unaware of. That companies like Oracle and SAP provide flexible work contracts to retain employees like Simon is helpful: if they didn't, Simon—and many others like him—would leave sooner rather than later.

But are all employees as proactive and open about their career ambi-tions as people like Simon? As we discovered during our Expat Study, not everyone pursuing a global career starts out wanting one, and this has major implications for eROI.

The Different Types of Global Careers

Global careers run the gamut from "company slave" to "free agent." What matters is not just the type of global career expatriates are pursuing, but whether their managers and mobility managers understand their career orientations and goals.

Global careers, as well as including various numbers of international boundary-crossings, are made up of two types of career moves—those that are *company-initiated* and those that employees *self-initiate*. The differences are shown in Table 5.1.

Company-assigned expatriates (CAEs) have been the mainstay of mobility programs for decades. Many CAEs are committed to their

Table 5.1. *Different Types of International Careers*[21]

	Company-assigned expatriates (CAEs)	**Self-initiated expatriates (SIEs)**
Initiated by	MNC	Individual
Reason	Company projects (specific)	Personal development (diffuse)
Funded by	Company expenses and salary	Personal savings and casual earnings
Career type	Organizational career	Boundaryless career
Known as	PCNs	TCNs

organization, bound by personal values of loyalty and security, and an employment contract that provides a generous salary, and in return are grateful for being offered an international career opportunity. CAEs are typically willing to allow the company, in exchange for a "safety net" of salary, benefits, and (if required) repatriation, to direct their international moves according to its needs. They thereby surrender a significant degree of control over their career progression to the organization, with their career moves unfolding in a single employment setting.[22] CAEs' deep company knowledge, long-term retention and career development often generates substantial long-term eROI.

Self-initiated expatriates (SIEs) enter the international labor market without company support, and forage, either before or after relocating, for such jobs as they can get.[23] Risk-takers by nature, they forego company "safety nets" and instead assert sole ownership of their international careers and make their own decisions regarding which locations to work in and which companies to work for.[24] Rather than being "organizational," their careers are "inter-organizational" and they pursue job opportunities as free agents and contractors. They can, and often do, provide substantial eROI to organizations, but it tends to be restricted to only the job they are employed to do now.

It is helpful to think of these two types of global careers as situated on a continuum. Between the "pure" types of CAE and SIE careers situated at extreme ends of the continuum (see Figure 5.1), many global careers will contain elements of both, although one will likely dominate. For example, an ostensible "loyal company servant" (CAE) may well initiate his or her moves through requests and applications, and may, like Eduardo (in Chapter 3), harbor an inner wish to "go it alone" when the time is right. Correspondingly, an SIE may eventually, in his or her travels, find a comfortable niche in a particular organization, staying there long enough to get promoted and perhaps even to undertake a move to a new location with that company. No employee is ever purely a corporate pool ball, able to be moved around at the company's whim indefinitely. Self-direction plays a part in every career move, and companies ignore individual career goals at their peril.

Figure 5.1. Global careers continuum.

While on the surface there may appear to be little difference between CAEs and SIEs, a simple distinction is that while both types of global careers entail movement across national borders and draw career validation from outside one particular country, self-initiated global careers are sustained by a continuing boundaryless future regardless of organizational membership, whereas company-assigned global careers are constrained by that same organizational tie.[25] As such, the motives for pursing CAE versus SIE are different. And it is these differences that create problems for MNCs.

Career Anchors

Career anchors are individuals' self-concepts of perceived abilities, basic values, and motives and needs as they pertain to a career, which evolve as a person gains life and occupational experience.[26] Career anchors concern such things as "technical competence" and "entrepreneurial creativity" that provide career direction. Recent research suggests that increasing numbers of individuals have an "internationalism" career anchor that involves an intrinsic, long-held desire to live and work in international environments and that this is a "built-in" preference that typically predates any international assignment experience.[27] American researcher Charlie Vance found in a study of 48 American expatriates in five major cities in East Asia that more than half had engaged in early self-initiated career strategies and activities during childhood or tertiary education for gaining valuable international experiences and as a means of preparing them for future expatriate experiences.[28]

An internationalism career anchor is important because it helps to explain why some people pursue global careers and others do not. But beyond establishing that expatriates possess this characteristic, there is the more compelling question as to why, if there are variable rates of return to be derived from a range of global career actors, organizations are still heavily focused on utilizing predominantly CAEs and to a much lesser extent the potentially higher returning SIEs? Further, what does it mean for eROI if one starts out as a CAE and becomes an SIE, or vice versa?

Changing Career Orientation

Under certain conditions, expatriates have the capacity to alter their career orientation, from CAE to something quasi-SIE. We illustrate this in Figure 5.2.

Conversely, and more rarely, some expatriates can shift from SIE to quasi-CAE status if circumstances dictate or an opportunity too good to pass up arises (illustrated in Figure 5.3).

Figure 5.2. Changing career orientation—from CAE to quasi-SIE.

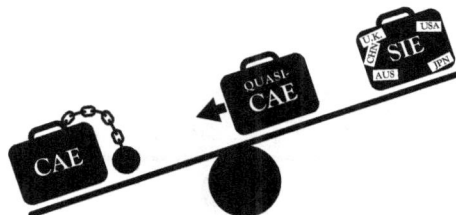

Figure 5.3. Changing career orientation—from SIE to quasi-CAE.

These shifts in career orientation take individuals to a place on the global career continuum that is not exclusively CAE nor SIE but somewhere in the middle, giving CAEs shifting to quasi-SIE status the freedom to explore new career choices without necessarily giving up the security of the MNCs employment benefits. For SIEs shifting to quasi-CAE status, there can sometimes be compelling circumstances, such as a special medical or educational need for a family member that necessitates a deep level of temporary organizational support.

In our Expat Study, we found it was far more common for CAEs to move part way along the global career continuum toward quasi-SIE status (i.e. Figure 5.2) than for SIEs to do the reverse (i.e. Figure 5.3). Further, while the shift to quasi-CAE status was almost always a temporary state of affairs for SIEs, CAEs in contrast viewed their shift to quasi-SIE status as nearly always a permanent move. This is because, to quote our participants, acquiring a "free agent" and "entrepreneurial" attitude about one's career is somewhat addictive: once (in their words) "my relationship with [the company] has matured" and "I've lost some of that naivety," employees are "not scared about leaving" because they have "learned quickly that loyalty to companies is actually not that important or that helpful." Many CAEs described their change in career orientation as being similar to "flicking on a switch"; once they had acquired the confidence and maturity to see their value on the international labor market, they could not—and would not—turn off the switch and go back to permanent CAE status.

The nature of these changes in career orientation leads us to label this middle ground on the global career continuum an "SIE orientation," which we depict in Figure 5.4.

Our use of the term "SIE orientation" departs from the existing view of expatriates as being in fixed categories: CAE *versus* SIE. The SIE orientation emerges in CAEs out of a combination of individual motiva-

Figure 5.4. SIE Orientation on the global careers continuum.

tions, company management processes, and labor market opportunities, with many CAEs changing their orientation because they feel compelled to consider the international labor market for career progression. They may not have intentionally set out to pursue global careers, or to become quasi-SIE, but once in the international labor market they tend to remain there because they gain immense benefit from doing so.

Further complicating matters is that one's career orientation can be dynamic, shifting over time from company-assigned to self-initiated tendencies and back again, as international experience increases and life circumstances change. This happens because mobility is influenced by a range of factors that combine but vary according to expatriates' age, stage of career, gender, family concerns, and assignment location.[29] Consequently, as priorities in their professional and personal lives change, career orientations also change so that at any moment a variety of factors may drive employee decisions about where they sit on the global career continuum.

Unfortunately, the shift by expatriates into a "no man's land" on a continuum between the categories of CAE and SIE is one that many companies are ill-equipped to cope with. Organizations tend to view expatriates in a somewhat rigid way, labeling them as either CAE (PCN) *or* SIE (TCN), with no wiggle room in between, and subsequently managing them according to a fixed, immovable status. The consequent ineffective management of expatriates may serve to further push them away—often permanently—from "pure" CAE status.

What, then, causes changes in career orientation for expatriates such that in knowing what these factors are companies are better able to manage expatriates with greater effectiveness?

Push Versus Pull Factors in Global Careers

To explain why expatriates change their career orientations we need to understand the push and pull factors that can cause movement along the global career continuum, most of which are linked to "individual ROI."

CAEs *pulled* from a CAE position toward an SIE orientation often do so because of their intentional individual decision to undertake career changes with multiple firms as part of a career path linked to personal and professional development. Although they may start out as CAEs, their SIE orientation may have been hidden from a company, whose subsequent offer of an international assignment then becomes an opportunistic launching pad for an international career. In other instances, an SIE orientation may develop during an international assignment where assuming expatriate status becomes such an "obvious part of their life that they cannot imagine any other kind of career."[30] In these circumstances, there is little that companies can do about it, other than to manage the competing priorities between itself and the assignee.

On the other hand, CAEs *pushed* toward an SIE orientation do so because they perceive their only choice is to begin self-initiating their own global career opportunities. In our Expat Study, the single most important factor creating a push toward an SIE orientation was a *lack of career management support*. Frustrations with career development opportunities in their current companies lead many expatriates to feel forced to self-initiate external job opportunities in order to advance their careers or to retain some control over it.

Obvious career issues emerge, from career decisions (in the words of some Expat Study participants) "being made at two or three o'clock in the morning in a bar," and there is also the problem of cronyism and "old boy's networks," seen by many mobility managers and expatriates as a major career enabler, or destroyer.

Our Expat Study and recent consulting work confirm other studies[31] in showing that, in many MNCs, career development and support for expatriates remain an ad hoc and reactive process. "Push" factors begin with failing to engage expatriates in "what's next" discussions as their assignments come to completion. One Expat Study participant talked about having "stumbled through a career … where most of the changes have happened through my own choice but a lot of it has been by chance." Other's talked about people on assignments not being linked to career progression where, "it's more or less, well there's a hole and just put somebody in there." For yet others, there are problems in not having plan B if plan A fails, in the risk of relying on one individual (who may leave or retire) to champion one's career, and the frequent lip service given to meaningful career management where promises and commitments are not honored.

The result of poor career management support is demotivation, unwillingness to "go the extra mile," and increased job searching. What most increases expatriates' willingness to seek other job opportunities is the hampering, by employing companies, of their efforts to build global competencies, a failure to provide long-term global career paths extending them across geographical boundaries, and a focus on repatriation as an end state of their careers.

Career Management Support by Employers

The types of support desired by expatriates represent a practical take on modern careers, where fluidity and flexibility are seen as essential. Consider the perspective of this Senior Executive and the way the talent management program at his global pharmaceutical company is run:

> Two weeks ago I've been interviewed by a headhunter employed by the company, went through interviews with HR people and so on, and then also with the President of Europe, so if you have been identified as a key person in the company then they look after you … they do discuss it with us and they know what my aspirations are … [so] long-term career planning is of paramount importance. This is a big company and we are a fishing pool for other companies who say, "ah ha, that's a very nice one, must be high potential because they've sent him abroad so let's just buy him," and if you're then in the middle of a period where you don't get the career perspective from [the company], you're an easy target.

Career management support for expatriates needs to include the following elements:

Career planning. Global talent review systems are crucial for managing global careerists, enabling all parties to know at what level assignees are operating so that business units can pinpoint people with potential and determine in what roles they should next be considered.

Talent management. It helps for organizations to identify a global talent pool with key positions, including successors for key executive positions, and high potentials. Assignees can then be monitored in terms of what they do, where they're moving to next, and how best to develop them.

Managing expectations. As we explain in the next chapter, expatriates' expectations in relation to global career development are crucial. When expectations regarding what expatriates are prepared to buy into, particularly for global careerists pursuing multiple assignments over many years, are clear from the outset, the commitment and retention rates of assignees are likely to be high.

Fostering committed and motivated assignees. Retaining staff is perhaps the biggest eROI pay-off of all. Well-motivated people, who are on assignments doing the job companies want them to do and who are well received and still considered talented when they come back or move to another assignment, sends a clear message that global careerists are valued and important.

Building relationships. Maintaining contact with assignees who are considered high potential and alerting them to new opportunities usually involves little effort for a substantial return.

Understanding expatriates' needs. When companies seek feedback from expatriates, the focus is all too often on process elements such as relocation assistance and the quality of the repatriation program. Rarely do companies seek feedback as to expatriates' personal satisfaction with an assignment and the outcomes they have derived from it. Questions that matter include whether assignees are happy with their new career? Whether they have plans to stay longer? And whether the assignment has helped their development?

Planning repatriation. Whether an expatriate is repatriating for good or intending to relocate again at some point in the future, the planning of repatriation activities emerged in our Expat Study as a major concern. Best practice for repatriation involves having an assignee pop up on a list 6 months or more before they are due back, and then identifying a job or at the very least entering into a discussion about what could be next. As obvious as this seems, many expatriates worry that they will slip under the radar and be made redundant, or stuck out in limbo because the employer has no jobs on offer. We found that these fears frequently resulted in a strong desire to avoid repatriation altogether and instead to re-assign to anywhere but "home," thus further pushing expatriates along the global career continuum to an SIE orientation.

Top management support. When top management does not support global career activities, expatriates *know.* Supportive senior managers, particularly those with their own global career experience, can therefore be pivotal in sending clear messages that international assignees are valued and that global careers matter, and in encouraging others in the company to focus on improving global mobility and enhancing global career opportunities.

In addition to the above best practices, organizations need to also recognize that some expatriates increasingly undertake "dynamic global careers," wherein repatriating to their home country is but one move that they make as they continue to build career-enhancing competencies. Here, re-thinking repatriation as "relocating back" with a view to expatriating again *after* repatriation, rather than repatriation to "end an international career," is important, along with the idea that for some expatriates a global career never truly ends. The global compensation model we explained in Chapter 3 fits well with the concept of dynamic global careers, where compensation for "international employees" as opposed to "expatriates" can alleviate some of the administrative burden associated with changes in status from the balance sheet to local status and back again once employees re-expatriate.

How Global Careers Affect eROI

Returning for a moment to our global career continuum, let's consider that by the end of an international assignment, or even before, a raw but loyal CAE may become a sophisticated mobile free agent, with obvious implications for long-term eROI as the assignee's employer finds the return on its investment being potentially reaped by another company. This is possible for any employee, not just expatriates, but it is especially important in the case of expatriates because of the much bigger and more unique investment typically made.

Retention can impact on eROI substantially. Given that CAEs maintain more long-term loyalty to their organizations, there is likely to be less eROI gained from short-term "passing through" SIEs than from long-term CAEs who represent a valuable competitive advantage to companies. Companies recognize this too, and in our MM Study, we found that many were heavily focused on improving their repatriation activities for traditional CAEs as a way to increase post-assignment retention.

But as we've shown, retention, especially for SIEs and those with an SIE orientation, is just as important, and in some instances even more important during an assignment than during repatriation. Expatriates of all orientations tend to value their international assignments in career terms: similar to other reports, 65% of participants in our Expat Study believed that undertaking an international assignment played a positive role in their career progression and global career advancement. But like other employees, expatriates operate in an *open labor market.* Over 84% of the Expat Study sample believed that their marketability to *other* employers had increased as a result of undertaking an international assignment, and over 40%, anticipating poor repatriation support and other career problems, were actively engaged in alternative job search activities during their assignments, being willing to change jobs *before the end of their contract* if the right opportunity appeared. Such job search activities include obtaining information about job opportunities, developing networks of contacts about job information, keeping an updated resume, getting external validation of remuneration from outside employers, giving attention to the next position that they desire, being involved in interviews with local or international competitors, considering job offers, or preparing to resign.[32] The following quotes provide examples of this growing problem:

> I got headhunted about six months ago for a job back in [the UK], a really good job and I got down to the final two and I missed it. So if someone comes to talk to me about something then definitely, I'll consider it.

> Absolutely I am seeking external job offers. I'm kind of getting to the point where to make that big jump I have to leave to do that.

I've just handed in my notice. I was head hunted and I've recently accepted, as in only like a few days ago … I missed out on a promotion in February, which I really felt that I deserved. I felt I wasn't getting the reward here … my boss said to me, "hang on, you'll get it next year," but I know I deserved it this year.

As head of this business I get a job offer a week and these range from being head at a big financial institution down to being head in the same industry, to being head at a big corporate. So let me put it this way—I have a standing offer from at least two [competitors] to join them the day I want to join them.

We conclude that expatriate management systems have not been designed or conceptualized to cope with turnover and its immense ramifications at any point other than at repatriation. Indeed, much recent research has been focused on losing global talent only at the point of repatriation.[33] There has been virtually no research on expatriates who leave during an assignment, on the basis that given their distance from the home country, their unfamiliarity with the local culture, and their contractual ties, it is implied that they just would never do so. We know from our Expat Study that this assumption is false because data suggest that the potential "leaver" pool is trending up and could now be as high as 40%, or more. Indeed, Brookfield's latest *Global Relocation Trends* survey reports the main reason for failed assignments as being "expatriates who leave the company during an assignment,"[34] with 19% of MNCs rating it as their top reason. In the context of recent talent shortages this is a very real problem, especially in Asia where there has been a rise in local executive salaries to a point where they now surpass those in Europe.[35]

If eROI is focused predominantly on repatriation, there are likely to be many lost opportunities in leveraging it at other points in time. We therefore believe that retention activities need to shift to another point during expatriation, anywhere but only at the point of repatriation. But what sorts of retention activities should be in place?

To retain expatriates, including global careerists, organizations need to make them committed employees. This can be achieved in a variety of ways such as focusing on the strength of expatriates' ties to colleagues and the job itself. What is the relative ease by which these ties can be broken? What would have to be given up in order for expatriates to leave a job? As we saw in Chapter 3, recent changes in expatriate compensation—from full packages to local-plus—has decreased not only the organizational ties that bind expatriates to their firms, but has reduced the financial sacrifices associated with international job changes, even *during* an assignment. To counteract this, better employment relationships are necessary; something we discuss in more detail in Chapter 6.

Career expectations also need to be met through open communication about opportunities and possibilities. When they are not, iROI is perceived to decline, with loyalty to the company likely to shift to loyalty to oneself. From this we can predict a natural decline in organizational commitment and a shift toward an SIE orientation as an inevitable outcome. Loyalty, then, is important not just in the long-term as we would expect from CAEs willing to undertake multiple assignments, but short-term loyalty as well, to get the job done on *this* particular assignment.

The trend we see here ties in directly to our view that repatriation, both as a measure of eROI and as a retention activity, is often a misguided activity. As we said earlier, *forget about repatriation*, including the recent focus on the repatriation "career wobble" which, in our view, is an outdated model.[36] We say this because our Expat Study shows that many CAEs do not wish to be repatriated, but instead prefer to leverage their career capital in another international assignment: the preferred or expected outcome for nearly 50% of the participants is re-assignment to another location. This may explain why "repatriation support" did not emerge as an area where expatriates were seeking improvements (cited by only 14% of participants), and why the need to avoid repatriation was so strong in comments such as, "repatriation doesn't fit into the scheme of my career," and "I think it's a dumb thing; it's holding me back in my view." One participant explained the futility of repatriation by saying, "the chances of me repatriating would be less than 5% with this company, and yet I'm still being managed as though I will be." Such comments reinforce the message that retention is a "whole assignment" objective, not just an "end of assignment" activity.

Why We Need Global Careerists

An *Economist Intelligence Unit* report in 2010[37] found that organizations view talent management as a key factor in business success (41%, ranked third), but that many remain unconvinced that they have strategies in place to achieve it. While the global war for talent is very real, conventional attempts to win it have failed. MNCs may be winning small battles but are losing the war because they don't understand global careers: why people pursue them, and how they can be leveraged to deliver to them the eROI they seek.

The future of global staffing will depend on global careerists as a valuable source of competitive advantage. Whether pushed or pulled into their career choices, global careerists and those developing an SIE orientation are part of an increasing and irreversible trend, given that more and more people seek "lifetime employability" through the development of global competencies and that the international labor market is able to support such an endeavor.[38] Global careerists will come to dominate the international labor market in the same way that PCNs/CAEs used to a decade ago, bringing with them many benefits.

> ***Global careerists widen the talent pool.*** In the global war for talent, nothing adds more value than finding the right people for the right job at the right time. Companies that need employees with global competencies often struggle to keep pace with the demands placed on them whilst also facing innumerable barriers to mobility among their own staffing pool. Global careerists employed as TCNs or foreign local-hires solve that problem: they represent an available, less expensive source of staff, particularly when deep local or regional knowledge and technical skill is required.
>
> ***Global careerists can cost less.*** It can be cheaper to employ some global careerists than more expensive CAEs because they have fewer ties to a home country. This then avoids having to remunerate them using a balance-sheet approach and makes them far more willing to accept host-based terms and conditions of employment. Being already located where a job vacancy exists, there are fewer relocation costs and other expenses that need to be spent.

Global careerists are willing to move. Global careerists actively seek mobility. They are self-starters, using the international labor market to their own advantage, looking for organizations to help them further their ambitions. If we add to the equation a global careerist with a family that is also willing to move, and which has likely acquired the rare and valuable "global family skill set," then more eROI is likely to accrue.

Global careerists self-manage their careers. Given the poor level of support provided by companies to manage expatriates' careers, it is not surprising that some firms favor individuals who are proactive in planning their own career steps. Global careerists are precisely the type of employees who do this, preferring to take charge of their destiny and be responsible for the development of their own career path. Because they seek psychologically meaningful work, they recognize that career opportunities often exist in inter-company self-development rather than one-company advancement.[39] And recent research shows that whereas organizational career management support and career self-management by the individual might lead to contradiction and conflict, they rather tend to support each other in leading to superior career outcomes.[40]

Global careerists often outperform CAEs. Global careerists' success and enjoyment comes from a genuine interest in how cultures operate, which energizes them (like Simon Haig, in our case). Because they embrace mobility and feel in control of their career, they often face fewer adjustment challenges: they can therefore "hit the ground running" with more ease than CAEs. Because they take risks, they drive innovation and creativity, fresh thinking and new ways of getting things done, often outperforming traditional expatriates. Although they may lack deep knowledge of the organization, they make up for it with deep knowledge of markets or cross-cultural interactions, business relationship building in key markets, or are true globalists who "get" what it is to work across time-zones, cultures, languages, and surrounded by diversity.

Summary

In this chapter, we have focused on global careers as a means by which much eROI can be gained for MNCs. In acknowledging that expatriate careers are not new, but that how they unfold and what people do with them is rapidly changing, we have shown that "organizational expatriates" have been replaced by "global careerists," a new type of international employee whose free agent mentality can have significant implications for global staffing. By exploring in this chapter why people pursue global careers, including "self-initiated expatriation" and "boundaryless global careers," we have shown that the frequent mismatch in expectations between expatriates and their employers can be overcome once the issues are understood. To offer further assistance as to how this can be done, we now move onto Chapter 6 where our focus on employment relationships offers considerable guidance.

CHAPTER 6

Expatriate Psychological Contracts

This has never been a hire and fire firm; it's been a considered, conservative organization which takes its time over building up staff resources, and equally takes its time if staff resources have to be wound down. That I think is part of the psychological contract that exists, and it's not written down anywhere, the mutual understanding between the company and its staff. It's not necessarily always looking up the letter of the law or the letter of the contract, but it tries to absorb some of the spirit of the situation, the spirit of the contract.

—Middle Manager, 39 years, Europe

Every expatriate working for an MNC is an *employee* of, or *contractor to*, that organization and, therefore, in an *employment relationship* with it. The relationship is formalized in an employment contract between organization and individual. The contract contains obligations on each party that are legally binding, specifying such things as the employee's duties and performance standards, his or her reporting relationships within the organization's hierarchy, the salary and conditions to be provided by the employer, and the terms of service. In the case of expatriate employees, as we have seen, some of these factors may be especially complex taking into account compensation plans, family support issues, dual-career challenges, and global career expectations.

But even more important than the legal contract between employer and employee is the *psychological contract.* We all have one, even though few have heard about it or realize how it impacts on their day-to-day working life. This was especially true in our Expat Study: few of the participants had any understanding as to what the psychological contract was, but once explained they readily recognized its nature and importance and spoke candidly about their experiences. Based on our research, we can safely say that the psychological contract is the biggest differentiator for organizations wanting to obtain a satisfactory eROI.

What Is a Psychological Contract?

A psychological contract is an indirect, unwritten, and often unspoken agreement between an employer and employee.[1] It is subjective, defined by the individual within the context of their employment, and *idiosyncratic*, or unique to each employee. The psychological contract represents an exchange agreement: organizations have expectations regarding performance outcomes and other actions from their employees, and employees have reciprocal expectations from employers regarding such things as support, communication, and equity. Because employment relationships can, and do, change, psychological contracts are perpetually evolving.

Psychological contracts can be *relational* or *transactional*, or a combination of both. A relational contract is based on a trusting, long-term relationship between parties: for example, a close employer–employee relationship might be reflected in the mutual (but unwritten) expectation that, provided the employee works hard and remains loyal for many years, he or she could expect to achieve promotion to a higher level, or a substantial gratuity on retirement, even if there has been nothing specifically promised in the written employment contract. A transactional contract, in contrast, is based on the short-term exchange of minor favors: "Yes, I'll put in the extra hours, on the explicit understanding that this is followed by a performance bonus."

In recent years, commentators have noted an insidious change in the nature of psychological contracts: an inexorable trend from relational (and permanent) contracts, to transactional (and temporary) ones. Some organizations bemoan the loss of loyalty by employees who now need a "quid pro quo" to secure their cooperation, just as some ex-employees bemoan the loss of loyalty by former employers, who, in difficult times, ignored their relational contracts and laid them off.

Psychological contracts are important to MNCs because they are critical to gaining the wholehearted effort from expatriates on which mutual success depends. Nothing shakes an expatriate's confidence and commitment like the feeling that his or her trust in the organization has, in a breach of the psychological contract, been betrayed or ignored. In the past three chapters, we have shown that expatriates have high expectations of their employing companies in the areas of compensation, care for their family, and long-term career development. An organization that fails to meet these expectations runs the risk of violating psychological contract fulfillment, often leading to major losses of employee commitment, and thereby of eROI.

In this chapter, we explore psychological contracts between expatriates and their organizations. Based on extensive data from our research and that of others,[2] we explain why psychological contracts are so important, what the psychological contract means to expatriates, and how psychological contract-based "new deals" can be used to get expatriates and their organizations collaborating productively about eROI.

Why Do Psychological Contracts Matter?

Although psychological contracts are not legally binding, their breach nonetheless costs MNCs millions of dollars each year in diminished employee engagement, low morale, and labor turnover. Especially troubling is that many MNCs often do not know that a psychological contract has been breached until an expatriate walks out the door and joins a competitor.

To get an idea of how the psychological contract works, consider the following story by a global careerist in the Middle East.

CASE: Building Relationships One Expatriate at a Time

Jackson Riley is a Canadian political correspondent for a large European news broadcaster, a veteran of 19 years in the field. At 42 years of age, he is on his sixth international assignment, having done "tours of duty" in some of the most dangerous locations imaginable—Somalia, Croatia, and Palestine to name a few—with other visits to "hot spots" such as Bosnia, Macedonia, Kosovo, Haiti, and the Middle East. Being in TV news, Jackson considers himself at the heart of what the company does: making the content on the front line.

Currently on an assignment in Egypt with his family, Jackson thinks that his current assignment—in Cairo in troubled political times—is inevitable. "After nearly 20 years doing this line of work, you do look at your life as a series of stories, and this one, the Middle East, is up there as one of the perennial 'must cover' stories that journalists do."

Jackson is deeply respectful of, and loyal to, his company: "Wherever they need me to go, I'll go. I'm open to pretty much whatever and wherever they need me to be."

Jackson's unique skill-set lies in dealing with hostile environments and diverse groups of people. But his choice of career and his acceptance of third-world locations, and of insecurity and danger, has caused both him and his Israeli-born wife and their two sons considerable hardship. Covering the war in Somalia, for example, brought with it unimaginable suffering from which he was lucky to escape with his life.

> We were asleep in our home, our son was only nine months old, and six local militia men broke into the house, beat me up, and we had a really horrible time of it, it was really rough (and) left me in hospital.
>
> Everyone in the company dropped everything they were doing and were all on the next flight to get to Africa, six or seven senior executives from around the world showed up in a one-week period. And within three months I was in a new job. The company said, 'We know that this isn't going to be easy for you, we admire the job you've done here, but we would quite understand if you wanted to move. Do you want to move?' And I said 'Yeah.' And they said 'Okay, fine, you're off to Paris.' That was them honoring the psychological contract. You know, 'You've put yourself at risk for us, and now we're going to stick our necks out for you.' And that's something that again, it was important, and it felt right.

So in terms of the psychological contract, it really does cement the fact that this company has always felt like a family. But I can see how difficult it would be if that went wrong, if they said 'Sorry to hear about that, but I'm busy with something else, so you handle it.' It felt like they did the right thing by me, and it then increased the motivation ... I have the motivation to actually go out and represent [the company], to not just treat it as a job. That sort of thing really inspires. It really gives you passion.

Jackson's love for his job and loyalty to the company lie mostly in his knowledge that the organization has always been full of professionals who treat each other with respect, and that means something: "If my boss, tells me 'Don't worry, we'll take care of it,' I'm not going to turn around and say 'I want to see that in writing,' because I know that they will."

"I'm doing what I set out to do, which is to travel the world from Afghanistan to Zaire and see incredible things along the way, and meet incredible people and witness incredible events. And then I get to record them for the world. I can't think of anything I would rather have done with my life so far."

Jackson feels that, on the whole, the company takes very good care of him and his family: "I am well paid and well treated. I feel like an adult, and feel that I have responsibilities I am trusted to carry out." But he is quick to point out that, despite his deep loyalty to the organization, he is not a slave who loves the company unconditionally. "They don't always get it right, like the last relocation when the whole accommodation side of things got really out of hand." But in comparing his employer with a previous one who, he says, "let you know very early on in your career that you were an expendable member of staff, and if you didn't want that job there were 30 people out there to replace you ... I wanted to get out of there pretty much within a year or so of starting, and I did. I left as soon I could make it happen. What's important is that I've never felt like that working here. I have put myself into perilous situations on the company's behalf because I see it as the purest journalistic organization out there."

In Jackson's psychological contract, what are his expectations and how does the company meet them?

A big plus is Jackson's evident love for what he does, his pride in performance, and his deep respect for his organization. That's a huge start: MNCs need to select expatriates who will love what the organization asks them to do and be aware that a positive company profile can make up for minor breaches of the contract.

Jackson has a *relational* contract: long-term, based on mutual respect and mutual loyalty, with no thought that any favor given by one side to the other needs to be reciprocated to an equal degree. One can almost feel the binding power of such a relationship.

Jackson's case also highlights a pivotal aspect of psychological contracts—that, through its fulfillment or its breach, it has the potential to substantially improve or harm the employment relationship.

Finally, it is of course not organizations but *people* who make or break psychological contract fulfillment: the senior executives who rushed to Jackson's side in his time of need did so as individuals who made choices about what was important. As another participant in our Expat Study acutely observed:

> My psychological contract isn't so much with the organization as it's with the individuals within it. There's a couple of people in this company I feel I'm morally obligated to, that I'm loyal to. They were incredibly supportive when I went through my separation and divorce, and they put me through one of the best universities in the world for logistics management and I mean that alone cost $100,000. So to me I look at the individuals that helped facilitate that.

What Psychological Contracts Are Like

What are the characteristics of any psychological contract?

Psychological contracts are implied and unspoken. The formal employment contract is only a starting point. Because psychological contracts are assumed rather than verbalized, a guessing game often goes on between employees and their organizations, sometimes complicated in the case of expatriates by thousands of miles of distance between the parties.

Psychological contracts are unpredictable. Unlike written contracts, psychological contracts have no official start and end date, and are subject to ongoing and constant re-negotiation. This often makes them difficult to manage because what doesn't matter to employees one day may suddenly matter months, or even days, later. For this reason, there may be little warning of a breach.

Psychological contracts are universal. They exist in *every* employment relationship from the janitor to the CEO. Because they exist everywhere, it makes no difference whether one is in a local or international role, a part-time or full-time job, or what language is spoken.

Psychological contracts are particularly important to expatriates. This is because they are geographically separated from the relative stability of headquarters, and therefore accrue higher levels of risk, cultural conflict, uncertainty, and disruption, and are therefore likely to place a greater emphasis on perceived mutual understandings and indirect support.

Psychological contracts are determined by employees. Psychological contracts are primarily controlled not by organizations, but by employees, who also decide whether, when and how the terms of their psychological contract have been met. More and more expatriates are therefore "calling the shots" in their employment relationship and indeed may seek to include individual needs and demands that may be self-serving and not aligned to the goals of the organization (see Eduardo's case study, Chapter 3).

Psychological contracts are altered by, and alter, the changing power dynamics in employment relationships. The increasing demand for high-quality expatriates, the emergence of the new millennial iROI-focused Generation Y we discussed in Chapter 1, and the increasing frequency of local-plus compensation and global careers have given expatriates more say about their professional lives. While MNCs may feel secure because assignees are bound by a written contract, de facto power rests more with expatriates, whose psychological contract expectations include iROI concerns. Because of iROI, the "power-over" tactics of the past, seen in traditional dictatorial expatriate management practices, no longer work. Today's expatriates expect a "power-with" approach that demands organizational leadership and creates and attracts *empowered* assignees. This has forced organizations to provide expatriates with more fulfilling psychological contracts, through support, communication, and clear organizational commitments.

Expatriates' psychological contracts are also becoming more transactional. These changes are evident in expatriates' shorter-term commitment to their organizations; their proactivity in navigating new forms of salary and benefits; and their willingness to accept early, but limited, career progression in order to acquire "symbolic" career capital (e.g. "high potential" status and prestige) that they can then leverage later in their careers with a second, third, or even fifth global employer. As today's expatriates negotiate and re-negotiate their opportunities, and invest in global mobility, their new patterns are beginning to shake the conventional wisdom of global staffing.

Additionally, because expatriates have become more confident about their worth on the international labor market, MNCs are increasingly compelled to manage them in new ways. The increased internationalization of work and the growth in career mobility has changed the playing field: today's expatriates seek a balance between the wealth they help generate for their organizations and the knowledge flows necessary to sustain their own long-term employability.

Fulfillment of the Psychological Contract

Fulfillment of the psychological contract comes down to an employee's perception as to whether promises and obligations have been met, and his or her trust that they will continue to be met.[3] Expatriates use their judgment to evaluate psychological contract fulfillment along a sliding scale of *met* and *unmet expectations*, *breaches*, and *violations* (see Figure 6.1).

When expatriates perceive that their expectations have been met, the psychological contract is considered to be stable and fulfilling, resulting in increased trust, loyalty and commitment, better performance, "going the extra mile," and perhaps a willingness to undertake further international assignments.

On the other hand, unfulfilled psychological contracts tend to invoke negative responses, such as disappointment, frustration, resentment, and

**Met
expectations**
Promises and obligations
have been fulfilled

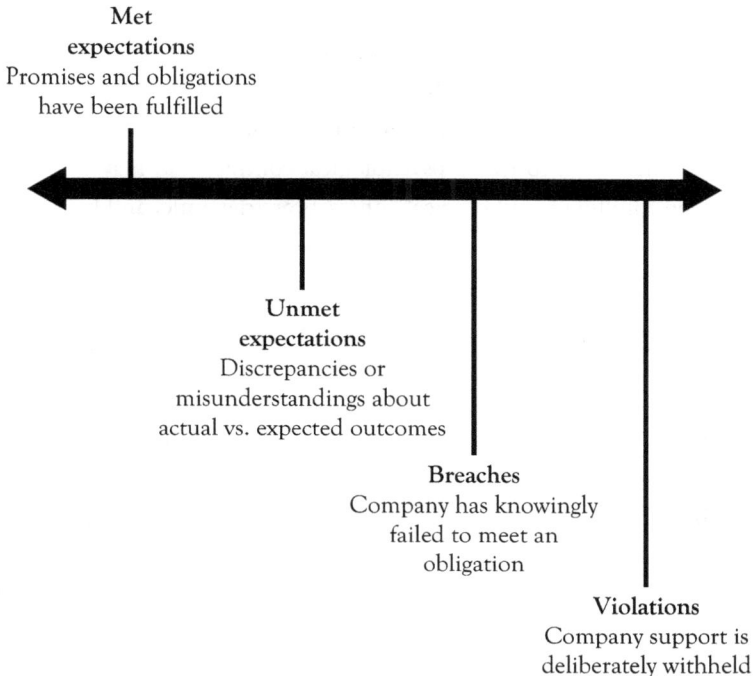

**Unmet
expectations**
Discrepancies or
misunderstandings about
actual vs. expected outcomes

Breaches
Company has knowingly
failed to meet an
obligation

Violations
Company support is
deliberately withheld

Figure 6.1. Sliding scale of psychological contract fulfillment.

anger, the intensity of which is dependent upon the meaning an expatriate attaches to the obligation or promise that has not been fulfilled.[4]

The least intense response to unfulfillment is *unmet expectations*—discrepancies or misunderstandings about actual versus expected outcomes. *Breaches* are slightly more serious wherein expatriates perceive that the organization has knowingly failed to meet an obligation, for example, by denying them the support necessary to achieve their professional goals. Contract *violation*, obviously, is a "worst-case" category arising when company support has been deliberately or intentionally withheld (e.g. a promotion), resulting in intense emotional responses including things like causing an assignment to fail or resigning and joining a competitor.

We cannot, however, ignore that some expatriates often have poor psychological contracts to begin with so that the contract itself is the source of dissatisfaction rather than a breach or violation arising from it. Further, self-serving biases often distort expatriates' perceptions as to how well they and their organization have fulfilled contract obligations; some assignees may perceive their performance or value as better than it is. Sometimes critical events, such an assignment's beginning, encountering language difficulties, or a medical emergency can trigger expatriates to assess psychological contract fulfillment according to how the event is handled, thereby distorting a psychological contract that may otherwise have been fulfilling. Psychological contracts are dynamic, and because of this they can be difficult to manage and assess.

"Currency" of the Psychological Contract for Expatriates

Expatriates' experiences of psychological contract fulfillment are linked to perceptions about the obligations and promises owed to them by their organization. This is the "currency" or "content" of the psychological contract, the "things that matter," and they generally fall into two categories.[5]

On the one hand, expatriates need and desire *economic* currency in benefits like tax equalization, bonuses, paid home leave, housing and education costs, and medical insurance. While these "material" items are usually explicit in the written contract, the amount of benefit that is offered, in dollar terms, is closely tied to psychological contract expectations. A good example is when a company falls short in offering a housing benefit or medical insurance that matches the cost of living in a particular location, necessitating that the assignee then has to kick in thousands of dollars of their own salary to make up the shortfall.

On the other hand, expatriates also need and expect *development* currency in the form of, for example, increased levels of job autonomy and challenge, and mobility opportunities (including re-assignment) that can help them build an international or global career. These development items are often more critical in psychological contract terms because they pertain to long-term, bigger picture "iROI" aspirations.

Strong psychological contracts have a positive impact on eROI, but building such strength can be tricky. One key feature of a contract's strength is its "malleability" in terms of how well expatriates tolerate deviations from their expectations, before they perceive that a breach or violation has occurred.[6] The "expandability" of the psychological contract pie—its capacity to shrink or grow in scope to accommodate the many aspects of expatriation—is therefore important.

Imagine, for example, that a managerial employee is offered an international assignment, whose compensation package is increased according to his or her new responsibilities, resulting in an enlarged psychological contract, including more emotional reliance on the organization for family and other support. Suppose that the same assignee, after 3 years of excellent performance, wishes to extend the assignment or re-assign to a new location, but is instead offered the choice of repatriation or, in order to stay in the host-location, a reduced "local-plus" contract that subsequently alters his or her "status" and reduces their salary benefits. Either way, the psychological contract will downsize. More importantly, has it been broken?

In our Expat Study, the above scenario was increasingly common, resulting in feelings that breaches of the psychological contract may have occurred. This then led to unforeseen consequences however unintentional the message sent by the organization may have been. For example, one expatriate accepted the offer knowing that, although their psychological contract expectations had not been met, sufficient trust existed that their organization would eventually "do the right thing." Another perceived that the downsizing of the psychological contract was an unjustifiable form of punishment and responded by exploring new employment opportunities with a competitor.

Data from our Expat Study provided evidence that some of the organizations we studied had "got it right," at least in the short-term. While only 11% of participants felt that expectations relating to their current assignment had been wholly *unmet* or their contract breached, just over half (59%) said that their expectations had been wholly *met* by their organizations. This result, of course, does not account for longer-term expectations arising from multiple assignments with the same or another employer, which, if it did, might alter expatriates' perceptions. The result may also be due to the realistic attitude of many expatriates about their employment relationship. For example, nearly one-fifth (18%) of the participants said they viewed the psychological contract as pointless because "there have been very few promises made anyway."

Of greater concern, however, is the remainder (30%), who sat somewhere in the middle, unsure that their psychological contract would, or could, be fulfilled, with some prepared to trust a while longer while others called it quits. These "fence sitters" create the most problems for eROI, because their loyalty and continued retention is dependent upon much more than what the written employment contract can provide. So, what can organizations do to convince expatriates that their expectations can be met?

Denise Rousseau, author of *I-deals: Idiosyncratic Deals Employees Bargain For Themselves*, gets right to the point when she says that "changing the deal while keeping the people" is one of the greatest challenges in today's employment landscape.[7] When companies reduce expatriate compensation, for example, they are shrinking the psychological contract pie by asking assignees to re-define their sense of worth, perhaps their lifestyle, and probably their commitment to the organization. But in the global war for talent, the resulting shifts in loyalty that arise from such changes are happening at precisely the wrong time. How then can organizations struggling to overcome talent shortages and increase eROI deal with the challenges that the psychological contract presents?

Relocation Support

Relocation support presents a classic example of how a psychological contract can, at the very beginning of an expatriate's foreign service, establish the psychological contract for years ahead, or derail it immediately. The requirement that the company will do all it can to welcome newcomers or transferees to their new locations and ensure a smooth transition is common to most expatriates' psychological contract expectations. Consider, for example, the case of this senior executive's relocation to Germany.

CASE: It's The Little Things That Count

Paul Schubert is executive vice president, marketing for a global pharmaceutical company headquartered in Switzerland. A year ago, he, his wife, and their four children relocated from Zurich to Berlin. Although the move has been good for his career, the handling of the relocation itself has been, in Paul's own words, "a debacle":

> Nobody ever explained to me a full picture of what I'm entitled
> to for the relocation. Some of the elements I've been discover-
> ing by myself and when I point it out, HR is coming back

with 'No, no, you're not entitled to get this', and then after I am taking this to HQ, they then come back with, 'oh well, yes, OK, we can do that for you now'. An example is school transportation for my kids—they use a public tram and they told me 'no, you cannot claim this for being reimbursed', and then after some email exchange with HQ, I finally got it. It's not worth a lot of money, but it's more the annoyance this is creating. I always get the feeling that they expect me to cheat on them and to claim something that I'm not entitled to, and so they really intimidate me to not claim. There is absolutely no openness with regard to that and claims I send in remain open for months without being answered. I personally find this a ridiculous strategy of the company, because by doing so they might be saving, I don't know, maybe five or six hundred, maybe a thousand Euros a year, but the damage they create, because the value which is at stake is a completely different order of magnitude, yes? It's ridiculous to annoy people with peanuts, sometimes putting at stake the motivation on a larger scale. Sometimes I end up sitting late in my office asking myself 'Well, why am I rushing like hell, for what am I doing that?'

Paul's situation highlights that perceptions of even trivial breaches can lead to destructive resentment among expatriates.

This case illustrates that relocation support matters because it is a symbolic form of indirect communication signaling how the organization will treat expatriates—not just in relation to the big things like compensation and career—but about the little practical things that often cause initial stress but which, when effectively dealt with, can also build trust.

More than half of the participants in our Expat Study rated the relocation support they received as "fair" to "non-existent."[8] For example:

There was no relocation support, nothing, I had to do everything myself. All the company did was give us names of three movers and said, "Ok now it's up to you." In my view, the global mobility department did nothing more than write down what we told them on a piece of paper and got us to sign it, and then created more bureaucracy around it.

In psychological contract terms, poor relocation support can create short-term tension and long-term resentment and make short-term cROI problematic: causing weeks worth of typical "setting up" tasks that could be handled by a personal assistant, distracting an expatriate from getting on with the job, and creating a feeling of abandonment by the company.

The provision of effective relocation support is not difficult and does not necessarily require companies to spend more money. Some areas where improvements can be made include the following:

Policy flexibility. When a relocation policy is too inflexible and rigid to meet a unique need, relocation benefits can make no sense. Fighting with a company to save it money on expensive pre-allocated temporary accommodation because a friend has cheaper accommodation that one prefers to stay in, or being denied reimbursement for ground transportation of a horse because it does not fit the technical definition of "domestic household pet" are some of the frustrations we heard about. Swapping one benefit for another or bending the rules in such a way that doesn't increase the overall relocation budget is good common sense, not because expatriates "win" a policy exception, but because doing so increases psychological contract "goodwill." In short, petty limitations help no one.

Get it right in the first 2 weeks. Despite an earnest—and often expensive—relocation effort that often extends into months after their arrival, what seems to matter most to expatriates is the relocation support they receive in the first 2 weeks. This includes help with setting up bank accounts, finding suitable housing (or at least a good real estate agent), navigating public transportation, and knowing where to find suitable medical care. Making expatriates jump through hoops over trivial matters, as Peter Schubert found himself doing in his move to Berlin, wastes everyone's time.

Provide one point of communication, two at most. Nothing irritates expatriates more—or sends them into a spin quicker—than having to deal with a dozen or more people to make their relocation happen. Going to procurement to ask for the car lease and some-body else about the housing contract not only takes up valuable time, it can also be confusing for a person who is not familiar with their new office environment. Here, outsourced relocation vendors such as Brookfield Global Relocation Services or Cartus—special-ists that provide a "one-stop shop" for international relocations—can be a great help, whose job it is to communicate directly with assignees about policy benefits, claims, arrival assistance, and other day-to-day issues. Monitoring the quality of vendor support is important to ensure that expatriates do not feel cut off from a com-pany process that is affecting their life deeply.

Having established that relocation support can be a good starting point, what else matters to expatriates?

Three Key Areas of Expatriate Psychological Contracts

We found that there are three critical "currencies" common to most expatriates' expectations that determine the relative strength of their psy-chological contract (see Figure 6.2). When companies understand what these are, they are then able to begin dealing with the challenges that the psychological contract presents.

1. Career Management Support

In a recent article, it was suggested that "career development is arguably the most important long-term concern of the individual in formulating his or her psychological contract with the MNC, in the context of an overseas assignment."[9] And as we discussed in Chapter 5, global mobility is at a crossroads, with more and more expatriates changing their career orientation in pursuit of a more balanced cROI versus iROI pay-off (i.e. a quid pro quo arrangement). The "fence sitters" in our Expat Study (i.e. 30% of the participants) who felt *unsatisfied* with their psychological contract are becoming the "loose cannons" of global talent management, "game changers" on an unprecedented level, because what they will do to overcome their dissatisfaction is an unknown quantity. Why does this problem exist?

**Career management
support**
Global career opportunities

Compensation
Local-plus, localization

Psychological contract
Met and unmet expectations,
breaches, violations

Family support
Socialization, adjustment,
dual-careers

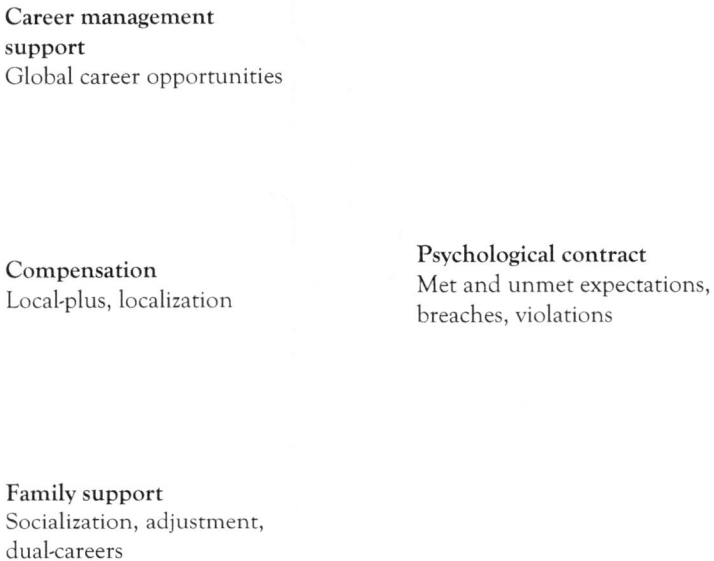

Figure 6.2. Currency of the psychological contract for expatriates.

For an increasing number of today's modern expatriates, companies are not rewarding and supporting them in ways that matter: few MNCs seem able to truly deliver what is needed via strong psychological contract fulfillment in relation to career management. The growing numbers of global careerists, in particular, cause new retention problems for companies because their external marketability to other employers is a recent form of development currency, tying in directly to expatriates' iROI. To be absolutely clear, turnover represents one of the strongest outcomes from psychological contract violation in terms of losing the talent upon which so much eROI is riding.

In short, if an international assignment is instrumental for advancing employees' careers, then improved communication about career planning and greater levels of career management support are required. As we outlined in Chapter 5, these include such things as having a global talent review system in place; professional career coaching; identifying a global talent pool with key positions; managing expatriates expectations;

building relationships and communicating career opportunities; planning repatriation as one potential move in an overall career; and top management support.

2. Compensation

For more and more expatriates, compensation is a "means to an end"—it matters only to a point. Most organizations are therefore mistaken in their belief that financial gain is expatriates' overriding motivation when they go abroad. In fact, in our Expat Study, we found that financial gain becomes most important to expatriates only when a sudden change in remuneration causes them undue hardship or when they are close to retirement.

As we saw in Chapter 3, because compensation is becoming increasingly transactional and does not necessarily feed into the relational aspects of the psychological contract that expatriates seek, traditional forms of assignee compensation cannot be used to the same extent as they have in the past to motivate expatriates to perform and to remain with the organization. In accepting this new reality about compensation, it is not then the type of compensation that matters most to expatriates, but the *process* by which compensating them takes place and how they are subsequently treated, because if the financial ties that bind them to their organizations is lessened by local-plus, or cut altogether as is the case with localization, then using only money to retain them seems somewhat futile. This is particularly true when competitor organizations can match or exceed an assignees existing remuneration package as a means of poaching them.

Our point is that it's not *just* about the money. In fact, for some millennial expatriates as well as those climbing the ladder to middle management, it's often *never* about the money. To secure a proper eROI, MNCs need something less transactional and more relational that engages and motivates their expatriates: this is where the psychological contract can have real power. Here, again, we refer back to Chapter 3, where we saw Eduardo in a situation of having his salary and benefits reduced during his assignment. In this example, he was not unhappy per se with being on local-plus, but deeply dissatisfied with the *process* around managing his *expectations*—when and how reductions in his salary were communicated, when the changes in benefits were likely to occur, and the alternatives that might be available to offset the inevitable financial shortfall in relation to his obligations and responsibilities as the family breadwinner.

There's something else here to consider: the power of the psychological contract is determined not by how much money is spent or thrown at a problem, but by the intent behind the actions or behavior. It costs MNCs nothing to treat their people well, by communicating with them openly and thereby fostering harmonious and committed relationships through mutual respect and understanding.

3. Family Support

Recent reports show that the majority of expatriates are married, and many relocate with their children.[10] But as we explained in Chapter 4, when family problems arise during an international assignment, the consequences can be devastating, not just for the family but also in eROI terms.

In psychological contract terms, family support during expatriation is immensely important because relocations affect everyone, not just the person employed by the company. When it is lacking, problems at home can be distracting to the expatriate employee and cause resentment among partners who often blame companies and/or their working spouse. The follow-on effects, as we saw with the Fletchers, can impact on one's physical health, psychological state of being, future relocation decisions, and even a marriage.

Families, and especially children, are vulnerable people during relocations because they are participating in a process over which they have little or no control. Much research, including our own,[11] shows that the psychological impact of relocating can be far worse than the practical issues that arise which, once dealt with, are often forgotten. In short, although psychological contracts exist between employers and employees, expatriation is a unique situation; it is not unreasonable to find that the partners of expatriates also have psychological expectations about how they and their families will be treated by a company, regardless of their non-employee status.

To illustrate our point, it was not Jonathan Fletcher—the company employee—driving the decision to repatriate to Ireland, but Julie, his wife. In Chapter 4, we discussed the fallout in eROI terms about their decision to enter into a split family arrangement and it bears repeating: had their family's expectations been met in terms of food and drug safety, practical support to assist in medical emergencies, professional support to address Julie's dual-career issue, and emotional support to deal with marital stress, there's no telling how much more resilient the Fletchers might have been to work through the various challenges they faced in China. As it was, Julie had lost faith in the company that it would honor verbal career promises made to her husband and that the next two moves abroad would benefit her and their children in ways that mattered.

How Psychological Contracts Impact on eROI

Creating psychological contracts that work isn't rocket science. At its core, good psychological contracts require a high degree of *manager–expatriate communication*, established via informal conversations and utilizing performance evaluations (e.g. 360 degree feedback) to develop mutually held expectations. Also important is *building a culture of trust*, particularly across international boundaries. Being responsive to expatriates concerns, questions, claims, and other queries, regardless of the distance between them and the headquarters or their boss, is paramount. In our Expat Study, we found that development currency could be offered by organizations in areas like career management support, performance management, and assignment support, for which expatriates appeared both "hungry" and grateful.

Although we have identified three of the most common "currency" items in the psychological contract, the reality is that there can be hundreds more that impact on eROI specific to individual circumstances, family size, the host-location, or economic instability. How companies respond to "shock events," such as the recent 2008/9 global financial crisis and the subsequent loss of jobs, reduced assignment activity, increased repatriations, and decreases in compensation arising from it,[12] is one good example.[13] But there can be others.

What matters for eROI is how much bigger the "fence sitter" pool we spoke about earlier is likely to grow, and whether and how psychological contracts can change not only the size of the pool, but its negative outcomes. If we consider, for example, that a change in career orientation (discussed in Chapter 5) is often a logical consequence of poor psychological fulfillment, then better management of the psychological contract becomes critical. The question all MNCs need to ask, then, is whether their expatriates are *pulled* by a deeply held desire to work and travel abroad over which they have no control, in which case short-term psychological contract management for short-term ROI gain would be the preferred course of action; or, as we suspect is more likely, whether better long-term management of the psychological contract can avoid expatriates being *pushed* to an SIE orientation and entering into job search activities with competitors, thereby leading to stronger organizational ties and longer-term ROI gain via their continued employment.

Summary

We began this chapter by introducing the concept of the "psychological contract" between expatriates and their organizations, explaining that the formal written employment contract is only a starting point in managing this important relationship. Initially, we explained what a psychological contract is and what it means to expatriates. We then outlined how psychological contract-based "new deals" for expatriates and their managers can facilitate discussions about employment relationships, and greater expatriate and assignment success, and provided a case study of an employee that illustrates how effective utilization of the psychological contract can assist in effective expatriation. Based on our research, we know that the psychological contract is the biggest differentiator for organizations wanting to obtain a satisfactory eROI, and in this chapter we explained why. Looking specifically at three of the most common "currency" items, we explained why career management support, compensation, and family support are critical pieces of the psychological contract "pie." Finally, we outlined best practices around how to create psychological contracts that work.

PART 3

Managing Expatriation Using ROI

CHAPTER 7

A New Model of Expatriate ROI

In Part 3 of this book, we return to ROI to show how the concept can be applied to expatriation. We achieve this by providing new strategically based practices for the management of expatriates, applicable in international organizations worldwide.

In this chapter, we build a model of eROI and demonstrate how we believe it should be measured, advocating for a proper strategic base for expatriation, and an integrated set of policies and practices. We then show how, and why, expatriation needs to be a strategic choice, and eROI a directing goal.

As we discussed in Chapter 2, an eROI approach is based on *strategic intent*. How do international assignments and the broader program of global mobility contribute to the organization's strategic goals? What is the purpose of international assignments? Why use global staff at all? Answers to these questions are driven by strategy as a key determinant of assignment purpose; it is important because knowing the purpose then moderates the costs and benefits arising from international assignments.

A Cost-Benefit Perspective

If the first necessary element in an eROI approach is strategic intent, the second is a *cost-benefit perspective*. By "perspective" we do *not* mean an exclusive focus on deploying metric devices—though this will help in moderation at various times subject to strategic intent—but instead the application of a rigorous eROI *philosophy and attitude*.

So, what *are* the costs and benefits arising from international assignments?

Financial Costs

These are often substantial. Though accurate estimates remain inconclusive, some evidence suggests that international assignment costs exceed US$1 million per assignee and per assignment—a substantial investment.[1] On average, the majority of firms spend between two and four times base salary to hire an expatriate employee, with the actual costs differing according to position and seniority, size of family, length of assignment, and destination location.[2] Take a look at the estimates in three UK companies from our MM study and decide for yourself:

> Our expats cost us between UK£1–2 billion a year [3300 expatriates].

> We came up with a price tag of US$300M [5000 expatriates].

> Total investment in our global mobility program is UK£60M annually, including base salary, benefits, assumed tax costs; it does not include shares and bonuses [817 expatriates].

Consider this: the average cost per expatriate across the three companies equates to between £149,000 (US$240,000) and £258,000 (US$410,000), according to whether the first company's costs are taken as £1 billion or £2 billion. But the vagueness of this company's estimate alone, and the fact that per expatriate costs varied from £60,000 (second company) to £606,000 (first company, higher estimate) suggest that these estimates are little better than guesses. Also, when assignments fail, costs can become absolute losses and this happens, according to numerous consulting reports, in 4–6% of all cases.[3]

Despite eROI being based on a combination of financial *and* nonfinancial costs and benefits, in our MM study we nonetheless found a consistent focus *only* on financial data, particularly the costs associated with hiring expatriates versus hiring local nationals. Yet, we found that although 82% of companies conducted budgets or cost projections as part of the assignment approval process, and 60% formally tracked financial costs during each assignment, only 22% compared the actual versus forecasted costs at the end of the assignment. So even though companies espouse cost control, they tend not to see it through.

In many companies, a paradigm shift is needed in turning their mind-set from cost to investment. A Compensation and Benefits Manager in Europe explained this well when he said, "it is still a battle. Too many managers are looking at cost without actually understanding the cost issue, and certainly never looking at the benefit in terms of developing managerial skills."

Furthermore, cost-reduction strategies rarely attain their intended out-comes without incurring some form of opportunity cost: during expatria-tion this is clearly seen when the localizing of expatriates causes subsequent changes in compensation, resulting in an inability to retain high-performing and talented employees who are unwilling to remain in a location under reduced benefits or local conditions. As we explained in Chapter 3, cost-reduction strategies can, and do, create ongoing retention issues.

Some companies however get it right: at least a couple of managers in our MM study clearly understood the cost versus benefit concept cen-tral to eROI. The Head of Global Mobility for a UK bank explained that although expatriate costs can be a big element in her company's eROI estimate, "when someone is out there doing billion dollar deals, a £500,000 expat package is effectively nothing." An oil company Vice President said much the same:

> One driller in, let's say, Azerbaijan, can effectively be generating, say, $100M of revenue a year for us, yet he is only costing us $300K. So I wonder about the cost because cost is important but even if I get that $300K down to $250K, to me it's "have I got the right person in the right place to generate $100M for us?" That is what I view as a success for us as a company.

Non-Financial Costs

Although these costs are harder to identify, articulate, and quantify, our research shows that non-financial costs can influence eROI as much as, if not more than, financial costs. For example, there are costs associated with back-filling home-country positions vacated by expatriates, as an inter-national assignee director in Switzerland pointed out: "If you send a good person out and the department he used to run falls apart because he isn't there, is that a cost you're willing to have? Is that a cost that is even assessed?"

There are also considerable risks associated with ensuring adequate performance in roles filled by expatriates a long way from headquarters, and then managing the fallout from failed assignments should they occur. What are the costs of failed assignments? As a starting point these typically include reduced performance by the business unit in which the failure occurs, disrupted relationships with host-country nationals, and damage to a firm's reputation and brand particularly in key emerging markets.[4]

Most managers try diligently to avoid failed assignments because the costs incurred are not counterbalanced by any benefits. Indeed, when failed assignments occur, there may be further unanticipated losses in a "ripple effect" that can continue to cause negative effects in the organization long after the expatriate has left the assignment, including increased barriers to mobility and reduced willingness-to-expatriate among potential candidates. Failed assignments can also affect expatriates' physical and mental well-being in terms of low self-esteem, loss of prestige amongst colleagues, weakening of the psychological contract, family problems, career path damage, and loss of promotion prospects.[5] All of these are non-financial costs that are rarely accounted for.

Financial Benefits

Data from our MM study show that, although problematic in other ways, the easiest method for determining eROI is to assess the financial benefits arising from international assignments. Here, we are talking about revenues, market share, profit and loss, and other "economic sustainability" measures of a business operation—data that all organizations hold and track and which is relatively simple to obtain.

In terms of financial benefits, substantial savings may be made by using expatriates to avoid the costs associated with hiring and training locals. This is particularly evident in firms where company-specific values are an important part of the business culture, and where training locals to adopt such values are seen as a more costly (and risky) exercise than using an experienced home-country employee.

On the other hand, some managers believe that because employees recruited locally afford access to important networks and are familiar with local customs, financial benefits can be gained by using expatriates to train locals, who can then replace the ongoing need for expensive expatriate employees when long-term assignments come to an end. In the eyes of a Global Expatriate Program Manager in the United States,

> part of the return is the business that the local person can now do ... it's a growth, a succession kind of thing that we create another talent [that] then is going to bring in business or do something that will affect the bottom line. Ultimately, it gets translated into a dollar number.

Non-Financial Benefits

The non-financial, strategic benefits of expatriation demands a paradigmatic shift from a traditional accounting-based (financial) perspective of ROI, to a broader focus on *strategic value*. Thus, while financial measures of eROI can be useful to assess the economic profitability arising from an international assignment, true eROI is much more about the overall *value* to the business, even when it is more difficult to assess. Consider, for example, the long-term value of an employee who goes to China, comes back to the United States, and now has a market association with the potential to win future work.

Non-financial benefits can be substantial because, as we showed in Chapter 1, the reasons for using expatriates are frequently intangible and/or strategic in nature: to fill a skills gap, to develop management expertise, and for control and governance purposes. This is not surprising given that the increasingly popular resource-based view (RBV) of the firm emphasizes the importance of viewing employees, and the rare and unique capabilities that they acquire, as a source of competitive advantage.[6]

The non-financial benefits of expatriation include: (1) increasing employees' inter-cultural awareness; (2) transferring skills and experience to local employees and thereby enhancing their careers; (3) developing global business awareness and thereby improving decision-making and resource allocation; (4) increasing corporate culture adjustment to accelerate performance in the host country; and (5) building a flexible and mobile workforce.[7] International experience can also increase (6) firm knowledge (e.g. knowledge of foreign markets); and (7) international competencies in the top management team.[8]

For individuals, the iROI benefits can include improved "career capital" resulting in career advancement opportunities with existing employers as well as improved career prospects with future employers.[9] There may also be beneficial "transformational experiences" that influence expatriates' identity and career goals.[10]

A New Model of Expatriate ROI

Having established the costs and benefits of an eROI approach, we now return to ROI to show how the concept can be applied to expatriation. In doing so, we will "work backwards" applying some basic principles from what we know (from our own studies, others' research, and our consulting work) of common practices and key issues in expatriation. We seek thus to create a *new eROI-based model of expatriation*, applicable in principle to any MNC. But for our model to succeed in practice, we must first recognize that global mobility practice today needs to move forward from a heavy focus on managing *work in fragments*, to more of a focus on managing *people holistically*. Why does it matter that expatriates are managed holistically?

A "people first" approach practice of management demands clear strategic objectives, oversight, and career paths and is the only way to ensure that scarce resources (largely people and their expertise) are allocated wisely. Furthermore, people management is inherently long-term, because people are long-term, their careers in the organization are potentially long-term, their commitment and expertise take a long time to acquire, develop, and leverage, and as a result they provide organizations with more lasting results.

As for "holistic," managing and measuring expatriation as a set of isolated activities—in a "silo" fashion—ignores the cumulative impact of synergies or conflicts on outcomes. It may be easier to manage expatriate activities in isolation both from each other, from other activities, and even from a broader firm-wide strategy, but in the long-term it doesn't work. *All* the activities surrounding expatriation impact on each other in "system effects." To make them work together we need to start to think not in terms of activities, but of *systems*.

A Systems Approach

Expatriation takes place within an *expatriate management system*. This is actually a sub-system within a wider organizational system and is defined as *a configuration of organizational activities, events, processes, policies, practices, and strategies that are directed at influencing the outcomes of international assignments, to impact the international concerns and goals of global firms*.[11] Many of the global mobility problems that companies experience arise from the fragmentation of the expatriation process, thereby resulting in expatriate activities (selection, training, compensation, and so on) being handled, and often measured, separately. Any evaluation of the outcomes from these separate activities seems acceptable: for instance, "Did pre-departure training take place at the expected cost? Did compensation exceed budget? Was the assignment successfully completed on time?" What's missing is that the *interface* between these activities is rarely examined.

As evidence in our MM study shows, few companies are able to "connect the dots" among activities in their global mobility program as well as with their company's broader strategic agenda. For example, even if expatriate training is completed, does it help the assignee to better understand the host-country culture, and does it improve intercultural performance? It is at such interfaces that collaboration is most needed, but also where our research and consulting work tells us most of the efficiency and effectiveness of global mobility is lost. Because of the focus on individual "dots" or separate activities, the organization can also lose sight of the totality of what is happening to individuals as they proceed "from dot to dot."

An expatriate management system is necessary for eROI because it operates at three levels according to: (a) the global staffing strategy, (b) the organization, and (c) the individuals within it. An expatriate management system can be influenced by factors both internal and external to the organization, resulting in "configurations" of factors that will vary according to these influences. Some configurations will obviously have a more dominant impact on eROI than others.

To appreciate why a systems approach to eROI is so important, let's briefly discuss two "building blocks" from the somewhat rarefied field of systems theory: *systems linkages* and *systems flexibility*.

Systems Linkages

First, it's necessary to apply "systems thinking,"[12] wherein the MNC needs to be seen holistically as a combination of many parts which are integrated in relationship to the whole. Systems thinking is focused less on the elements (e.g. expatriate activities) that constitute a system and more on the relationships between components of the system that *link together* to facilitate a stated goal. For some companies, this might be evident in the desire to link global mobility activities to graduate recruitment or talent management programs.

Expatriation may be one sub-system within a larger management system, where expatriate processes interact not only with each other but also with other systems in the MNC, such as market expansion strategies. Our argument here is that a systems approach to eROI views expatriation as an *integrated* process that enables managers to focus on the interrelationships across a range of activities that exist during *all* stages of an international assignment.

Systems Flexibility

Because organizational systems are linked and they evolve as a result of their interactions with other systems (what some commentators have called "organizational ambidexterity"),[13] changes in system structures can be expected to impact performance outcomes. The problem with system change, however, is often not the change in and of itself and the challenges it creates, but how a change in one system triggers a compensatory response in another. For example, a company might change its expatriate recruitment strategy to employing external candidates (such as TCNs) rather than selecting and deploying internal staff (PCNs): but if deep internal knowledge of the organization is essential for promotion to top jobs, this change in approach is likely to impact on another system—succession planning.

To be successful in achieving its aims, an expatriate management system has to be sufficiently *co-ordinated*, *dynamic*, and *flexible* so that companies can adequately "buffer" the impact of external factors as well as internal operational changes, many of which occur despite, or independently of, the organization's strategic intent. Again, this is organizational ambidexterity in action, enabling firms to adapt to a changing environment.

But system flexibility also comes at a price. While unpredictable situations (such as economic downturns) require innovative solutions, these can often be in contradiction to firms' broader strategic intent. For example, if a company repatriates a large cohort of expatriates in response to an economic downturn, this can lead to poor strategic alignment because it ignores or overrides longer-term talent management initiatives. How can companies deal with this? Being clear about when the opportunity cost of flexibility is too high is a good place to start: while some strategic changes can allow for a more explicit and robust eROI framework to emerge thereby enabling managers to address future challenges with greater clarity, reactive changes can create more problems than they solve.

The Expatriate Management System

To build a new model of eROI, we need to conceptualize the components of an expatriate management system, on the basis that the full system more fully explain ROI outcomes than single activities can in isolation. What does an expatriate management system consist of? Figure 7.1 below is our starting point.

How can, and should, this model, developed by academics, be used by practitioners dealing with the nitty-gritty of expatriation in their organizations? As well as enabling a conceptual understanding of the vast array of inter-related factors affecting expatriation, and the way they interact with each other, it has a very useful *checklist* function. If you feel so inclined, get out a notepad as you read the remainder of this chapter. After each section, think, in quite a concrete way, about *How does this work in my organization?* At the end, you should have a useful summary, perhaps worth editing into a memorandum (for your own use? for others?) of some of the key issues affecting expatriation management in your organization.

Global Staffing Strategy

An expatriate management system ideally begins and ends with a "global staffing strategy." "Global staffing" represents *the critical issues faced by*

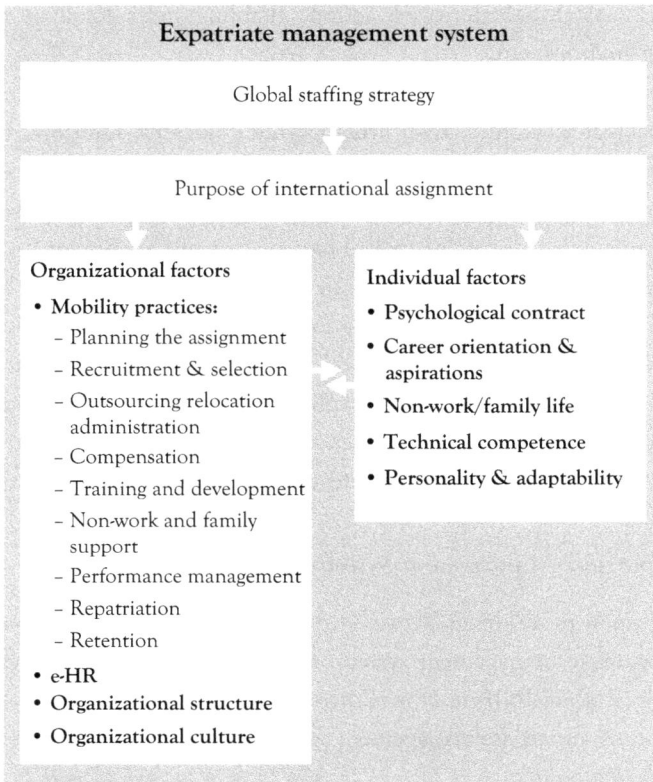

Figure 7.1. Components of an expatriate management system.

MNCs with regard to the employment of home, host, and third-country nationals that are required to fill positions in their headquarter and subsidiary operations.[14] A global staffing strategy is concerned with how best to utilize employees—PCNs, TCNs, and HCNs—in various contexts and under differing conditions to support a broader international strategy. There are generally three broad global strategies that companies can adopt.[15]

An ***adaptive staffing strategy*** is one in which there is no transfer or exchange of the headquarters philosophy, policies, and practices to the offshore subsidiary. This results in a "polycentric" staffing approach (i.e. hiring TCN or HCN staff). In relation to eROI, local staff may be less expensive in the short-term, but there can be longer-term implications for knowledge transfer as well as management development and organization culture.

An ***exportive staffing strategy*** involves heavy reliance on PCNs and the wholesale transfer of the headquarters entire HRM systems to offshore subsidiary operations. It is likely to result in an ethnocentric staffing approach. In relation to eROI, the choice of PCNs to facilitate management control and the transfer of headquarters knowledge may achieve a degree of organizational development in the long-term, but is expensive.

An ***integrative staffing strategy*** combines the characteristics of both an adaptive and exportive strategy to allow for shared decision-making and transfer of practices between headquarters and off-shore subsidiary offices. Global staffing is likely to include a mix of PCN, TCN, and HCN staff appropriate to the demands of the business. In relation to eROI, this approach perhaps best illustrates the organizational ambidexterity that is required to develop an optimum expatriate management system, in which the movement of components in and out of the system depends on striking a balance between global integration and local differentiation (i.e. being "glocal").

Organizational Factors

In an expatriate management system there can be literally hundreds of organizational factors impacting on eROI outcomes, but we narrow them down to a core set of what we call "*mobility practices*," along with three other factors, with the potential to significantly influence international assignment outcomes.

Information from our MM study and others' research[16] suggests that there is a set of core mobility practices that represent inter-related strategic activities linked to the needs of a company's business. We briefly explain each of the mobility practices, showing causes and effects.

Planning the assignment. Knowing the purpose of an international assignment is critical because its absence may result in unforeseen costs. In order to feed into the success of other systems, such as talent management and increasing leadership capabilities, international assignments need to meet clear business needs and have clear business goals.

Selection and recruitment of expatriates. Once careful planning has been established, companies then need to develop a selection process (with criteria and assessment methods) to find suitable candidates. Our MM Study shows that inadequate recruitment and selection practices continue to plague many firms, representing in some cases little more than a "coffee machine" approach.[17] Other studies have consistently shown that the rushed and reactive selection of expatriates leads to decreases in performance.[18] In fact, Mercer found in its *2011 Worldwide Survey of International Assignment Policies and Practices* that 62% of companies rate "poor candidate selection" as a major cause of assignment failure. The problem is that a lack of "best fit" between strategic intent, assignment purpose, and expatriates' skills and abilities (e.g. language expertise relevant to assignment location, relational abilities, and spouse and family considerations) is likely to result in an assignment not achieving its stated objectives.

Outsourcing administration of the relocation program. An expensive component of an international assignment is the considerable costs associated with physically relocating the expatriate (and their family) to a new location. We found in our Expat Study that the *lack of relocation support to conduct a move* is a major complaint, largely because many companies rely heavily on local HR staff in offshore locations to assist with international relocations. Although utilizing local HR staff represents cost savings in the short-term, savvy companies recognize that outsourcing the administration of their relocation program to independent specialists provides a better ROI in the long-term. This is because companies such as Brookfield Global Relocation Services and Cartus (relocation and destination-services experts) can (1) ensure greater cost savings through better negotiations with relocation suppliers; (2) gain access to vendor expertise the company could not otherwise provide, and (3) allow the company's HR staff to focus on its core business activities.[19]

Compensation. We explored expatriate compensation in more detail in Chapter 3. Just as in domestic operations, effective expatriate compensation packages are necessary to ensure high performance. When expatriate compensation includes mobility premiums, hardship allowances, and other benefits in addition to base salary, it is a financial cost that influences eROI. To avoid some of these costs, many firms use standardized compensation packages which are less costly to administer and control and which give (at least) the appearance of equity. But these types of packages often do not account for differences in assignment objectives or cultural conditions, where compensation and reward systems can be a critical factor in motivating expatriates not only to accept assignments, but also to perform well in difficult locations.

Training and development. This may involve not only expatriates but also their family members and include cross-cultural preparation and language programs appropriate to the assignment's location. Training typically represents a significant financial cost to firms in the initial stages of an assignment. The costs include the direct costs of the training itself as well as the opportunity costs associated with the employee attending development sessions for a future role. But there are also significant benefits to be gained in terms of better performance and cultural adjustment. Further, training and development programs that are customized according to an expatriate's past international experience, the assignment's objectives, the intended location, and the needs of the relocating family are likely to be more effective than generic training and development programs. Better training can lead to more realistic expectations, higher levels of cross-cultural adjustment, and better overall performance.

Family support. We discussed family support in more detail in Chapter 4. To reiterate, we know from consulting reports[20] and our own research that family support practices are critical during expatriation to facilitate adjustment. But here we need to consider the hard evidence. In a 2010 survey of 196 organizations in North America, Europe, and Asia, it was found that firms' interest in improving spouse and family assistance is waning, with only 13% making it a priority for the next 3 years, down from 19% in 2007.[21] It was also found to be the least important priority overall in a list of seven priorities, and when asked to list the greatest mobility challenges in terms of future impact on their organization, MNCs listed nine challenges, yet spouse and/or family issues did not warrant mention.

With so little attention paid to this important aspect of expatriation, it is no surprise that "family and personal circumstances" and "partner's career" remain the most significant reasons for employees refusing to accept an international assignment, and that the three main reasons for failed assignments continue to be "family concerns," "partner dissatisfaction," and "inability of spouse to adapt."

Performance management. This can influence eROI in two ways. First, when a performance evaluation is conducted during an assignment it can provide firms with (1) the ability to assess whether the objectives of an assignment are likely to be met; (2) an opportunity to address problems before they result in assignment failure; and (3) insights into the effectiveness of other HR activities, including training and compensation packages, in promoting performance. But performance management appraisals need to also be *customized* to account for differences in assignments' purposes and the types of jobs expatriates perform. As obvious as this seems, the Expat Study showed large-scale and widespread dissatisfaction with performance review processes among both mobility managers and expatriates. This is largely because appraisal programs tend to be based on domestic review processes that fail to account adequately for the international context in which expatriates live and work. Doing so will likely result in improved employee motivation because performance can then be linked to incentive systems, such as compensation and promotion.

Repatriation. Because the end of an assignment is where expatriation can often deliver considerable benefits to many companies, if the benefits of repatriation are lost, it can significantly affect eROI in terms of the potential loss of employees to competitors and the subsequent depletion of international skills and abilities. Yet, although many companies use expatriates explicitly to acquire international expertise and knowledge *and to leverage it on their return*, repatriation remains the most challenging and poorly managed aspect of expatriation in nearly every firm we have studied. Compounding the problem is a difficulty indicated by evidence from the Mercer 2011 survey that 80% of companies do not offer returning expatriates post-assignment guarantees of employment at the same level or above: they thereby increase the likelihood of turnover, even before an assignment has ended, and the loss of key skills and abilities.[22]

Retention. Finally, if an expatriate management system is perfectly managed, yet a company is unable to retain the talent in which it has invested millions of dollars in time, money, and effort, then, from an eROI perspective, poor retention rates can be extremely costly as well as devastating to companies' longer-term competitive advantage. There are many factors contributing to expatriate turnover, including compensation inequities, family difficulties, poor career management support leading to increased career uncertainty, and perceived or actual downward job mobility and status during repatriation (see Chapters 3–6). However, retention only matters when the loss is unexpected and a company loses high performers considered pivotal to achieving its long-term strategic objectives: when poor performers leave, labor turnover may not always be unwelcome or as costly. Expatriate retention therefore needs to be approached as a carefully managed combination of *functional retention* and *functional turnover*, in which high performers are retained and low performers are lost as part of a larger strategic plan. Under these circumstances, the strategic replacement of poor performers during international assignments may not be as costly to firms in the long-term, while the longer-term impact on eROI may be minimized.

Although our focus here is mainly on mobility practices that support expatriation, there can be other factors that also impact on eROI outcomes. For example:

e-HR. The use of technology in HR (e-HR) is recognized by many mobility managers as helping to increase organizational innovation, resulting in greater efficiencies and reduced costs in areas, such as selection and recruitment, training, HRM supply chain management and shared service models, knowledge management, and global networks. In streamlining and speeding up certain processes, and improving the quality and accuracy of assignment data and information, eROI can be enhanced.

Organizational structure. Whether an MNC has a centralized or decentralized/flat structure can determine: (a) how expatriates are managed from a network perspective; (b) the co-ordination and co-operation between regional business units as they strive to achieve a desired level of organizational capability; (c) how international moves are logistically handled; and (d) whether strategic assignment objectives can be supported. For example, centralized organizations in which assets, resources, responsibilities, and decisions are tightly controlled via a central hub or headquarters can provide companies with economies of scale and improved value chain linkages, thereby improving eROI outcomes. On the other hand, decentralized firms that are controlled locally within a region or country-specific location, with informal headquarters control over operations, are able to more fully meet the needs of local customers and penetrate local business networks, but may also find it difficult to co-ordinate costing and other global staffing data that is essential to managing expatriate costs and determining its benefits.

Organizational culture. Organizational culture captures the underlying attitude an organization adopts toward its employees, which is manifested in how it treats them on a day-to-day basis. Where a company is supportive of expatriate employees, there are likely to be better quality, and more consistent, mobility practices during international assignments (e.g. good-quality career management support), which in turn can improve the retention of strategically important employees. Our MM study shows that a common barrier to implementing eROI programs is an organizational culture that lacks support or buy-in from senior management, including a lack of ownership of, and accountability for, international assignments. This is a special problem in organizations where there is a lack of co-ordination across functions and regions, or a tendency toward a strong operational rather than strategic focus toward global staffing.

Individual Factors

The final set of factors that make up an expatriate management system is personal characteristics specific to particular expatriate employees.

Career aspirations. We discussed expatriate career issues in more detail in Chapter 5. These are concerned with why expatriates undertake international assignments and whether their motives are aligned with those of the organization, as well as their longer-term career orientations and objectives, including whether they are more inclined toward a "free agent" type of career or stronger organizational commitment. What matters is how far these are in line with a company's broader global staffing strategy. For understanding and managing expatriates' career expectations, the level of career management support provided by the organization is an important consideration.

Non-work and family life. We devoted Chapter 4 to further consideration of these issues. It includes consideration of the welfare, cross-cultural adjustment, and happiness of the expatriate's partner and children, the dual-career issue, children's education, and family and friendship networks. Expatriates' non-work and family life has been shown to be an important contributor toward willingness-to-relocate, assignment success, retention, and repatriation adjustment.

Professional and technical competence. Here we are talking about the multiple competencies expatriates are expected to possess when selected to undertake their international roles. Traditional notions of expatriates' competence have evolved from considering only technical, functional, and managerial skills, but now also include managing conflict, power, influence and control, commitment, and trust building.[23] Do expatriates have the skills to be successful in their international roles, and how can these skills be acquired?

Personality and adaptability. For expatriates, this relates to their expanding inter-cultural responsibilities, and the corresponding cross-cultural adjustment and job satisfaction that leads to improved performance. For example, *emotional intelligence* (e.g. empathy, social responsibility, and social relations), and *cultural intelligence* (the specific ability to adapt attitudes and behavior to new cultures) are important personality traits for expatriate managers as predictors of intercultural adjustment and assignment success.[24]

The psychological contract. This is at the heart of individual ROI outcomes. As we explained in Chapter 6, the psychological contract, consisting of mutual expectations between an organization and expatriate regarding their respective obligations and responsibilities, if mutually agreed and fulfilled, is likely to lead to more positive employee attitudes and actions, better performance, and increased trust and organizational commitment. These positive outcomes can, in turn, influence turnover intentions, as well as the career orientations and adjustment of international assignees.

The eROI Model

Having established what an expatriate management system looks like, what its components are, and why it matters from an eROI perspective, we can now begin to build a new eROI model. To do this, we conceptualize three additional components that feed into, and are in turn influenced by, the expatriate management system: *external factors*, *eROI outcomes*, and a *feedback loop*. These are shown in Figure 7.2. Let's discuss each component in turn.

External Influences on eROI

No expatriate management system exists without being influenced to some extent by the external environment in which the MNC operates. External factors need to be constantly monitored and taken into consideration in determining and modifying the global staffing strategy, including the purpose of an international assignment, and the various practices that may be deployed to support expatriates.

One obvious consideration is the *host-location* to which expatriates are sent and the challenges or opportunities it may create for individuals as well as for companies doing business there. For instance, the decision to use PCN expatriates may be dictated by the degree of corruption in a host location:[25] where it is high, corporate governance and control may necessitate using a more experienced, more senior, company-assigned— and by default, perhaps a more expensive—assignee. Economic transformation may be equally important. Is it, for example, an emerging economy such as Malaysia, or a co-ordinated economy such as France or Australia? How easy would it be for an expatriate to live and work in China where guanxi[26] is a pre-requisite for business interactions? What about the political orientation of the host-location and the influence of labor unions, trade associations, and labor legislation, as well as laws and

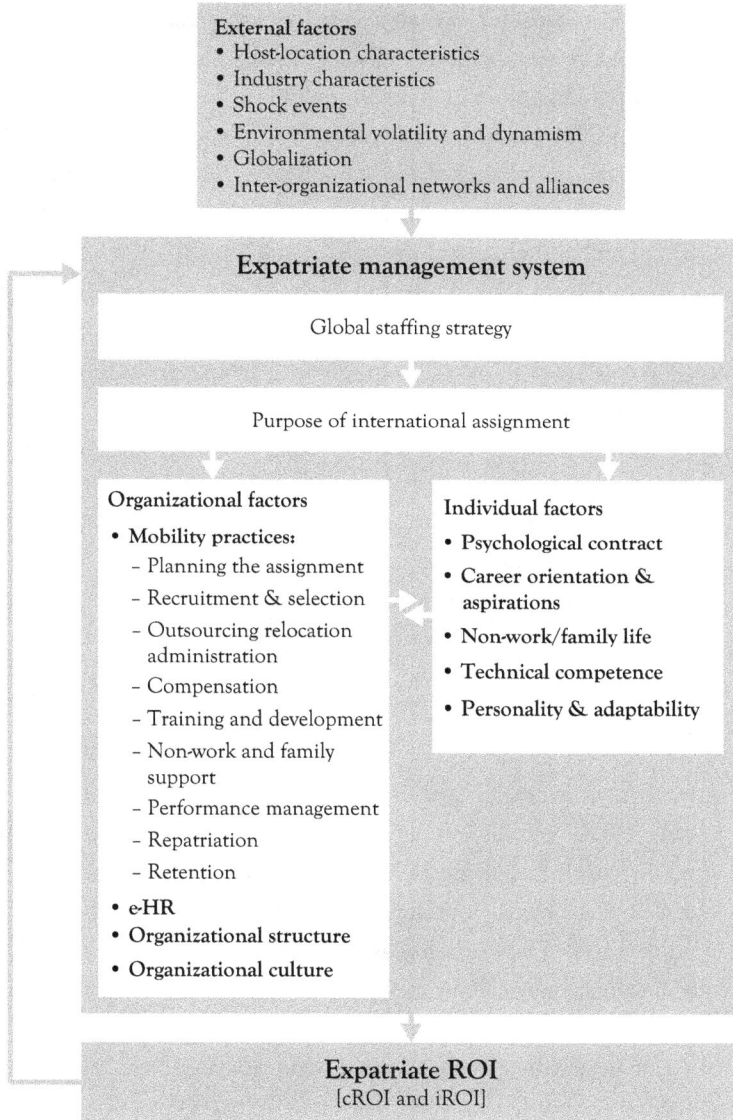

Figure 7.2. Conceptual model of expatriate return on investment.

institutional frameworks that guide the relationship between the organization and its external environment? To what extent does the national culture of a particular country present challenges for expatriates, particularly women, in terms of religious customs, restrictions, socialization, adjustment, and language barriers?

We must also consider ***industry characteristics*** particular to certain types of global firms, including legal, cultural, and economic factors relating to different sectors or types of operations (e.g. health services or manufacturing). For example, manufacturing firms may be influenced by seasonal fluctuations in market demands, wherein the demand for expatriate staff in certain locations may as a result increase or decrease, requiring a shift in global staffing strategy.

Another critical factor is the influence of ***shock events*** which we introduced in Chapter 6. Shock events can occur at the macroeconomic level (the 2008/9 global financial crisis), within regions (the 2003 SARS outbreak in Asia), or within industry sectors (the 2001 Enron corporate governance scandal). What makes shock events particularly challenging for organizations is that they are unpredictable, yet their effects often continue for indefinite periods of time. Such volatility can impact a company's competitiveness depending on its ability to cushion the impact.

Shock events typify ***environmental volatility and dynamism*** as being ever present in an organizations external operating environment. Because of this, many companies grapple with how to respond effectively to external pressures (e.g. unstable currencies or political systems), as well as the increasing demands of global staffing. A case in point is the dynamism of the business environment in emerging economies such as Brazil, Russia, India, and China (the "BRIC" economies), where uneven industrial development and variations in governmental decision-making place complex demands on firms, as well as influencing the strategic directions of parent companies.

Needless to say, ***globalization*** as a whole creates challenges, particularly abrupt organizational changes that, in time, could undermine firm stability, and employee trust and commitment. For eROI, the effects of globalization are evident in the complexities associated with transferring knowledge across borders as well as the effective management of international assignments across multiple locations.

Lastly, ***inter-organizational networks and alliances*** (e.g. business alliances, political affiliations) are increasingly relied upon by global firms and their expatriates to generate new resource capabilities in order to support both organizational and individual international business efforts. Even though these networks frequently operate outside the firm, they nonetheless play a vital role in "getting business done."

Expatriate ROI Outcomes

The end result of an effective expatriate management system is, of course, positive eROI outcomes. We defined these in Chapter 2 as the calculated financial and non-financial costs and benefits of the international assignment to the firm, and outlined there what they may be. In the next chapter we will show how they might be measured. These outcomes are determined in large part by the purpose of an assignment and the stated assignment objectives. We say "in large part" because international assignments can, and do, produce other unexpected outcomes, sometimes beneficial but sometimes not.

The Feedback Loop

The final step in building the eROI model is to put in place a *feedback loop* because the value of an eROI outcome lies not just in having achieved it but also in having the result then inform and assist future decision-making. Without a feedback loop between international assignment outcomes and strategy, eROI is not likely to improve, nor is the assessment of eROI likely to be of any long-term benefit to an organization. Thus, *eROI only becomes truly meaningful when it feeds back into the overall expatriate management system at the strategy level*, to impact on and improve future global staffing initiatives. This requires the organization to constantly gather information about all the factors in the model, so it can control these feedback loops rather than being controlled by them.

In practice, a feedback loop asks and answers questions such as: Were the outcomes in line with what was expected? If so, which factors need to be replicated to produce similar results from future assignments? If not, which factors are problematic and require more careful management and thought? Are there specific factors that require higher levels of expertise (e.g. consultancy advice) to deal with more effectively?

There is another benefit to the feedback loop which is often overlooked: it shows clear evidence as to how strategy may be developed in response to practice, for example, how a global staffing strategy could be developed, improved, or adapted in response to external, organizational, and individual factors. In Chapter 1 we showed that the various types of international assignees may alter the global staffing strategy to account for a wider diversity of candidates that includes traditional (PCN) expatriates as well as TCNs, inpatriates, HCNs, and returnees.

Our point is that the feedback loop gets to the heart of eROI in principle and in practice: that *being attuned to eROI and managing it* is just as important, or even more important, than measuring it. The effectiveness of an eROI program, then, is not just in its formulation—the getting of an eROI statistic—but in how the program is implemented, linked to policy, managed in practice, and improved at the strategy level among all the "learning" that subsequently takes place.

Summary

So, where have we got to in this chapter? First of all, we considered some of the specific costs and benefits arising from expatriate assignments, but stressed that the philosophy of evaluating eROI is more important than the actual measures. We built on this foundation by then outlining, as background to good eROI practice, a new model of expatriate ROI, including an explanation of the expatriate management system that is key to its effective utilization.

We end this chapter by briefly re-stating why a systems approach is so essential to building an eROI program. If we reflect on the NexCorp case introduced in Chapter 2, we can see there are two main problems it is facing: escalating mobility costs and not knowing what to do with assignees when their assignments are over, both of which point to the much larger problem of not having a proper strategic plan in place for the talent management of expatriates. To overcome the problem, this financial services firm needs to address not just one aspect of its global mobility program in isolation, but a *system* of activities (e.g. approval processes, policy development, tracking and costing data, and organizational culture) to better improve the return it hopes to gain from expatriates. In doing so, NexCorp will reap the benefits from utilizing a more effective *expatriate management system* to explain increases and decreases in eROI outcomes, taking into account that some combinations of factors will have a more dominant influence over others according to a variety of situations and contexts.

CHAPTER 8

Evaluating Expatriate ROI

This is a "*how*" chapter: How, specifically, might one measure eROI, and insofar as eROI has been assessed in the past, how has that been done? What particular metrics have been used, and what are their pros and cons? What new metrics are being developed, or might be developed in the future?

Some readers will be eagerly anticipating our answers to these questions: managers always want to know *how*! But every *how* question must logically be preceded by a *why* question, the answer to which will bear critically on the *how* methods that are considered. Part of the problem MNCs face is that in the past those professing expatriate management expertise have often been too pre-occupied with how and rather negligent of why. In Chapter 2 and then later in Chapter 7, we systematically addressed the "why" question. Here, in this chapter, we want to make it clear that while it is important to find the best available metrics to assess eROI, obsessing about these is counter-productive: what matters is less the method than the *philosophy*. So, in the first section of the chapter, let's examine what the metrics can, and cannot, do for eROI by considering some of the methods currently used to measure it, and the issues these created in a specific case.

How Do Managers Currently Measure eROI?

What formal attempts have firms made to measure eROI? Although obtaining such a measure has been a high priority for many companies for at least the past decade,[1] the short answer is "none." When we first began our research over 10 years ago, we found this surprising. If firms investing millions of dollars annually into global mobility programs do not have this discipline, on what basis do they make critical decisions about global staffing?

What we discovered is that while formal measures of ROI do not yet exist, there are numerous informal measures that have been used, predominantly in an attempt to measure *something*, even if that something isn't particularly meaningful in terms of guiding future decision-making. To illustrate our point, let's consider the problems at SimiCorp.

CASE: Misleading Metrics at SimiCorp

In 2003, SimiCorp, a food and beverage conglomerate with subsidiary offices in 23 international locations, including 15 offices in Asia Pacific, reported an annual international assignment failure rate of 38%, a significant increase on prior years' statistics of around 4–6%. The problem was immediately diagnosed as poor on-assignment cultural adjustment leading to assignment failure, and to counteract it the CEO immediately approved a new cross-cultural training (CCT) program that cost the company an estimated $1.2 million in additional expenses. As it turned out, the cause of failure was *not* cross-cultural adjustment, and the new CCT program, whilst welcome, did nothing to decrease the number of failed assignments the following year, which remained constant at around 32%. Consequently, the CCT program was significantly scaled back.

The head of international assignments at SimiCorp, Margarita, was extremely busy during this time repatriating a large number of expatriates, many of whom were returning early from their assignments, with a particularly large cohort leaving Asia. When the CEO, in 2004, demanded to know why the costly CCT program had not delivered its intended result, Margarita needed to delve more deeply into the problem: what was causing assignments to fail and, more importantly, how was the failure rate statistic being determined?

In stepping back from the busyness of repatriating SimiCorp's many assignees, Margarita realized there was a connection between the high rate of failed assignments and the high rate of repatriated employees leaving Asia. As it turned out, SimiCorp predominantly defined assignment failure as "premature return," a category into which more than 90% of the recently returned Asia-based expatriates could be placed. Further investigation showed, however, that the reason for their premature return had nothing to do with their adjustment or performance; instead, all were coming back early out of concern for their, and their families', health and safety due to the 2003 outbreak, in Asia, of SARS (Severe Acute Respiratory Syndrome), a life-threatening infectious disease.

It became apparent that the misuse of "assignment failure" designated a measure of international assignment effectiveness in an effort to "connect the dots," was meaningless, and indeed, misleading to the company's subsequent decision to implement the costly CCT program. The proof was in the pudding: in 2005, the failure rate at SimiCorp dropped to an all-time low of just 3%—in the absence of the now-withdrawn million-dollar CCT program and with the easing of the SARS threat in Asia.

The problems at SimiCorp are numerous: the use of ill-defined informal measures; observing only a few behaviors, factors, or outcomes within a limited context (e.g. assignment failure); and ignoring the possible inter-relatedness of various factors that simultaneously impact on eROI. Furthermore, focusing only on isolated factors and their outcomes tends to focus too much attention on the expatriation program alone, rather than on other wider organizational and international forces. In consequence, inappropriate data on their own reveal very little about *why* certain outcomes occur.

What we learn from the SimiCorp case is that existing measures of eROI do not account for the total *expatriate management system*. This is a major failing because such a limited focus prevents managers from reframing international assignments in the broader context of an organization's overall strategic capabilities. At best, such "measures" give the perception that measurement is in some way driving the desired organizational actions expected from expatriates, even if the impact is not visible or is misleading. At worst, careless measurement may drive the wrong actions and create long-term problems of improper resource allocation and increased costs.

To illustrate our point, let's examine the five informal types of eROI measures that have been used: (1) anticipated outcomes; (2) short-term financial measures; (3) short-term functional measures; (4) long-term strategic measures; and (5) individual measures. In Table 8.1 we provide examples of these informal measures, and, from our MM study, their levels of usage by organizations and sample quotes about them from various mobility managers interviewed in the study.

Table 8.1. *Informal eROI Measures Used by Mobility Managers*[2]

Informal measure	%	Sample quote
1. **Anticipated outcomes:** Expected ROI calculated in a paper-only exercise as a decision-making tool	24	By the time we find someone who is going on an assignment it is a done deal. The estimate and the approval process is just a formality.
2. **Short-term financial:** Determine whether costs of assignment exceed budget or revenues increase	30	In terms of ROI … we're able to determine it from apportioned revenue from the individual in what they charge … it's relatively easy for us to determine how much somebody bills and offset that against assignment costs and look for baseline data to determine ROI.
3. **Short-term functional:** Immediate benefits assessed in local objectives met (e.g. knowledge transferred), local successor groomed, repatriation turnover, premature returns/failures, among others	41	It comes down to really the success in the assignment, are they actually doing the job … it's got to be the fact that we increase sales by X or we design something new or we do whatever we needed to do … the actual fundamental job you sent them to do.
4. **Long-term strategic:** Benefits assessed beyond end of assignment in long-term retention rates, promotion rates, talent management and succession planning objectives being sustained, building career expats, increasing brand recognition and relationships, and overall value gained	31	We looked at the psychometric profiles of expats going out and those returnees coming back … it's very clear in which areas they have grown and developed and improved. So that to us is a return on our investment, on an unquantifiable side. The return on investment would be that we continue to have a viable talent which is enhanced by the overseas experience … somebody who is able to get the job done, but who is now more culturally savvy and can be counted on again for an assignment.
5. **Individual measures:** Benefits accruing to expatriate employee rather than firm (e.g. career capital enhanced, financial gain)	12	Mobility has very much more to do with what is the net cash position going to be to the employee and are we doing the right thing by the employee.

Note: Managers provided multiple responses, so percentages do not add up to 100.

We are highly critical of most of these measures because we found overwhelming evidence in our MM study that the reported outcomes arise largely from ad hoc data and subjective perceptions of reality, much as occurred at SimiCorp. Indeed, most mobility managers admitted that their eROI assessments were based on "intuition," a "feeling," a "belief," or an (often biased) interpretation of an actual outcome, as one informant admitted:

> We have all the data in the systems which are trackable, all the costs are trackable, and that's no issue because we can call them out of the system without much difficulty ... it's not difficult to do. But we don't do it I'm afraid to say ... it's all basically perception.

An additional problem is that these informal measures relate to past performance and provide only retrospective data as observed once the assignment has been terminated, thereby diminishing managers' ability to obtain predictive information upon which they might act. In this light, many existing eROI measures such as those shown above are unsuitable for guiding future decision-making and helping managers sustain long-term strategic success.

A further problem is that, because informal measures are easier to obtain, they typically produce quantitative indices (e.g. turnover rates and failure rates) that, as the SimiCorp case shows, often lead to inferences about unobserved relationships. Another good example is the use of promotion rates: some companies justify continued investments in global staffing on the basis that expatriates are promoted at a faster rate than non-expatriates, but there is little evidence to support their conclusions. For example, if time in a domestic role is 3–4 years for a non-expatriate, the length of an international assignment is pretty much the same; for a lot of expatriates, the next move is probably going to be a promotion but the key question is: *Was being on an international assignment what made the difference?* We would argue no, not in all instances. Thus, the usefulness of measuring promotion rates is questionable.

To further explain what we mean, let's discuss the pros and cons of four of the most common measures of eROI.

Repatriation Turnover

Avoiding "repatriation turnover" (defined as the proportion of former expatriates who resign from the company to take up a job elsewhere within 2 years post-assignment) is often treated as an indicator of successful mobility programs. But as recent reports show many companies no longer provide post-assignment repatriation guarantees,[3] so the loss of these employees during or soon after repatriation may be inevitable and may even be functional. Additionally, in some instances repatriation turnover may be due to factors other than expatriate dissatisfaction or performance, including short-term external influences such as market conditions (e.g. redundancies or downsizing). For example, the 2008/09 global financial crisis led companies to reduce the number of expatriates, typically increasing the rate of repatriation before assignment completion.[4]

Low repatriation turnover may also be misleading: for example, the loss of even one expatriate may be strategically devastating for a business unit if that particular individual is pivotal to achieving a vital objective and is considered a high performer whose retention is a specific objective of an international assignment. Similarly, the loss of poorly performing expatriates during repatriation may be welcomed as functional turnover. Here, context matters: measures of repatriation retention and turnover will have varying degrees of relevance to the eROI assessment that must be factored in accordingly. Furthermore, in our view, the emphasis on repatriation as a criterion of success needs to be re-thought, because, as we discussed in Chapter 6, the importance of repatriation in its traditional form is declining. For all these reasons, repatriation turnover as a measure of ROI is, in our view, a mistake.

Assignment Failure

Perhaps the most popular measure of all, assignment failure is also the easiest statistic for managers to obtain. Yet, failure rate data have consistently shown to be inadequate and unreliable, resulting in "efficiency" measures that are mostly subjective and intuitive. Failed assignments are difficult to define leading to estimates of failure that are grossly exaggerated, ranging up to 75% but accepted as fact.[5] Such a statistic is highly misleading for guiding future decision-making because it fails to account for the context within which failure occurs, for example short-term economic downturns or unforeseeable shock events (such as in the SimiCorp case). It therefore results in generalized data that neither depicts the "true picture" nor is region specific.

In the rare cases when assignment failure is properly identified, data can provide useful diagnosis of organizational dysfunctions in the processes that support expatriates, such as poor career management support, or gender discrimination. Doing this elevates the tracking of failure rate statistics beyond "measuring to report" to providing meaningful data that can be used to manage and improve expatriate policies and practices. In practice, however, this is rarely the case: the failure rate can, for some mobility managers, be an embarrassing statistic even when it is relatively low, as one informant explained: *"it's not something you want to advertise … so we buried it."* We saw this sentiment reflected in the fewer than 10% of companies in our MM study that were formally tracking failure rates on an ongoing basis.

We do not advocate assignment failure rates as an appropriate eROI metric because we view it as a lazy measure, frequently used as a scare-mongering tactic to sell third-party vendor services. This is because the myth about high failure rates has been around for so long that no one questions it any more. We recognize this is a bold statement, but it needs to be said. To understand why, let's delve deeper into the psychological fear behind failed assignments.

We know from our MM and Expat Studies that a failed assignment can sometimes de-rail a company's strategy, and maybe even send it spiraling backward in terms of competitive advantage, especially in emerging markets where it may be difficult to get expatriates to go in the first place. The fall-out can be deep, for example, in Asia where business is based almost entirely around personal relationships with locals, thus creating a ripple effect that can be difficult to recover from in the short-term. If companies can then be convinced that assignment failure is high across a particular industry or region, they can more easily be persuaded to buy consulting services that will supposedly help them avoid having failed

Table 8.2. Assignment Failure Rates Among MNCs[6]

	Percentage of companies reporting failed assignments	N = 19
Less than 5%	89	17
5 to 20%	11	2
More than 20%	0	0

assignments. Common sense dictates, however, that companies with high failure rates would go out of business—period.

The reality is that failure rates are *relatively low*. Our MM Study shows that under normal business conditions, companies report fewer than 10% failed assignments, with most ranging from 4 to 6% annually, a statistic consistently supported by consulting reports for more than 20 years,[7] including our own research.

Based on the data above, it is time to stop buying into the illogical conclusion that international assignment failure is high and to start seeing this measure for what it is: one frequently used in isolation from other measures and assignment outcomes, plagued by poor construct definition and inconsistent data collection, that mythologizes the impact of expatriation on a company's strategy and is clearly a weak measure of eROI.

Assignment Success

To most managers, the success of an international assignment is the embodiment of eROI. After all, if the assignment achieves what it is supposed to, then what better return can there be? The problem is that because companies still struggle to define not only why they have expatriates but what benefits they expect from expatriation, assignment success is as slippery a concept to define and measure as assignment failure.[8] In our MM study, only 52% of companies said they set clear objectives at the commencement of an assignment that were documented as part of the approval process. Only 20% then checked against those objectives at the end of an assignment to determine whether they had been achieved. Further complicating the situation, assignment objectives often change due to a management or strategy shift (e.g. from a joint venture or merger).

How then are assignment objectives monitored and assessed? What about short-term objectives assessable as soon as the assignment is completed, versus long-term objectives, the benefits of which may not be visible for some years? We contend that although knowing how to define assignment success in terms of the *real* value to the organization remains a considerable challenge, what matters more is *having clearly defined assignment objectives* from which assignment success can be determined at various stages during an assignment, and after it is completed.

Our and others' research suggest that possible criteria for assignment success include cross-cultural adjustment, job performance, organizational commitment, assignment completion, and achievement of assignment objectives. Numerous consultancy surveys report further complexities. For example, a 2004 report by Cendant found amongst a cohort of 146 global mobility managers worldwide that companies use three different assignment success measurement approaches: (1) bottom line assignment costs; (2) business generated from the assignment; and (3) justified expense as part of a long-term globalization strategy.[9] A 2005–06 report by Mercer based on a survey of 160 MNCs found that success measures also include: (4) development of local competencies; (5) development of a pool of skilled, experienced managers; and (6) increases in market share in the host location.[10]

Job Performance

Job performance is perhaps one of the most critical short-term measures of eROI because it can be directly linked to an assignment's purpose. If an expatriate's performance against agreed on-assignment objectives is deemed to be satisfactory, then assignment success is almost guaranteed— and who could want more than that?

Unfortunately, expatriate job performance assessment is handled poorly by many companies, being viewed too often in terms of adjustment rather than expected job outcomes. This is especially the case in academic studies, where an extensive focus on adjustment to facilitate performance has impeded the more important focus on actual international assignment performance outcomes.[11]

Furthermore, job performance as a component of assignment success must be based on a specification of assignment objectives. Yet, consistent with earlier studies and our own, a 2005 GMAC report showed that only 32% of organizations monitored expatriate performance against clear objectives,[12] while a 2006 ORC report stated that nearly 40% of home-country business units responsible for setting, monitoring, and measuring expatriate performance objectives did not clearly understand what those objectives were.[13] Part of the problem is inconsistency in the use or enforcement of performance appraisals. In addition, various cross-cultural factors make it difficult to implement, monitor, and manage expatriate performance on a global scale.

Job performance also tends not to be given high priority when assessing assignment outcomes. For example, the most recent Brookfield report[14] shows that of those companies that do attempt to measure eROI, "completing assignment objectives" is the third-ranked criterion, *behind* "international assignee compensation costs" and the "cost of relocation support."

Expatriate ROI Metrics

The perceived critical role of "metrics" and the heavy focus on finding a measureable "magic bullet" for managing global mobility programs have pre-occupied the relocation industry for a long time. Mobility managers have tended to believe that the right metric would solve all their problems—gauge assignment success, justify their own job of managing the mobility function, secure continued investments in mobility and more internal funding for global staffing, and elevate their status as true deliverers of value based on unquestionable rock-solid metrics much like the accounting department can do. But this search for tools has distracted managers from focusing on what really matters: the *approach*, the *mindset*, the *philosophy*, and the *culture* that lives and breathes eROI. What do we mean by this?

Metrics are superficial—for a small cost, they can be bought in any number of management books.[15] But what cannot be bought is the more difficult-to-achieve and elusive goal of "lasting organizational change." This may explain why so many instead chase after the metric—it's easier and it says, "I'm doing something," even if that isn't much, and has no real value. It proves mobility managers are active, even if the activity is misplaced.

In this chapter, we will not develop or promote an extensive list of metrics per se because there are many that can be used which are easily available elsewhere.[16] Our core message is that metrics are useless if companies don't get the basics in place first—the "basics" being an *eROI philosophy*. Beyond a list of examples that follow, we leave the metrics to other consultants because our focus is bigger than just measuring: our focus is in helping you understand *why* you get the ROI that you get, and what you can do to improve or repeat it.

Example Metrics

Drawn from "*12 key PricewaterhouseCoopers Saratoga human capital metrics*," the five examples below represent a set of metrics with agreed global definitions that enable companies to report their human capital profile to shareholders and other relevant stakeholders.

- Revenue per FTE[a]   → *defined as* → Revenue/total FTEs
- Profit per FTE   → *defined as* → Profit before tax/total FTEs
- Cost per FTE   → *defined as* → Total costs/total FTEs
- Remuneration/cost   → *defined as* → (Total compensation + benefits)/total costs
- Human capital ROI   → *defined as* → (Revenue – non-wage costs)/(total compensation + benefits)

---

[a] *FTEs* = Full Time Equivalents (Employees)

HCROI can be particularly useful in eROI terms because the ratio indicates how much revenue is generated for every dollar spent on, or paid to, an expatriate. But because HCROI does not factor in turnover costs, when added these will make the HCROI ratio smaller.

Source: Saratoga and PricewaterhouseCoopers' 2006 and 2010 "Key trends in human capital: A global perspective."

We don't mean to suggest that developing metrics is unimportant—it is a very critical step in implementing ROI when the right metrics are used, though here we will go so far as to suggest that some companies will not even require additional metrics to achieve a satisfactory eROI, provided that they have the right eROI philosophy and framework in place. Doing this may be enough if senior management is realistic that lasting change is more than just the metric and has invested sufficient time, money, and thought in implementing a proper eROI philosophy. As the Senior VP at NexCorp, our case in Chapter 2, found out, metrics was not likely to deliver the change that was needed; instead, going straight to the root of the problem—in that particular case the organizational culture around approving international assignments—is the likely place where solutions can be sought.

Building an eROI Evaluation Framework

Having established that metrics are important to many companies, we can now begin to build an evaluation framework to guide both the choice of eROI metrics (vertical fit/strategic alignment), and how eROI measurement should be approached (horizontal fit/operationalization). Again, our core message is that eROI is not so much a measure as it is a philosophy, one that requires metrics but requires a robust *framework* even more. In Figure 8.1, we outline two phases with five criteria that can help companies build an evaluation framework. Here, we explain in more detail what each critical step in the evaluation framework involves.

PHASE 1: *Vertical Fit/Strategic Alignment*

Phase 1 is a necessary part of strategic alignment and is based on the systems approach that is essential to proper eROI management (see Chapter 7). When a clear reason for calculating eROI is known, mobility managers will be better equipped to determine what needs to be measured, and to manage expatriate activities so that appropriate data are collected and reported to relevant stakeholders.

[1: ASK]. In Phase 1, we are concerned with the vertical fit of eROI metrics to a company's broader strategic objectives. Here—before deciding on actual metrics—we first determine how senior management across all business units (and not just the HR or mobility department) intends to use the information arising from the chosen metrics, and the purpose it will serve in the broader scheme of achieving organizational-wide objectives.

The point of Phase 1 is to ensure that the choice of metrics is linked to an assignment's purpose. Doing so ensures that only relevant data are

PHASE 1

VERTICAL FIT
Strategic planning
and alignment

1. ASK

Ask: How does manager intend to use information
resulting from expatriate ROI outcomes?

Expected outcomes:
- Help determine what needs to be measured
- Collect appropriate data
- Report findings to relevant stakeholders

**Link measures
to assignment
purpose**

PHASE 2

HORIZONTAL FIT
Operationalization
of measures

2. MIX

Use mix of financial and
nonfinancial measures

Expected outcomes:
- Shifts ROI calculation
  beyond functional/
  financial to strategic/
  non-financial focus as
  appropriate to assignment
  purpose
- Non-financial measures
  allow inclusion of criteria
  which might otherwise be
  overlooked
- Non-financial measures can
  have greater predictive
  power re long-term
  profitability

3. USEFULNESS

Use clear, feasible,
and useful measures

Expected outcomes:
- Clarity = well defined
  measures, avoids
  ambiguity
- Feasibility = manager
  can actually collect
  appropriate data
- Usefulness = resulting
  calculation has meaning
  to manager/firm

4. SIMPLICITY

Avoid overly prescriptive
measures; avoid measuring
every mobility activity

Expected outcomes:
- Measure overall impact
  using a few important
  measures based on clear
  intention for use of
  resulting data and purpose
  of the assignment

5. TIMING

Conduct ROI assessment
at appropriate time

Expected outcomes:
- Enables benefits to be
  assessed beyond time period
  when financial investment
  occurred (if appropriate to
  purpose of assignment)

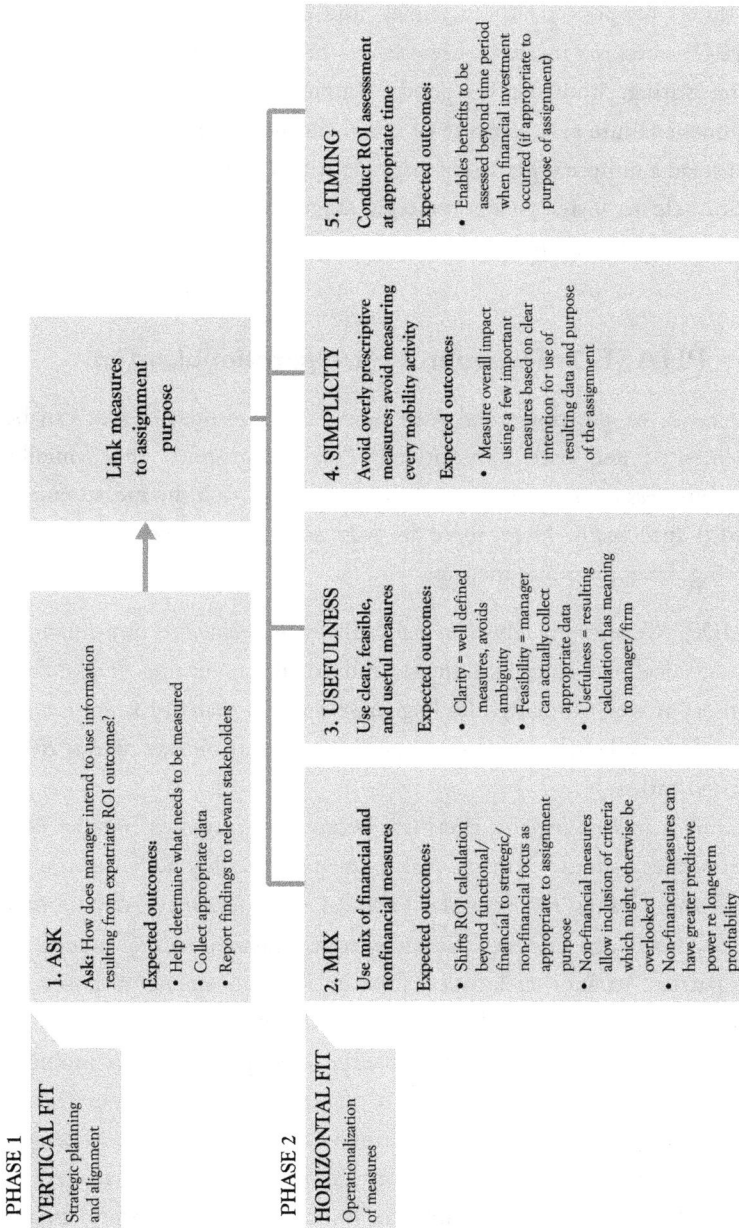

Figure 8.1 Criteria for building an eROI evaluation framework.

captured to assess the costs and benefits arising from any particular international assignment. When metrics are linked to assignment purpose, two things happen: (1) the accuracy, and by default the reliability, of the eROI outcome increases because the metric is appropriate to what it is measuring. SimiCorp is a good example of poor reliability, wherein assignment failure as a measure of eROI did not measure *actual* failure but instead a temporary concern arising out of a shock event; and (2) the metrics help to foster greater strategic alignment of global mobility to other areas of the company.

PHASE 2: *Horizontal Fit/Operationalization*

In Phase 2, we are concerned with how to choose metrics that can be implemented and used appropriately "on the ground" (horizontally, across business operations), as well as how to approach the measurement of eROI specifically. Here, there are four additional criteria to assist in choosing the appropriate metrics.

[2: MIX]. We strongly advise using a mix of financial and non-financial metrics, ideally a combination of traditional accounting (e.g. salary expenses) as well as intangibles (e.g. development gains). Example metrics could be adaptations of *remuneration/costs* and *human capital ROI*, discussed earlier.

Using a mix of metrics is critical because a company's broader corporate strategy should demand that a range of mobility activities is used to determine value, for example, financial revenues, successful transfer of tacit knowledge into explicit knowledge, reassignment of a successful expatriate to another location for career enhancement purposes, or retention of a key individual for succession planning. Furthermore, if we consider that eROI is based on outcomes arising from many mobility activities, then it is logical that a mix of metrics stands a better chance of accounting for outcomes from the total *expatriate management system*.

The benefit of using a mix of metrics is that it pushes managers to capture eROI value beyond only the (much easier to measure) financial costs associated with deploying expatriates, thereby allowing criteria to be assessed that might otherwise be overlooked. This is particularly important for assignments where the main purpose is to achieve intangible or "softer" results, such as acquiring intercultural capabilities or enhancing leadership skills. Because the inclusion of non-financial metrics does not restrict perceived assignment value to only the period in which the corresponding outlay of investment (expense to fund the assignment) occurs, it also provides greater predictive power in relation to longer-term profitability.

[3: USEFULNESS]. In choosing metrics that can be implemented and used appropriately "on the ground," a third criterion is to choose metrics that are *clear, feasible,* and *useful.*

Clarity requires that any eROI metric is well defined and avoids ambiguity, trivialization or irrelevance through too few or too many, or the wrong metrics being used.

Feasibility assesses whether a manager can actually collect the required data that a metric demands in a systematic and chronological manner. As we saw in Chapter 2, one of the main barriers managers face in making progress on eROI measurement is a lack of available time and resources; when data are too difficult to collect, managers are less inclined to bother. In the same chapter we also saw that data collected in an ad hoc manner holds little value for longer-term planning; thus the ability to collect data consistently, over time, in a chronological manner, is critical.

Usefulness implies that outcomes stemming from the eROI metrics can be utilized effectively. Here, we are concerned again with strategic fit: if an eROI metric has clarity and is feasible but the outcome itself will not tell a company what it needs to know about the value gained from international assignments, then the metric itself has little meaning. For example, if *revenue per FTE* or *profit per FTE* is used to assess financial gains, but the global staffing strategy is tied up in expatriates' developmental gains, then the usefulness of such metrics is questionable.

[4: SIMPLICITY]. The next criterion is to avoid being overly prescriptive by attempting to measure the impact of *every* global mobility activity or *every* outcome expected from international assignments. This is important because we know from our MM study that mobility managers are busy people who are frequently overworked and understaffed, leaving them with fewer resources and more time constraints. It therefore makes more sense to measure carefully selected mobility activities using just a few key metrics, ensuring a greater likelihood that there is a clear intention for the *use* of the resulting data, given that less—but the most important—data will be collected.

[5: TIMING]. The final criterion is to measure eROI at the appropriate time, recognizing that the outcomes to be expected from expatriates may not be fully realized for several years. This is particularly true for assignments where predominantly non-financial benefits are expected, in areas such as building leadership and succession pipelines, and talent management programs. Assessments of eROI can also be made at more than one point in time: for example, during the assignment (via performance reviews); at the immediate conclusion of the assignment; during and/or after the point of repatriation (if appropriate); and in subsequent years as the benefits accrue. The timing of the eROI assessment is critical because it shifts the measurement of eROI beyond the traditional accounting approach that expects assessments of value to be conducted in the same time period in which the initial financial investment occurs. Instead, eROI can, and should, be assessed when the value that is gained is expected to be most apparent.

Advantages of an eROI Evaluation Approach

A key benefit of the evaluation framework we outline here is that it elevates the mobility manager from an internally focused and program-based "advisory" role and makes him or her accountable for *business results*. By capturing and combining hard outcomes such as sales and profits, and soft outcomes such as developing expertise and building leadership, the accuracy of eROI assessments improves, thereby improving global staffing decisions.

It also proposes a "paradigm shift" from using only one "best" measure to assess outcomes from every type of assignment, to instead using a mix of metrics that better suit the purposes and expected outcomes of each type of assignment. By accounting for differences in assignment purposes, including different assignment types (short-term, long-term, commuter, and so on), the resulting eROI outcome is far more accurate.

Furthermore, the framework is sufficiently flexible to be adapted when new trends and learning needs emerge and therefore to account for changes in organizational priorities over time, particularly in relation to changes in a broader corporate strategy.

Additionally, our focus on *evaluating*, rather than "measuring," is likely to avoid metrics that are not relevant, timely, or useful. After all, it is not the measurement of eROI itself but what we *do* with the insights gained from the measures that matters and drives business performance.

Summary

Our goal in this chapter has been to advocate how eROI measurement might best be achieved. We began first with a case about SimiCorp that identified problematic approaches to eROI measurement, and then continued by critiquing existing measures of eROI derived from our MM study and explaining the pros and cons of each. We came to the conclusion that many of the measures in use today are flawed and misleading, being incapable of providing predictive information upon which managers might act to improve their mobility programs. This often results in careless measurement of eROI that may drive the wrong actions and create more long-term problems for companies. Next, we outlined some example metrics to illustrate how it can assist in evaluating eROI in the right context. But our central message is that while it can be important for some companies to use metrics, for others it may not, where the metric matters less than the *philosophy* that drives satisfactory eROI outcomes. To end the chapter, we presented, as an alternative approach to measuring eROI, *an evaluation framework*, that guides both the choice of eROI metrics and how eROI measurement can be approached.

CHAPTER 9

Five Core Principles for Effective eROI

What can we do to raise awareness in our organizations that eROI matters? How can we ensure that an eROI approach to managing expatriates is sustainable? This book began with the idea that achieving an acceptable expatriate return on investment is not only essential, but entirely possible when expatriates' needs are better understood and they are managed more effectively. Issues of compensation, career, family, and psychological contracts are changing not only the employment relationship between expatriates and their organizations but the very landscape of global mobility. How we navigate these changes is critical for both immediate and long-term eROI returns, as well as for global staffing initiatives that are essential to many companies competitive advantage.

In prior chapters, we have explored the basics of expatriation and the many facets of eROI, including both its corporate (cROI) and individual (iROI) components. We have discussed four key issues for expatriates to provide an in-depth understanding of the lives they lead and the challenges they face, and how their aspirations are impacting on global mobility in new and complex ways. We have built a model of eROI to demonstrate how the measurement of eROI should be approached, and advocated for a proper strategic base and an integrated set of policies and practices. And we have illustrated many of the pitfalls to eROI evaluation, along with best practices for gaining maximum value from international assignees.

In this final chapter, we combine what we have learned about eROI in Part 1 and Chapters 7 and 8 with what we know about expatriates from Part 2, to offer a roadmap for executing and sustaining an effective eROI program. We do so by translating the points raised in prior chapters into five "core principles" that can assist mobility managers to restructure and realign expatriate management to ensure an appropriate return on the company's expensive investment in expatriate employees. For many companies, this involves "getting back to basics" to re-define and re-structure their global mobility program. For other companies, much less change may be necessary. But to illustrate our point, let's return to the NexCorp case that we first looked at in Chapter 2 to determine where your organization sits on the road to improving its eROI approach.

CASE: Getting Back to Basics at NexCorp

When we left NexCorp, the company faced major, apparently intractable, issues caused by a decade-long, unfocused, laissez-faire approach to global mobility, particularly in its use of international assignments. To recap, these issues included inconsistent policies as well as the use of international assignments for personal purposes rather than organizational goals. This had resulted in an international assignment "blow-out"—too many assignments, extended for too long, and going over budget. Talent development was in a bigger mess because it attracted the wrong people to both the global mobility *and* talent management programs.

To resolve the issues, senior management at NexCorp decided to adopt an eROI-based approach, stemming from "getting back to basics." This required the company to (a) build a mobility program with eROI in mind; (b) understand the barriers, and the work required to overcome them; and (c) evaluate eROI in a meaningful way.

Senior management at NexCorp realized that in order to reduce the number and cost of assignments and increase the firm's eROI, it was necessary to bring more rigor to the selection and approval processes for international assignments, greater alignment between assignments and the firm's talent and business priorities, and greater visibility to mobility costs. To achieve these goals, the first step was to articulate the firm's overarching objectives for its mobility program: to give NexCorp's most talented people a truly global mindset; to ensure diversity of leadership and thinking; and to support key business priorities. These explicit objectives set a clear direction for career and talent development for line managers, business units, and heads of departments.

With the intent that NexCorp's new approach would be implemented via a multi-year initiative, as well as through an evolutionary process of changing the firm's culture and management, the Senior Vice President (SVP) of mobility and his team then identified a number of key actions to build the new eROI program. Work began in earnest on designing and implementing various major changes to the way the mobility program was structured and managed.

Standardized Policies

Building on earlier work to streamline expatriate benefits, NexCorp implemented four standard policies to cover all expatriate assignments— two for long-term assignments, one for short-term assignments, and one for permanent transfers. The policies detailed explicit terms and conditions for each assignment type, including remuneration and employment conditions, relocation assistance and services, and assignment-related benefits. In addition, a legacy policy transitioned existing expatriates into one of the four new policies. "Exceptions" were outlawed. The driver of this change was cost containment.

Assignment Approval Process

NexCorp then launched its first formal approval process for new international assignments. In effect, the approval process now requires managers to submit a proposal that documents the following information about a proposed assignment:

- *Reasons for creating the assignment*, including (a) the assignment role, (b) the specific purpose of the assignment, (c) the business justification for the assignment, and (d) why a local employee is not the preferred option.
- *Anticipated investment and benefits*, including (a) specific, measurable and dated objectives for the assignment, and (b) projected assignment costs against which actuals can be assessed.
- *Talent considerations*, including (a) strength of the preferred assignee in terms of latest performance rating, and (b) a development plan for the assignee. Company guidelines

now state that only top performers—candidates with a
"1" or "2" performance rating out of a possible "5"—can
be considered for international assignments. Similarly,
there is a new emphasis on ensuring that the most talented
employees are the primary source of new assignees.

Once completed, assignment proposals are reviewed by a regional
head of international assignments as well as the SVP of mobility and
other members of the firm's senior management team. If any of these
believes the proposal needs a more robust business case or a stronger
career development plan for the assignee, the proposal is returned to
the requesting manager in the business unit.

An HR team member then enters the information from approved
proposals into an Excel spreadsheet, which currently serves as a rudi-
mentary international assignment database for documenting, tracking,
and ultimately evaluating assignment success. On a very practical level,
the new approval process, while perceived by some as bureaucratic,
forms a "back to basics" approach for building a measurement culture
for eROI at NexCorp that is well worth the time and effort.

Integration with eHR

As part of the multi-year evolution of the mobility program, the SVP
of mobility developed new software for a global HR database that
automatically captures data via the intranet from every assignment
proposal submitted to HR; captures much more data *during* an assignment; and includes repatriation or further assignment actions to better
reflect the full life cycle of an assignment. A global assignee payroll that
integrates with the global HR database has also been implemented.
This is to ensure that expatriates paid on host-country payrolls still
feed into the company's global HR system, making it easier to track
and report ongoing payments and allowances.

Although NexCorp recognized that the development and imple-
mentation of new mobility software required bringing in outside—and
costly—consultants with expertise in this area, it viewed this expense as
worthwhile given that its international operations are spread across many
countries and regions, and co-ordination problems can be a challenge.

Review of Existing International Assignments

In tandem with the launch of the new assignment approval program, NexCorp also embarked on a company-wide review of all existing international assignments to ensure that they could still deliver the greatest value possible to the company. Those in doubt would need to be culled.

The process began by requiring business managers to justify each active assignment and to develop specific action plans for the assignee, detailing such information as why they were on assignment, what they were currently doing, and where they could expect to be within the

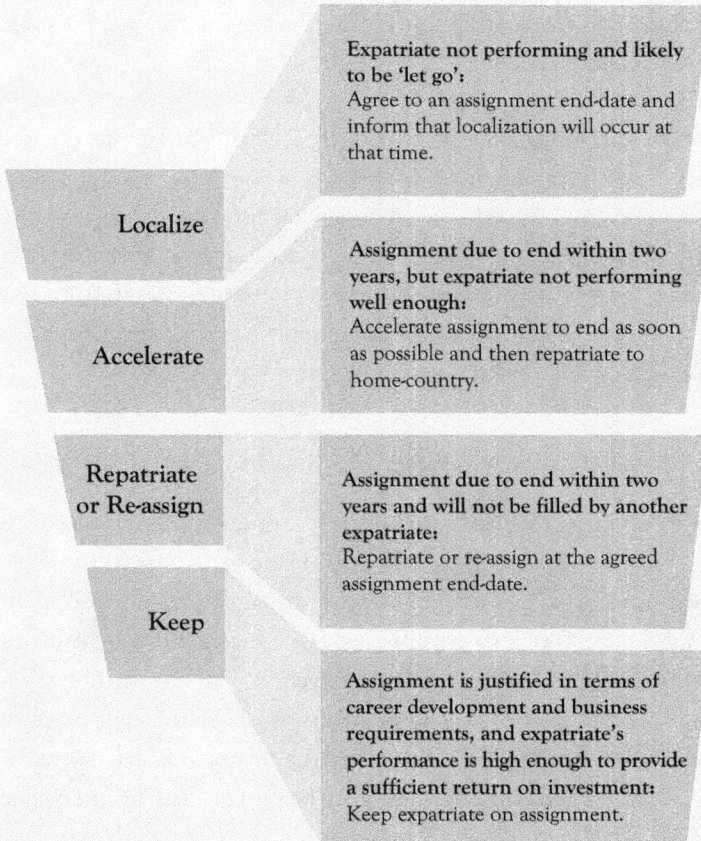

Localize

Expatriate not performing and likely to be 'let go':
Agree to an assignment end-date and inform that localization will occur at that time.

Accelerate

Assignment due to end within two years, but expatriate not performing well enough:
Accelerate assignment to end as soon as possible and then repatriate to home-country.

Repatriate or Re-assign

Assignment due to end within two years and will not be filled by another expatriate:
Repatriate or re-assign at the agreed assignment end-date.

Keep

Assignment is justified in terms of career development and business requirements, and expatriate's performance is high enough to provide a sufficient return on investment:
Keep expatriate on assignment.

Figure 9.1. Flow chart for international assignment review.

next 2 years. Using a flow chart (see below), managers were required to choose one of four possible exit strategies from the mobility program for each existing assignee, with a specific end date attached to the strategy.

As one would expect, the process of choosing an exit strategy for assignees played out quite differently across the various business groups. Some managers in smaller groups were quite happy to give up a number of expatriates without replacing them (a form of "functional turnover"), though this begged the question of why the particular assignments existed in the first place. Managers in larger business groups, however, were more reluctant to let go of assignees: many cited the importance of these assignments to maintaining standards of performance, and the attraction of an international career as a reason for people to join NexCorp.

In the end, the business units agreed to a 45% reduction in the firm's total number of expatriates over 2 years. To remain on track toward the 2-year goal, regular meetings to report on mobility volume and activity were established between the SVP of mobility and the top 15 executives in the company. Two key agenda items for these meetings were (1) comparison of reduction numbers against business unit targets, and (2) reports on the number of new expatriates added since the previous review period.

Capturing and Monitoring Costs

The next step required a thorough examination of NexCorp's third-party vendor responsible for reporting relocation expenses for international assignees to the mobility manager. Was it tracking and monitoring costs adequately to provide data that could then be used to determine eROI? As it turned out, the vendor had not been capturing out-of-pocket assignee expenses, which instead were being processed by expatriates through NexCorp's internal expense management system. This resulted in relocation costs being reported by the vendor that did not reflect the actual costs paid by the company; thus, it was impossible to get a clear picture of the total expenditure.

To make assignment costs more transparent, NexCorp implemented a new process whereby all relocation costs were to be processed through its third-party vendor, utilizing a central auditing system with increased reporting capabilities: this resulted in more accurate, traceable, and manageable data.

ROI Champions

As expected, NexCorp faced considerable internal resistance, particularly from long-tenured senior management who had benefitted from the legacy program, to the changes now being made to its mobility program. To overcome this challenge, the company has installed "ROI champions" throughout the firm who act as torchbearers for the strategic value of the new mobility agenda and the good progress being made toward its goals. The most visible champion is the relatively new CEO, a passionate manager prepared to make the tough decisions in order to succeed. "When push comes to shove," says the SVP of mobility, "we rely on the CEO to bang the table and say, "Okay, guys, why aren't you doing this?"

NexCorp has made substantial progress in dealing with major dysfunctions in its global mobility approach. It has done so by developing a new process that rigorously applies the idea of eROI to all aspects of expatriate management, thus replacing an uncontrolled, free-for-all program with a system that is more strategic, objectives-driven, and consistent.

Much like NexCorp, companies serious about measuring eROI need to recognize that a "back to basics" approach—often with an initial *absence* of metrics—is an essential first step. Devoting time and resources to this effort is critical. Identifying areas of weakness and seeking expertise—both internally and externally—help to provide guidance as to what needs improvement, who might be tasked with doing it, and the expected benefits. What helped NexCorp were a number of necessary first steps devoid of metrics: strategic analysis, policy formulation, procedural change, and the gathering of top management support. It was not metrics that turned NexCorp around, but management determination to implement change, and the policy framework of which metrics is the likely next step.

The reasoning behind such an approach is simple: metrics may tell NexCorp *what* it got, but it won't tell the company *why* it got that particular result! And if the company doesn't know why, it will not be able to improve or repeat those practices that have helped it achieve some measure of lasting return from the global staffing program. When there is no underlying mindset to metrics' usage—no eROI philosophy applied to the choice of measure and what value the metric can ultimately deliver, as we saw countless times in our MM study—then the measures can be somewhat meaningless, ill applied, and, in some cases, quite misleading as we saw, for example, in the SimiCorp case in Chapter 8.

The reality demonstrated by the NexCorp case is that the determination of eROI is not as complex and sophisticated to implement as most companies might think: relatively simple steps can move an organization into a practical eROI program. Strengthening or overhauling an existing infrastructure for managing assignments as a first step—planning, selection, approvals, and reporting—through small, targeted steps can significantly increase a firm's capabilities to better align assignments with business and organizational objectives, and to assess the success of assignments in terms of costs and benefits in order to improve future assignment effectiveness and ROI.

Utilizing the targeted activities driving the change at NexCorp, we now translate these into five core principles that most companies looking to effectively transition into better eROI management can adapt. Let's examine each of them in turn.

Five Core Principles for Effective eROI

Principle 1: Re-Frame Your Thinking—From "International Assignments" to "Global Mobility"

Expatriation practice today has evolved considerably from what it was even 5 years ago, moving remorselessly from "international assignments" to "global mobility." Such change has been driven by the steady growth in globalization, the rising importance of the international labor market, and changing international employment relationships. Many employees at NexCorp, for example, joined the company specifically for the opportunity to develop an international career, but their aspirations caused long-term problems for the organization. Such "global careerists" (discussed in Chapter 5) will present ongoing challenges for MNCs, as well as providing substantial benefits for savvy companies who "get" what they are about and the value they potentially bring.

In Table 9.1, we outline many of the changes apparent in modern expatriation caused, in part, by the emergence of global careerists, but also by other important areas such as those outlined in Chapters 3, 4, and 6, including that expatriates are now increasingly demanding rewards beyond only financial remuneration and that the prestige of an international assignment has been replaced by the normalization of global mobility as a "routine" step on the career ladder.

Table 9.1 illustrates that companies need to focus away from repatriation and on to re-assignment, that global careerists are the new expatriates, and that lifetime employability is driving the emergence of iROI as a catalyst for downplaying corporate interests. In short, expatriation has evolved from a focus on international assignments, to one that demands global mobility as a growing—and necessary—expectation.

Furthermore, because the changes we see are *inevitable and permanent*, it is crucial that companies recognize, appreciate, and embrace the evolution of expatriate management and view eROI as an "all or nothing" game. Having one foot in the future and another stuck in the past is counterproductive, as is sticking one's head in the sand and ignoring the signs. Both will lead to unexpected costs because of an inability to adapt which, compared to NexCorp, whose agility to proactively manage and adapt their global staffing practices in response to a changing international environment, has set it apart as an eventual winner in the "war for talent."

Principle 2: Champion eROI

As we saw in the NexCorp case, to achieve superior eROI the philosophy outlined in Part 1 of this book has to be embedded organization-wide, through every business unit dealing with expatriates. Reforming only the mobility department is a necessary but not sufficient condition for a successful eROI program. An effective program needs to be driven, as in NexCorp, from the top down, from the CEO to the most junior HR staff member, and all the way back again. This gets the kind of attention eROI deserves.

Table 9.1. Evolution of Expatriation: From "International Assignments" to "Global Mobility"

International assignment	→	Global mobility
Organizations		
Repatriation	→	Reassignment
One–off assignment	→	Global career employees
Full expatriate remuneration (relational contract)	→	Local-plus and localization (transactional contract)
Individual candidate selection	→	"Bench" mentality (candidate pool)
Building talent, e.g. PCNs	→	Buying talent, e.g. HCNs, TCNs/local foreign hires, returnees, and inpatriates
Global staffing workforce consists of elite cadre; international presence optional	→	Global staffing workforce consists of "international" employees; international presence essential
International assignment as reward for high-potential employees	→	Global mobility "normalized" as essential for employees' careers
Social security and pension location-specific	→	Pension and retirement schemes harmonized globally under "umbrella company"
Minimum or no international work-related travel during assignment	→	"Flexpatriate expatriates," i.e. extensive international work-related travel while on assignment
Individuals		
Company-assigned expatriation (company ownership)	→	Self-initiated expatriation (individual ownership)
Permanent and semi-permanent loyalty (long-term)	→	Temporary opportunistic engagements (short-term)
International assignment as a unique once-in-a-lifetime opportunity	→	International mobility as a routine lifestyle choice
Easily identified home country	→	Global citizen
International assignment #1 value = tangible benefits (financial gain)	→	International assignment #1 value = intangible benefits (career and personal development)
Barriers to mobility = dual careers, cost of living	→	Barriers to mobility = environmental degradation, cultural discrimination, political risk
International assignment for promotion and job security	→	International assignment for (multi)lateral job changes
Temporary migration (employment visa)	→	Semi-permanent migration (permanent residency and/or dual citizenship)
International schools as interim education solution	→	International and/or host-country (local) schools as long-term education choice
Lifetime employment (one firm)	→	Lifetime employability (many firms)

To achieve an eROI philosophy, most companies need one or more *eROI champions*—senior managers or directors passionate about global mobility, who probably have personal expatriate experience and are supported by top management in terms of time, energy, resources, and influence within the organization, to support large-scale change for however long it takes. If eROI matters, then finding the right person to build it, implement it, and own it also matters. NexCorp charged the mobility manager with this task and last we heard he was doing an excellent job of delivering the necessary changes. Key to his success was the CEO's involvement to encourage, or even enforce, compliance. Who in your organization has the skills and passion to drive a new eROI initiative?

Principle 3: Think Long-Term, Act Short-Term

While long-term planning has its place, short-term results can also be advantageous. To achieve superior eROI, companies are in need of long-term strategies and short-term "wins"—outcomes that feed into eROI evaluations on a quarterly or annual basis but do not disrupt 3-, 5- or 10-year plans. We illustrated in Chapter 5, for example, that TCNs and other locally hired foreigners can provide strong short-term eROI results because their employment is usually tied to "on-assignment" gains and because they are cheaper, whereas PCNs can provide more extensive longer-term eROI gains because their employment is often tied to succession and talent management planning.

The combination of "think long-term, act short-term" is becoming a new reality for many MNCs as they struggle to staff their offshore subsidiaries, not because they feel compelled to give up the long-term strategizing that is an effective part of their eROI approach but because, for some companies, short-term ROI is their only means of achieving true eROI success. Our point here is that putting all our eROI eggs into one long-term basket is a mistake: short-terms gains are an essential *shared* reality for today's world of global mobility.

A good illustration is the changes at NexCorp, which are intended to deliver both short-term and long-term outcomes. While NexCorp's underlying strategy remains long-term, it nonetheless requires immediate short-term results to kick-start the program and show it means business, and has achieved this by reviewing the existing international assignee population and culling "dysfunctional" assignees. By making short-term decisions about re-deploying, repatriating, and localizing expatriates, NexCorp is also solving a longer-term problem of spiraling costs and a too-flexible approval process and has set a stake in the ground for the future. Thus, NexCorp demonstrates strong alignment between its short-term outcomes and long-term goals.

Expatriates, too, experience the "think long-term, act short-term" approach but in a different way. Most, as we found, know that their current assignment is going to benefit them immediately through economic or development rewards (as outlined in Chapter 6). But many are also long-term career planners, who really want to know how the next assignment and the move after that—even if it means repatriating—will feed into a "bigger picture" career plan that boosts their iROI. But with mergers and acquisitions, buy-outs, bailouts, and bankruptcies commonplace in the global business economy, it is hard for companies to plan or predict with confidence, or guarantee, long-term benefits. Global careerists' mentality is that they need to know, if at all possible, how *today* factors into *tomorrow*. Thus, when organizations are able to align their longer-term planning with the short- and long-term outcomes expected by their expatriates, the resulting synergy can have significant implications for talent management, which leads us to our next principle.

Principle 4: Embrace Global Careerists

Careers, including international careers, are not what they used to be. As we explained in Chapter 5, most people now have many different jobs and employers during their career, involving times of major and intense *transition*—between jobs, organizations, types of work, levels of responsibility, projects, employment and self-employment, periods of work and periods at home with family—and even between countries. In other words, having a career involves frequently *crossing boundaries*, and the concept of the "boundaryless career," which indicates a progression of career moves across multiple employment settings and borders, has become prominent in careers thinking.

And of course expatriation brings another, new boundary into the frame, as careerists cross *international* and *cultural* boundaries with increasing frequency.[1] With each boundary they cross, even as CAEs, expatriates have to re-invent their careers, and parts of themselves, taking control of their own careers and seeking to direct their own lives. As "global careerists," these expatriates are active participants in the wider global economy and seek to develop skills and networks that are valuable in that economy.[2] More importantly, they are a new, permanent feature of the international labor market.

On the other hand, MNCs also have interests to protect that are vested in their expatriates' careers. Like all organizations they dislike excessive labor turnover, especially among their most talented employees. Because MNCs typically invest huge amounts of money, they too want an ROI— an eROI not an iROI—from the employment relationship. But over the long-term, what it takes to derive eROI for the organization may not be compatible with what the employee needs, or expects, his or her iROI to be given that, as the careers world in which expatriates live changes, assignees are also changing. Today's expatriates are more gutsy than ever, buoyed by an international labor market that increasingly supports their movement outside of the safety of the MNC. And of course the impact on eROI, particularly in relation to staff retention and the longer-term eROI each expatriate holds, can be huge.

How can these incompatibilities be adequately dealt with in the world of expatriate management, particularly if global careerists are not only here to stay but, as we discovered in the Expat Study, their numbers are also on the rise?

In our view, it's about working *smarter* but not necessarily harder. Savvy companies have learned to embrace and use global careerists to their advantage by leveraging what they have to offer. These companies recognize that many already exist in the organization despite their covert nature, identify where they are among their ranks, strive to understand what makes them tick, and then leverage their skills and talent in the short-term without losing sight of longer-term opportunities. Rather than be victims of the global war for talent, these companies act as facilitators of expatriates' careers, unafraid to engage in power-shared employment arrangements in exchange for guaranteed short-term benefits, and poten-tially longer-term gains if the employment relationship can be sustained.

In eROI terms, this type of approach makes a lot of sense because when all is said and done, the short-term eROI that global careerists are guaranteed to deliver, particularly as SIEs or those with an SIE orientation, is a valuable proposition that does not require the massive investment their CAE counterparts demand. In short, global careerists can impact the bottom line faster and with more impact than CAEs/PCNs. And in today's cost-cutting environment, that's not necessarily a bad thing. Here's why:

- global careerists represent a less expensive source of talent because a large majority will accept local or local-plus terms and conditions
- global careerists facilitate organizational agility—the ability to source the right talent quickly—because many are already in, or near, the locations where talent shortages exist
- global careerists desire power-shared employment relationships, thereby instilling a higher level of maturity that is often missing in "owner occupied" PCN assignments
- global careerists want to be global, want to succeed, and they strive hard to achieve both
- global careerists want to have influence over the terms of their employment and in doing so are more invested in the outcomes
- global careerists are not driven only by financial gain because their motivation rests largely in *being* global; these are professionals educated and trained in one country who *choose* to develop their careers elsewhere.[3]

We consider that more value can be gained by having a cohort of global careerists in the global staffing mix than by using any other type of expatriate (particularly PCNs). We further predict that the most successful MNCs in the coming decade will be those that utilize a smaller cohort of PCNs in favor of global careerists as the dominant part of their international talent pool, not just because they are less expensive to employ but because, over time, there are likely to be more of them available on the international labor market making them easier to find.

We know, for example, that the senior executive talent war is particularly fierce: top-tier executives are in hot demand, with those in emerging economies receiving three to four times more job offers annually than their developed economy counterparts.[4] The relatively new phenomenon of employing foreign executives in local organizations (FELOs) further ties into this type of approach to global staffing.[5]

An important take-away here is that organizations can no longer rely solely on "pull" factors such as higher earnings and a better standard of living to draw in global talent.[6] More is needed to attract individuals willing to undertake the unprecedented level of global mobility that is required as companies enter new markets and expand their operations. One way to attract global careerists is to invest in the employment relationship because their mobility is a personal issue, not necessarily a money issue, where the psychological contract matters most of all. As illustrated in Chapter 6, today's expatriate employment relationship is no longer dominated only by the interests of the organization as it ruthlessly directs, incentivizes, and rewards assignees to its own advantage.

Remember the case of Eduardo, the MOVER Inc. expatriate whose story we described in Chapter 3. Eduardo has hassles with his employer due to unilateral cuts it makes in his remuneration. With each new hassle, Eduardo comes closer to leaving the company and finding another career opportunity, possibly in a new location, where he can make a fresh start and leverage his existing skills and talents. Potentially, he is changing, psychologically at least, from being a "loyal company servant" to being a ship-jumper, an SIE, a "global careerist." Eduardo knows that he has developed huge personal knowledge resources that are of ongoing value, not just to his employer but with other MNCs as well. MOVER Inc. needs to be very careful in the way it deals with him.

We cannot forget that global careerists are individuals with "long-term personal agency" who can sustain global careers that involve multiple moves over multiple locations, but not necessarily with the same employer. What attracts global careerists is a feeling that their global aspirations are understood, and that mobility is a valid personal goal as well as a valid corporate objective. A policy then needs to be put in place that balances their interests with those of the organization.

Principle 5: Acquire a Dynamic Talent Pool

In eROI terms, talent flow matters. Where expatriates are sourced from, when and how they are deployed, and whether they stay or go can impact on eROI in significant ways, much as NexCorp discovered. Building a dynamic talent pool and deploying it to where it is most needed is no longer a nice-to-have but is a necessity, a critical "decision science" to assist in global staffing decisions.[7] As we outlined in Chapter 1, this means no longer being reliant on only traditional expatriates, that is PCNs, but instead having a sufficient number of qualified candidates drawn from a range of assignee types that includes TCNs, inpatriates, returnees, and HCNs. Flexibility to widen the talent pool is essential in a tightening international labor market.

Yet the connection between global mobility activities and talent pool acquisition remains weak: many companies continue to use international assignments without linking them to developing future global leaders or to meeting their assignees' career development expectations.[8] Nonetheless it is these same companies that espouse the hiring of foreigners as broadening their organization's understanding of global markets and helping it to develop a global mindset.[9] Our point here is that while hiring and deploying international staff frequently costs more in recruitment and wage expenses, labor mobility per se widens the talent pool, enabling companies to engage in the hiring of better quality people. Critical to achieving a larger talent pool is the ability to strike a balance: avoiding underinvestment in expatriates' global career aspirations which can lead to turnover and a depleted talent pool, and conversely avoiding overinvestment which can lead to unnecessary budget blowouts to fund activities and training that employees might otherwise invest in themselves.

Widening the talent pool does not necessarily mean hiring or deploying only "star" talent or "A level" players as advocated by McKinsey in the late 1990s.[10] This strategy often backfires because while this elite group of employees typifies "high impact" they can also be high maintenance individuals with complex needs.[11] While we cannot ignore that "star" talent frequently drives a disproportionate share of an organization's business performance and shareholder value[12], talent is nonetheless needed at different levels for different reasons. Behind the top 10% of the high-achieving workforce lies a bigger pool of "B level" employees— just as intelligent as their "A" level colleagues and also steady performers, but perhaps with less ambition and more desire for work–life balance.[13] When we widen the talent pool, we no longer ask "do we have enough expatriates?" but "do we have the right mix of people?"[14]

All of which is to say, while it is one thing to pay lip service to "finding the right talent" to build a dynamic talent pool, it's another entirely to go out there and actually find it. How do we do this?

One way to develop a talent pool, of course, is to *buy* talent, which often saves time and is less expensive than building talent internally. Here, global careerists and TCNs can play a crucial role as global staff already in the international labor market, who can be recruited and compensated differently—and less expensively—than PCNs, and are often more willing and better able to get into the global mobility game. While global careerists are certainly more temporary than traditional assignees (PCNs), and many are little more than short-term resources, on the flip side they also take more responsibility for their own careers, expect less support from their employers to relocate, and are able to "hit the ground running." As noted earlier, local-plus is often their preferred compensation because it provides enough flexibility for them to still have control over where they go and what they do, thereby avoiding long-term commitments to pensions and share plans as would be expected for PCNs. As we saw in Chapter 5, these expatriates are also highly proactive in managing their careers and motivated to fast-track it wherever the right jobs are.

Where do we buy the talent we need? First, we can look to competitors in our industry. We know from our Expat Study that a reasonably large—and unhappy—talent pool exists in many MNCs, with expatriates interested in searching for new job opportunities during their assignment and at the approach or onset of repatriation or re-assignment. While these employees do not actively advertise their availability, many are open to opportunities—and the opportunistic behavior of competitor companies—that arise through networking at sporting, social, and chambers of commerce events. Others will answer the phone when the headhunters call: nearly half of the participants in our Expat Study, for example, were pursued by international recruiters during their assignment.

Another approach is to "think regional." The rise of the "Asian leader" over the past decade, for example, has transformed how and where talent can be sourced. Regional talent flows in Asia Pacific are increasing, with many companies fulfilling their talent needs from within the region using HCNs, local foreign hires, or returnee candidates.[15] Specialization in a particular skill, to a professional network, or within a specific location has become "highly prized," not just by employers but also by *employees*.[16] Our point here is that talent is not necessarily defined by race or passport or even age (consider, for example, that some executives close to retirement are showing up in China to help establish foreign operations[17]), but by regional expertise from years of experience living and working in Asia or some other part of the world, with many expatriates having arrived in these locations in their early to mid-30s.

An alternative to buying a dynamic talent pool is, of course, to *build* the talent that already exists in one's organization. Although we predict that a decade from now global careerists will dominate the international employment scene, company-assigned expatriates such as PCNs nonetheless remain an extremely important part of the global staffing mix, because they bring with them stability and security, and can be counted on to still be around when the global careerists have moved on to other opportunities. Furthermore, although finding the "perfect candidate" for any given role is ideal, sometimes it comes down to deploying the best *available* person, even a second or third choice. In crunch time, when talent is short, this is often when PCNs are most in demand and can be counted on to deliver.

But building talent requires more than just putting in place a talent "structure"; it also requires developing, motivating, and retaining employees identified within it. One way to build talent is to open up previously invisible opportunities for young opportunity-seekers (e.g. graduates) and localized professionals who are often considered to be involved only in other processes and functions unrelated to a company's international or global staffing strategy. Another is to inpatriate HCNs to the headquarters location, or re-expatriate expatriates of host-country origin (returnees).

Developing and motivating expatriates is trickier. As we demonstrated in Part 2, expatriate employment relationships can be especially complex, particularly in relation to career management support. If little expertise exists internally to provide this, consider funding executive coaching and mentoring for expatriates, which has been found among millennial employees in particular to be a valuable part of their expected training and development.[18] This isn't about helping them find a job with a competitor, but about managing expectations and helping them find ways to overcome some of their career frustrations while sustaining existing employment relationships.

Lastly, once we have bought or developed talent, what do we do with it, and how do we counteract talent loss and brain drain? We believe that an objective of every eROI program should be the retention of assignees. But the measure of retention is beyond "turnover": numbers don't tell us much about why expatriates leave, nor their commitment to the organization, particularly during an economic downturn when fewer assignees are likely to leave. Nor does it measure the different specific potential of each particular member of the pool, potential which may have been subsequently lost. Whether the goal is short-term on-assignment retention from bought talent, or long-term succession planning for talent that is built internally, the goal has to be to keep the people one really needs long enough to achieve the specific objective that made the organization want to employ or deploy them in the first place.

To get the best out of global talent, Deloitte suggests a shift of focus, away from just the end points of talent management—finding and acquiring it, and then trying to keep it—and on to the intervening processes of deploying and developing it,[19] because if organizations are not managing the talent at their disposal, they're liking doing nothing more than churning through time and dollars in an endless cycle of acquisition. Furthermore, at a time when even strong internal talent development does not guarantee freedom from talent shortages, the combination of buying and building talent is likely to be a more successful global staffing approach than focusing on one strategy in isolation. In China, for example, the supply and demand of available managers to run the estimated 50,000 new MNCs that enter the China market each year is running on empty: for every qualified Chinese manager, there are predicted to be nearly eight available positions.[20]

We recommend that for organizations to acquire the dynamic talent pools they seek, it is essential to retain a mix of global staff. This will involve actively recruiting and developing different types of expatriates, being collectively intelligent about staffing choices and embracing global careerists, and engaging workforce diversity (e.g. by utilizing the inpatriation of HCNs and employing more women and other non-traditional expatriates). An organization's future is dependent on its current talent pool and its mechanisms for enlarging and developing that pool and encouraging the pool's members to develop themselves. This makes our fifth key principle perhaps the most important of all.

A Final Word: Expatriates as Heroes

Nearly 20 years ago, US academic Joyce Osland wrote an insightful book on expatriation, *The Adventure of Working Abroad: Hero Tales from the Global Frontier*. Considered by some to be ahead of its time, her book was based on qualitative research, "tales told by expatriates," similar in some respect to the anecdotes and cases we have included in this book. Osland used Joseph Campbell's theory of "the myth of the hero's adventure" to show how the expatriate can be viewed as a hero, in the manner of, for example, Odysseus: the hero is called to adventure, to a great quest for a huge trophy or victory, heeds the call, crosses the threshold into the unknown, and reaches a place with the potential for the hero to achieve transformation and spiritual rebirth. After a series of trials and ordeals— but aided by "magical" gods, guides, and mentors along the way—the hero crosses back across the return threshold, now the master of two worlds instead of one.

What are the implications of considering today's expatriates as heroes? As with Osland's heroes, the call to expatriate is experienced as drama on an international labor "stage," and creates both excitement and anxiety as actors enter and exit through various roles. Crossing boundaries into new cultures provides physical tests and obstacles that demand maturity and courage to navigate the unknown. "Magical" assistance often comes from local mentors outside of the organization who can interpret the culture and provide guidance through it. Transformation takes place as the hero lets go of previous frames of reference, accepts new roles, norms, and customs, and becomes somewhat "addicted" to the novelty of new experiences and the learning that takes place.

But the biggest implication of acceptance of the expatriate as hero is that a true mythical hero is not a pawn who does as directed by corporate masters, but is a proactive, empowered individual who makes things happen because he or she has a personal agenda in which self-development is a key part. Heroism, in other words, is mostly based on an iROI rather than an eROI model.

Beyond this, however, we are forced to conclude that expatriates, though they often possess heroic qualities, are not pure heroes in the Odysseus mold, because in the end their quest is not only for their own development and victories but also for the purposes of their organizations—cROI added to iROI.

If we can accept that expatriates are not pure heroes in the classical sense, they are nonetheless heroic in their aspirations, demeanor, and self-understanding; in their pursuit of power-shared, respectful employment relationships; and their gutsy take-no-prisoners approach to acquiring international careers. As we have seen, increasingly they do not necessarily return, as Odysseus did, in due course to their own "home" shores: instead, in global careers, they cross boundaries to new locations, new organizations, and new goals. For those that do return "home," their heroism is not "switched off" but continues and adapts in new circumstances.

Read again the story of Craig Phillips, the Vietnam-based expatriate with whose story we started this book: there's something wonderfully heroic, as he progresses from assignment to assignment in ever less familiar cultural settings, in his constant search for problem solutions and new learning. Heroic, too, is the by-product of his actions, along with others' like him whose stories we have told: the transformation of expatriation from its traditional beginnings to its modern interpretation, the evolution of which is unprecedented for the sheer enormity of what is at stake for the global mobility function, the extent of the changes unfolding in a burgeoning international labor market, and the ramifications that will arise from it for decades to come. Because of Craig, and other "heroes" like him, expatriation as we once knew it will never be the same.

Clearly, today's world is less magical and more complex than Odysseus's. Expatriate heroes can't do it on their own, yet somehow the corporate framework within which they operate must not smother their heroism but support it. It must help them to focus on it, facilitate when and where they need help, and recognize the preciousness of their heroic quality. It must reward them so as to retain heroic commitment, look after the partners and families who travel with them, synchronize with their own developing long-term aspirations, and keep the faith. Most of all, it must find ways of ensuring that the two great quests—corporate and personal, or cROI and iROI—are always in focus as guiding stars and always compatible. As the world, its organizations and its people continue to globalize, that in itself is a heroic mission worth the attention of many.

APPENDIX A

Mobility Managers Study

"MM Study" for short, this study involved interviews with 51 global mobility managers who work directly with expatriates or manage mobility programs, who were drawn from 51 global firms.

The objectives of the study were to understand how organizations define and measure expatriate ROI (including any barriers they may face in using or developing effective ROI measures), and what, specifically, causes expatriate ROI to change, i.e. to increase and/or decrease according to a range of internal and external organizational factors.

Interviews (ranging in length from 45 min to 2 h) were conducted over a 2-year period from August 2004 to August 2006, mostly by phone (96%) with the remainder (4%) being face-to-face, to allow for time-zone and geographical differences. All interviews were recorded (with permission), and later transcribed. The interviews generated nearly 700 pages of transcripts.

The majority of the 51 firms are classified as a Fortune 500 company; consequently these are very large, well-established organizations that have utilized expatriates for a long time. Eighty percent are public companies representing 18 different industries. The participating firms have extensive regional coverage with headquarters in North America, Europe, UK, Asia Pacific, and the Middle East/Africa. This is a truly global study in which firms are represented across six continents.

In total, the 51 firms represent approximately 76,000 international assignees, with more than 52,000 long-term assignees. The average number of expatriate employees was 1,503 per firm, and the average number of long-term assignees was 1,029. The expatriate population of each firm represents between 0.02% and 23.80% of the total headcount for employees worldwide. Table 1 provides background data on the 51 firms in the MM Study.

Table 1. Sample Characteristics for the MM Study

n = 51	%	n = 51	%
Industry		*Number of employees*	
Energy & utilities	15	Less than 10,000	12
Financial services	9.5	10,000–49,000	37
Computer products & services	9.5	50,000–100,000	20
Banking	8	More than 100,000	31
Consumer products manufacturers	8		
Pharmaceutical/healthcare	8	*Number of expatriates*	
Business services/consulting	6	Less than 100	8
Food and beverages	6	101–500	8
Insurance	6	501–1,000	8
Aerospace & defense	4	1,001–5,000	19
Automotive & transport	4	More than 5,000	8
Metals & mining	4		
Chemicals	2	*Number of long-term assignees*	
Electronics	2	Less than 100	15
Industrial manufacturing	2	101–500	57
Media	2	501–1,000	4
Telecommunications services	2	1,001–5,000	20
Transportation services	2	More than 5,000	4
Company type		*Fortune 500*	
Public	80	Yes	63
Private/partnership	12	No	37
Subsidiary	4		
Government	2	*Total no. employees*[a]	3,762,400
Joint venture	2	Mean	73,772
		Lowest	2,600
Company structure		Highest	346,000
Global/MNC	94		
National	6	*Total no. expatriates*[a,b]	76,676
		Mean	1,503
Headquarters location		Lowest	30
North America	51	Highest	19,000
Europe	23		
UK	12	*Total no. long-term assignees*[a]	52,483
Asia Pacific	8	Mean	1,029
Middle East & Africa	6	Lowest	15
		Highest	15,000
Gender of mobility manager			
Female	56		
Male	44		

[a] These are employee numbers, not percentages

[b] Expatriates include all types of assignments and assignees, that is long-term, short-term, one-way transfer and commuter, and PCN, HCN, and TCN.

We used computer-aided qualitative analysis software (NVIVO version 7) to analyze data, hierarchical categories to reduce, sort, and cluster the data and then derive key themes, and content analysis to determine how strongly the themes are manifested.

To reduce researcher bias due to Yvonne McNulty's insider status in the expatriate community, an inter-rater reliability procedure was used. An independent researcher conducted a preliminary round of scoring of the categories, themes, and sub-themes on 10 randomly selected transcripts, giving an initial inter-rater reliability score of 93.5% based on an established formula. After consultation and discussion, a second round of scoring resulted in a much higher score of 98.5%. The minimum acceptable inter-rater variation is 80% which is consistent with the reliabilities achieved.

APPENDIX B

Expatriate Employees Study

"Expat Study" for short, this study involved interviews with 71 "company-assigned" expatriates, drawn from five firms with headquarters in the United States, UK, and Europe, representing four industries: financial services/banking, pharmaceuticals, transportation services, and media/communications.

The objectives of the study were to understand how expatriates define expatriate ROI, the measures they perceive are being used to assess ROI from expatriation, and which factors cause ROI to increase and decrease.

Interviews with expatriates were conducted between January and July 2008, by telephone, and recorded (with permission). The interviews generated over 1,000 pages of transcripts. Interviews ranged in length from 45 min to 3 h, with some expatriates being interviewed twice. All expatriates had been on a (current) long-term international assignment for a minimum of 6 months.

Eighteen percent of the expatriates were women. Regional representation by host country includes 44% of expatriates currently assigned in Asia Pacific, 38% in Europe, UK, Middle East, and Africa, 13% in North America, and 5% in South America. Expatriates include junior and technical staff (14%), middle managers (49%), and senior vice presidents, CEOs, managing directors, partners, and country managers (37%). More than half of expatriates (52%) were on a second or subsequent international assignment. Table 2 provides background data on the 71 expatriates in the Expat Study.

As in the MM study, computer-aided qualitative analysis software (NVIVO version 7) was used to store, cross-reference, and clarify new understandings as we progressed through data analysis. Hierarchical categories and content analysis assisted us to derive key findings. An initial inter-rater reliability score of 89% was achieved, after which consultation and discussion resulted in a higher second round score of 94%.

Table 2. Sample Characteristics for the Expat Study

Case firms (n = 5)			
Total participants per firm	n = 71	*Total number of employees*[a]	653,000
Financial services	19	Average	130,600
Banking	10	Lowest	15,300
Media/communications	11	Highest	346,000
Pharmaceutical/healthcare	18		
Transportation services	13	*Total number of expatriates*[a,b]	3,767
		Average	753
Firm company type		Lowest	180
Public	4	Highest	1,240
Private/partnership	1		
		Total number of long-term assignees[a]	3,341
Headquarters location of firm		Average	668
North America	2	Lowest	125
Europe	2	Highest	1,200
UK	1		
Participants (n = 71)			
Gender	%	*Home-country by region*	%
Female	18	North America	25
Male	82	Europe	21
		UK	28
Position in firm		Asia Pacific	18
Junior staff	14	Middle East & Africa	2
Middle manager	49	South America	6
Senior VP, country manager	37		
		Host-country by region	
Tenure		North America	13
1–5 years	21	Europe	21
6–10 years	31	UK	9
11–15 years	18	Asia Pacific	44
16–20 years	18	Middle East & Africa	8
20 years plus	12	South America	5
Age		*Last time lived in home country*	
Under 30	7	1 year or less	28
30–39	37	2–4 years	47
40–49	39	5 or more years	25
50 plus	17		
		Children	
Number of prior assignments		Yes	62
0	48	No	38
1	24		
2–4	24	*Partner*	%	*Accompanied*	%
5 or more	4	Yes	78	Yes	93
		No	22	No	7

[a] These are employee numbers, not percentages

[b] Expatriates include all types of assignments and assignees, i.e. long-term, short-term, one-way transfer and commuter, and PCN, HCN, and TCN.

APPENDIX C

Trailing Spouses Study

"TS Study" for short, this study involved surveying 264 trailing spouses on assignment in 54 host countries.

The objectives of the study were to understand the barriers to mobility that prevent expatriate families from undertaking an international assignment; the types of organizational support that assist trailing spouses' adjustment to the host-location; and the factors that cause, and the impact arising from, marital stress during expatriation.

Trailing spouses were surveyed over a 4-year period (between 2001 and 2005), using an online questionnaire accessible at www.thetrailingspouse. com. Completed questionnaires were submitted to an email address owned by Yvonne McNulty, with no identifying information about participants being captured electronically (e.g. IP address). The survey data generated more than 3,000 pages of responses, notes, and direct quotes from which we derive key findings.

The majority of survey questions were formatted to a five-point Likert scale ("very important" to "very unimportant" or "strongly agree" to "strongly disagree"), along with several open-ended questions to draw out the trailing spouse experience in participants' own words.

The typical trailing spouse in this study was married (97%) for at least 4 years (72%), female (91%) with children (57%) and under 40 years of age (54%). Table 3 provides background data on the 264 participants in the TS Study.

Responses to Likert-scale questions were analyzed using means analysis, frequency distribution scores, and individual item analysis. Responses to open-ended questions were analyzed using NVIVO version 8 to code and derive key themes, and content analysis to then determine how strongly key themes were manifested.

Table 3. Sample Characteristics for the TS Study

	n = 264	%		n = 264	%
Gender			*Questionnaire response*		
Female	241	91	Online	258	98
Male	23	9	Paper	6	2
Respondent's age			*Number of children*		
21–29	10	4	0	115	44
30–39	122	46	1	34	13
40–49	83	31	2	78	30
50–59	44	17	3	30	11
60 and over	5	2	4	6	2
Number of relocations			*Children living with you (n = 148)*		
1	97	37	Yes	97	66
2–4	133	50	No	39	26
5–7	20	8	Some	12	8
8–10	10	4			
More than 10	4	1	*Number of languages spoken*		
			1	109	42
Length of marriage			2	83	32
Less than 1 year	13	5	3	39	15
1–3 years	59	23	4 or more	31	11
4–10 years	75	29			
11–20 years	68	27	*Time since lived in home country*		
More than 20 years	40	16	Less than 1 year	75	30
			1–5 years	116	46
Marital status			6–10 years	47	18
Married	257	97	11–15 years	6	2
Engaged	3	1	16 years plus	10	4
Defacto, same-sex	4	2			
			Longest time in one location		
Home-country region			3 months to 1 year	28	12
North America	101	38	1–2 years	50	20
South America	3	1	2–3 years	67	27
Middle East/Africa	7	3	3 years plus	100	41
Asia Pacific	61	23			
Europe/UK	92	35	*Number of countries lived in*		
			1	106	42
Host-country region			2–4	115	46
North America	63	25	5–7	24	9
South America	28	11	8–10	4	2
Middle East/Africa	25	10	More than 10	1	1
Asia Pacific	55	22			
Europe/UK	80	32			

To promote research "trustworthiness", an audit trail was maintained about the processes and complexities of the study, along with peer debriefing (passing several drafts and notes from the coding process to other researchers and practitioners in the field for their review and feedback) and member checking (via an "industry report" of the findings which was compiled and sent back to as many participants as possible).

Notes

Introduction

1. Cartus (2012); KPMG (2011); Mercer (2011).
2. Brookfield Global Relocation Services (2012).
3. If the meaning of these terms is unclear, see our Glossary.

Chapter 1

1. Salt (2008).
2. Salt (2008).
3. PricewaterhouseCoopers (2010a).
4. PricewaterhouseCoopers (2010b).
5. Brookfield Global Relocation Services (2012).
6. PricewaterhouseCoopers (2010b).
7. Scullion and Collings (2006); Collings, Scullion and Dowling (2009).
8. Meyskens, von Glinow, Werther and Clarke (2009).
9. Tungli and Peiperl (2009).
10. See Harvey and Moeller (2009) for an excellent overview.
11. Goby, Ahmed, Annavarjula, Ibrahim and Osman-Gani (2002).
12. Arp (2012).
13. Harvey, Speier, and Novicevic (1999).
14. Thite, Srinivasan, Harvey and Valk (2009); PricewaterhouseCoopers (2010b).
15. McNulty, De Cieri and Hutchings (2013).
16. PricewaterhouseCoopers (2010c).
17. Harvey and Novicevic (2006).
18. Inkson and Myers (2003).
19. Parker and Inkson (1999); Thorn (2009).
20. Linehan and Scullion (2004).
21. Süssmuth-Dyckerhoff, Wang and Chen (2012).
22. GMAC, NFTC and SHRM Global Forum (2003–2004); Brookfield Global Relocation Services (2012).
23. PricewaterhouseCoopers (2008b).
24. Malewski (2005); The Straits Times (2013).
25. Vance (2005).

Chapter 2

1. Porter (1987); Perlmutter (1969); Bartlett and Ghoshal (2002).
2. Buytendijk (2007).
3. Scullion and Collings (2006).
4. Brookfield Global Relocation Services (2012).
5. McNulty and Tharenou (2004).
6. Hippler (2009); Economist Intelligence Unit (2010); Richardson and McKenna (2003); Dickmann and Harris (2005).
7. McNulty, De Cieri and Hutchings (2013).
8. Dickmann, Doherty, Mills and Brewster (2008); Stahl, Miller and Tung (2002).
9. Cartus and Primacy (2010).
10. See Yan, Zhu and Hall (2002) as a good example.
11. This term is attributed to Gardiner Hempel, Partner at Deloitte Touche Tohmatsu, in a conference presentation entitled "20:20 Foresight" at the Deloitte Asia Pacific Global Services Employer Conference, Hong Kong, 16–19, September 2008.
12. Larsen (2004); Cappellen and Janssens (2010).
13. Thomas, Lazarova and Inkson (2005).
14. McNulty (2013).

Chapter 3

1. Mercer (2012).
2. Diez, Kothuis and Chua (2012).
3. Ernst & Young (2010).
4. Hippler (2009); Dickmann, Doherty, Mills and Brewster (2008).
5. Sims and Schraeder (2005); Herod (2009); Neijzen and De Bruyker (2010).
6. Stanley (2009).
7. For assistance in calculating local-plus packages, see AIR Inc.'s Local Plus Calculator (LPC) at www.air-inc.com/tools.html.
8. Leung, Wang and Hon (2011).
9. Warneke and Schneider (2011).
10. Herod (2012).
11. HSBC Bank International (2010).
12. Phillips and Fox (2003).
13. AIRINC (2010); ORC Worldwide (2008b).
14. McNulty, De Cieri and Hutchings (2013).
15. Mercer (2010).
16. Phillips and Fox (2003).

17. Salimaki and Heneman (2008).
18. Feldman and Ng (2007).

Chapter 4

1. Cartus and Primacy (2010).
2. Andreason (2008); Cartus (2010); Ernst & Young (2010).
3. Patterson (1988, 2002).
4. McNulty (2012).
5. Glanz, Williams and Hoeksema (2001).
6. Shaffer and Harrison (2001); Cole (2011).
7. Thomas and Lazarova (2006); Lazarova, Westman and Shaffer (2010); Fish and Wood (1997).
8. Brown (2008).
9. McNulty (2012).
10. Shaffer and Harrison (2001).
11. Harvey (1985); Harvey, Novicevic and Breland (2009).
12. Brookfield Global Relocation Services (2011).
13. Brown (2008).
14. Selmer and Leung (2003).
15. Cole (2012).
16. Permits Foundation (2012).
17. ExpatExpert and AMJ Campbell International (2008).
18. Hyslop (2012).
19. Pascoe (2003).
20. McNulty (2012).
21. Beatson (2009).
22. ABC News (2012).
23. ORC Worldwide (2008c).
24. Cartus and Primacy (2010).
25. ORC Worldwide (2008c); Cartus and Primacy (2010).
26. AIRINC. (2012).
27. Attridge and Burke (2012).

Chapter 5

1. Inkson and Arthur (2001).
2. Makela and Suutari (2009).
3. Arthur and Rousseau (1996).
4. Boatman, Wellins and Neal (2011); Süssmuth-Dyckerhoff, Wang and Chen (2012).
5. Guthrie, Ash and Stevens (2003).

6. Cole and McNulty (2011).
7. Hutchings, French and Hatcher (2008).
8. Brookfield Global Relocation Services (2012).
9. Fischlmayr and Kollinger (2010).
10. Selmer and Leung (2002).
11. Paik and Vance (2002); Lowe, Downes and Kroeck (1999).
12. Gedro (2010).
13. Inkson and Myers (2003); Tharenou (2003); Andresen, Biemann and Pattie (2012).
14. Vance and McNulty (2013).
15. Doherty and Dickmann (2009).
16. Nahapiet and Ghoshal (1998).
17. Sullivan and Arthur (2006); Inkson and Thorn (2010).
18. Thomas, Lazarova, and Inkson (2005); Dickmann and Baruch (2011).
19. McNulty (2013).
20. McNulty, De Cieri and Hutchings (2013).
21. Adapted from Inkson, Arthur, Pringle and Barry (1997).
22. Jokinen, Brewster and Suutari (2008).
23. Inkson, Arthur, Pringle and Barry (1997).
24. Inkson and Meyers (2003).
25. Carr, Inkson and Thorn (2005).
26. Schein (1996).
27. Suutari and Taka (2004); Lazarova and Cerdin (in press).
28. Vance (2005).
29. Inkson and Thorn (2010).
30. Suutari and Taka (2004), p. 842.
31. Stahl and Cerdin (2004); Dickmann, Doherty, Mills and Brewster (2008).
32. Kossek, Roberts, Fisher and Demarr (1998).
33. Lazarova and Cerdin (2007); Kraimer, Shaffer and Bolino (2009).
34. Brookfield Global Relocation Services (2012).
35. Mercer (2012).
36. PricewaterhouseCoopers and Cranfield (2005).
37. Economist Intelligence Unit and Stepstone Solutions (2010).
38. Altman and Baruch (2013)
39. Parker and Inkson (1999).
40. Sturges, Conway, Guest and Leifooghe (2005); Inkson and King (2011).

Chapter 6

1. Rousseau (2005).
2. See, for, example, Inkson and King (2011); Haslberger and Brewster (2009); Granrose and Baccili (2006); Pate and Scullion (2010); Rousseau (2004).

3. Ho (2005).
4. Morrison and Robinson (1997).
5. MacNeil (1985).
6. Thomas and Feldman (2009).
7. Rousseau (1996).
8. For a recent study showing similar results, see Stahl, Chua, Caligiuri, Cerdin and Taniguchi (2009).
9. Yan, Zhu and Hall (2002).
10. Brookfield Global Relocation Services (2012).
11. McNulty (2012).
12. Brookfield (2009) reported a 50% drop in expatriate activity for 2009, and ORC Worldwide (2008a) found that the crisis had caused most companies to review their global staffing, mostly by localizing expatriates and reducing housing benefits.
13. The Expat Study was conducted in early 2008 in the months before the official global financial crisis began on 15 September 2008, as reported by *The Wall Street Journal*.* The concerns expressed by expatriates demonstrated the effect to which the global financial crisis had already begun affecting global firms at around the same time as the collapse of Bear Stearns on 16 March 2008, and some months before recessions, rising unemployment, and job losses were announced in the media.
* Lehman files for bankruptcy; Merrill is sold, *New York Times*, 14 September 2008. Retrieved 19 March 2009 www.nytimes.com/2008/09/15/business/15lehman.html

Chapter 7

1. Mercer (2011).
2. Deloitte (2010).
3. Brookfield Global Relocation Services (2012); Cartus and Primacy (2010).
4. Bhaskar-Shrinivas, Harrison, Shaffer and Luk (2005); Stroh (1995).
5. Shaffer, Harrison, Gregersen, Black and Ferzandi (2006); Guzzo, Noonan and Elron (1994).
6. Morris, Snell and Wright (2006).
7. McNulty and Tharenou (2004).
8. Harzing (2001).
9. Jokinen, Brewster and Suutari (2008).
10. Bossard and Peterson (2005); Osland (2000).
11. Taylor, Beechler and Napier (1996); De Cieri and Dowling (2006).
12. Von Bertalanffy (1972).
13. Jansen, Tempelaar, van den Bosch and Volberda (2009).
14. Scullion and Collings (2006).

15. Taylor, Beechler and Napier (1996).
16. McNulty and Tharenou (2004).
17. Harris and Brewster (1999).
18. Anderson (2005).
19. Cartus (2006).
20. Brookfield Global Relocation Services (2012); Permits Foundation (2009, 2012).
21. Cartus and Primacy (2010).
22. Mercer (2011).
23. Harvey and Novicevic (2002).
24. Thomas and Inkson (2009).
25. PricewaterhouseCoopers (2008a).
26. Guanxi describes an individual's network of contacts upon which he or she may depend when something needs to be done and through which he or she can exert influence on behalf of another.

Chapter 8

1. Doherty and Dickmann (2012); Brookfield Global Relocation Services (2012).
2. Adapted from McNulty, De Cieri and Hutchings (2009).
3. Mercer (2011); Brookfield Global Relocation Services (2012).
4. ORC Worldwide (2008a).
5. For an excellent critique of failure rates, see Harzing (1995).
6. Data sourced from The Mobility Manager Study.
7. Brookfield Global Relocation Services (2012); Cartus and Primacy (2010).
8. For a recent study that develops an empirically derived multidimensional measure of expatriate success, see Hemmasi, Downes and Varner (2010).
9. Cendant (2004).
10. Mercer (2005–06).
11. Takeuchi (2010).
12. GMAC, NFTC, and SHRM Global Forum (2005).
13. ORC Worldwide (2006).
14. Brookfield Global Relocation Services (2012).
15. See, for example, Fitz-enz and Davison (2002); for an excellent summary of the business case for human capital metrics, including traditional approaches to its measurement, see O'Donnell and Royal (2010).
16. Although we do not endorse any specific metric for measuring eROI, readers may find some of the following sources useful: Fitz-enz (2002); Becker, Huselid, and Ulrich (2001); PricewaterhouseCoopers (2010a).

Chapter 9

1. Banai and Harry (2004); Tung (2008).
2. Cappellen and Janssens (2010).
3. Carr, Inkson and Thorn (2005).
4. Economist Intelligence Unit and Stepstone Solutions (2010); Ernst & Young (2012).
5. Arp (2012).
6. PricewaterhouseCoopers (2007).
7. Boudreau and Ramstad (2007).
8. Cartus (2009); Minbaeva and Collings (2013).
9. KPMG (2009).
10. Chambers, Foulon, Handfield-Jones, Hankin and Michaels (1998).
11. Robertson and Abbey (2003).
12. Deloitte (2008).
13. DeLong and Vijayaraghavan (2003).
14. AON Hewitt (2011).
15. Desmarescaux (2011), Diez and Vierra (2013).
16. PricewaterhouseCoopers (2010b), p. 21.
17. Caldwell (2005).
18. PricewaterhouseCoopers (2008b).
19. Deloitte (2008).
20. Farrell and Grant (2005).

Glossary

assignee: an employee of an organization who voluntarily chooses to be sent from their country of origin and/or permanent residence to a foreign country to work temporarily but does not take up citizenship of that country; see *expatriate*.

assignment failure: when the deliverables expected from an international assignment fall short of a company's expectations; failure is typically defined as "premature return" but also includes under-performance and repatriation turnover, among others.

back to basics: an approach that emphasizes simplicity and adherence to the most important things.

balance-sheet approach: a compensation approach that links the base salary of an expatriate to the salary structure of their nominated home country with the intention of "keeping them whole," i.e. not disadvantaging them compared to living standards in their home country; often referred to as "full package."

best practice: a method that has consistently shown superior results, often used as a benchmark by which others are guided or aspire to attain.

boundaryless (global) career: the progression of career moves across multiple employment settings and multiple borders.

brain drain: when skilled individuals leave their home country temporarily or permanently.

brain gain: when societies that lose skilled individuals through emigration gain replacements in the form of permanent immigration.

career anchor: an individual's self-concept of perceived abilities, basic values, motives, and needs as they pertain to a career, which evolve as a person gains life and occupational experience.

career capital: competencies that add value to an individual's career, in the form of *knowing-how* (career-related skills and job-related knowledge which accrue over time), *knowing-whom* (a range of intra-firm, inter-firm, professional, and social relations combined in a network), and *knowing-why* (fit between an individual's identity and career-related choices).

career expatriates: re-assigned expatriates that spend most of their careers in assignments in countries other than that of their citizenship or of the headquarters country of their employer.

"coffee machine" approach: phrase coined by Harris and Brewster (1999, see references) suggesting an informal/closed selection procedure for expatriates that takes place among senior/line managers at the "coffee machine" or "water cooler"; the approach implies that expatriate selection is ad hoc and reactive, and that an organization's formal processes are brought in to play to legitimize an informal selection decision that has, in effect, already been taken.

company-assigned expatriates (CAEs): a traditional type of expatriate whose international career moves are controlled and directed by an organization to allow it to match organizational and individual needs toward improving a firms competitive advantage over time. CAEs' careers typically unfold in a single employment setting, i.e. within one firm, with the goal of helping individuals improve their career advancement within one company.

corporate expatriates: employees engaged as expatriates in business (for profit) organizations; excludes non-profit, military, missionary, education, and foreign service sectors.

corporate ROI: the return on investment to companies from expatriation.

cost-of-living allowance (COLA): payment by a company to compensate an expatriate for differences in daily living expenses between their nominated home and host country. Examples include the cost of transportation, groceries, furniture and appliances, medical care, and domestic help.

dual-career: a situation where both members of a couple seek to pursue careers in employment simultaneously.

exceptions: see *policy exceptions.*

expatriate: an employee of an organization who voluntarily chooses to be sent from their country of origin and/or permanent residence to a foreign country to work temporarily but does not take up citizenship of that country.

expatriates of host-country origin/returnees: permanent resident of the parent country but belongs to ethnicity of the host country and is hired and/or transferred by the parent-country organization to the host location on a temporary assignment or permanent transfer.

expatriate management system: a configuration of organizational activities, events, processes, policies, practices, and strategies that are directed at influencing the outcomes of international assignments, to impact the international concerns and goals of global firms.

expatriate return on investment: a calculation in which the financial and non-financial benefits to the firm are compared with the financial and non-financial costs of the international assignment, as appropriate to the assignment's purpose.

foreign executives in local organizations (FELOs): foreign individuals at the executive level who hold local managerial positions supervising HCNs in local organizations where these organizations have their headquarters.

foreign local hires: see *third-country nationals.*

foreign subsidiary: a partially or wholly owned company that forms part of a larger corporation that is headquartered in another country.

functional retention: when good performers remain employed (retained) by an MNC, as opposed to *functional turnover* when poor performers leave without being fired or dismissed; its opposite is *dysfunctional retention* (when poor performers are retained) versus *dysfunctional turnover* (when good performers leave).

geocentric: when an MNC takes a global approach to its operations wherein staff are drawn globally based on ability rather than nationality.

global careerists: individuals that engage in an evolving sequence of work experience that, over time, takes place in more than one country; global careerists are typically not linked to any particular home country.

global firm: represented by business units that span more than one country and whose activities require co-ordination and integration on varying levels; the term global firm represents a range of substituted terms, including multi-national corporation (MNC), multi-domestic, and transnational firms.

global manager: an individual who works for a company, or owns a business, that operates across national borders, i.e. internationally.

global mobility: the movement and relocation of a workforce from, to, and through various countries, facilitated by a *global mobility department* that supports the human capital needs of a business.

global nomads: refers to people who are living an international lifestyle, characterized by high mobility.

global staffing: the critical issues faced by MNCs with regard to the employment of home, host, and third-country nationals that are required to fill positions in their headquarter and subsidiary operations.

global war for talent: the difficulties companies face in attracting and retaining highly skilled and capable staff, otherwise known as "highly talented" or "high potential" individuals.

glocal: a phrase that captures "think global, act local" representing the combination of global and local, i.e. locally rooted and globally connected.

hardship premium: a salary premium (typically calculated as a percentage of base salary) offered by companies to induce employees to accept an international assignment to a challenging or undesirable location in terms of physical, cultural, social, or other conditions, e.g. China, Russia, and South Korea.

high potential employee: identified as having the *potential* ability, organizational commitment, and motivation for successive leadership positions within a company, often with unique and talented skills; high potential employees are distinct from high *performing* individuals who have already demonstrated superior ability, organizational commitment, and motivation.

home country/parent country: country of origin from where an expatriate has been recruited prior to undertaking an international assignment; the home country may or may not be the headquarters country of the organization, just as it may or may not be the country of citizenship of the expatriate.

host country: country to which an expatriate is temporarily assigned, but for which they usually do not have citizenship.

host-country nationals (HCNs): mostly non-expatriate employees residing in the host-location as citizens of that country.

home leave: a provision whereby employers cover the expense of one or more trips (often annually) back to the home country for expatriates and their accompanying family members.

home sale reimbursement: monies reimbursed to expatriates by their company for part of the loss incurred from the sale of their home when electing to sell their primary residence in the home country as a result of relocating abroad.

housing allowance: a monetary provision whereby employers provide expatriates with a specified monthly sum to cover all or part of their rental accommodation costs in the host-location; the monthly sum is typically determined by family size and job level and paid directly to the expatriate or the landlord.

human resource information system (HRIS): a systematic procedure for gathering, storing, maintaining, retrieving, and revising human resource data; typically a computer-based application that allows HRM staff to assemble and process data related to the management of their people.

human resource management (HRM): the management of an organization's workforce, or human resources, including hiring and developing employees.

individual ROI: the return on investment to expatriates from expatriation, defined as the perceived benefits that accrue to expatriates arising from international assignment experience in relation to professional and personal gains.

inpatriate/inpatriation: HCNs (local managers) and TCNs of a subsidiary sent to the parent-country headquarters on an international assignment.

international assignment: the project or temporary role in another country to which an expatriate is dispatched by his or her employing organization in service of corporate goals, typically for a period of 1 to 5 years.

international commuting: employees who work in a foreign country typically unaccompanied by their family members who remain in the home country to where the employee returns with some frequency because the principal residence is located there.

international human resource management (IHRM): refers to the management of people in an international context and is concerned with human resource management (HRM) activities (e.g. selection and recruitment, compensation), national or country characteristics (e.g. home, host location), and different types of employees (e.g. expatriates, frequent business travelers, commuters, cross-cultural team members, and other specialists involved in international knowledge transfer).

international itinerants: employees characterized by a career identity that is independent of an employer, who take charge over their careers, and are employed by a minimum of two independent organizations in at least two countries; also known as *global careerists* or referred to as individuals pursuing a *boundaryless (global) career.*

international labor market: defined as the total global supply of the labor force (the number of people in a particular country or area who are able and willing to work) that interacts with the world of commercial activity ("capital flows") where goods and services are bought and sold; relies on an exchange of information between employers and job seekers about wage rates, conditions of employment, level of competition, and job location, and represents the "invisible" factors of production associated with human capital (people) that contribute to corporate and national performance. Companies and countries compete on the international labor market to attract the best and brightest "highly skilled labor" and "knowledge workers."

inter-regional transfers: transfers between different regions (e.g. Asia and Europe).

intra-regional transfers: transfers between different countries in the same region (e.g. transfers among Asian countries).

localization: an expatriate employee who is switched to *permanent transferee* status after a period of time in the host country, usually at the employer's request; localization almost always involves replacing (and reducing) an expatriate package (e.g. base salary, incentive compensation, allowances, perquisites, social security, and retirement plans) with compensation comparable to that offered to host-country nationals (HCNs) or other locally hired employees.

local-plus compensation: an approach in which expatriate employees are paid according to the salary levels, structure, and administration guidelines of the host location, as well as being provided, in recognition of the employee's foreign status, with special expatriate benefits such as transportation, housing, and the costs of dependents' education.

long-term assignment: an *international assignment* of between 1 and 5 years duration.

millennials: a term used to describe individuals that are members of "Generation Y," that is those born between 1982 and 2000.

mobility managers: people who manage the movement and relocation of a workforce (expatriates) from, to, and through various countries on behalf of organizations, determine a company's international staffing policies, and implement international assignment management.

multi-national corporation (MNC): a company operating in at least one, or several, countries but is managed from one home or headquarters country.

paradigm shift: a fundamental change in an individual's or a company's view of how things work, or should work, in business.

parent-country nationals (PCNs): citizens of the headquarters country location of a company, from which they are then sent abroad.

permanent transferee: an employee who resigns from his/her home-country office and is hired by the host-country office of the same MNC at the time of relocation, but for which there is no return to the home country and no promise or guarantee of repatriation or re-assignment elsewhere; employees are expected to operate as a "local" in the host country—also known as "one-way moves."

perquisites: a payment, benefit, privilege, or advantage over and above regular income, salary, or wages paid to expatriates as a special right or privilege arising from their position.

personal agency: individuals that initiate, execute, and control their own volitional actions in the world for which they also take responsibility.

policy exception: approval of a deviation to a mobility policy (benefits) at the discretion of the MNC, usually for extenuating circumstances or to induce willingness to relocate; exceptions often include an item or service not otherwise covered by the mobility policy, an item or service not eligible to an expatriate due to their personal circumstances or lack of seniority, or both.

psychological contract: an indirect, unwritten and often unspoken agreement between an employer and employee.

re-assignment or **sequential expatriation:** an international assignment that is undertaken at the immediate conclusion of a prior international assignment without an intervening period of repatriation.

region-centric: when an MNCs structure is based on a geographic strategy, for example, staff are recruited and deployed regionally but not necessarily globally.

return on investment: a financial ratio that expresses profit in direct relation to investment; in accounting terms, an investment is defined as something worth doing or buying because it may be profitable or useful in the future, whereas a *return* is defined as the profit expected from a capital investment which is usually expressed as an annual percentage.

repatriation: the re-integration of an expatriate into their original home operation from whence they undertook their (first or only) international assignment.

rotational assignments: work assignments that involve an employee commuting from the home country to a place of work in another country for short and specified periods of time, returning periodically to the home country to rest; typically unaccompanied by family members.

self-initiated expatriate (SIE): qualified people who move to new countries of their own volition, without company support, and seek to "see the world" or develop their careers there.

shock events: events that impact a company but which sometimes originate from outside it; characterized by uncertainty and unpredictability, and the absence of "historical paradigms" from which to co-ordinate relief.

short-term assignment: an *international assignment* of between 3 months and no more than 12 months duration, usually unaccompanied by family members.

short-term business travel: frequent international business trips undertaken by employees for more than 30 days but less than 180 days per year; also known as "extended business travel."

single-status assignment: an international assignment whereby an expatriate is not accompanied by his/her family members, who remain in the home country or a nominated third ("other") country—also known as a "split assignment."

split family assignment: see *single-status assignment.*

social capital: contacts and ties combined with norms and trust that facilitate knowledge sharing and information exchanges between individuals, groups, and business units.

symbolic capital: in career terms, the perception, understanding, and recognition of the value attributed to social, cultural, and economic capital; typically embodied in prestige, renown, reputation, and personal authority.

talent flow: the temporary and permanent migration of individuals from, to, and through countries.

talent management: the strategic management of people identified as having the potential for high performance as a critical component of an organization's business success, including their recruitment, selection, identification, development, and retention.

tax equalization: a compensation approach for calculating an expatriate's share of their worldwide tax burden by striving to ensure that he/she is financially no worse or better off than they would have been had an assignment not been undertaken and they had remained in their nominated home country.

third-country nationals (TCNs): also referred to as "foreign local hires," TCNs originate from neither the home country where corporate "headquarters" is located, nor the host country where they are employed, but a third country where they have lived either temporarily or permanently before agreeing to move to the host country.

third-party vendor: an outsourced company that provides services or performs a function previously performed within an organization, e.g. relocation, property management, tax, and immigration.

trailing spouse: a companion to an expatriate who is included in the definition of family for the purposes of obtaining international assignment benefits, whose status may be married or unmarried and same or opposite gender; the trailing spouse is the person in a relationship for whom an international assignment is *not* offered and whose job does *not* effect the move abroad. Also known as *accompanying spouse/partner* and sometimes referred to as "domestic partner."

umbrella company: a "holding" company that acts as an employer to employees on serial assignments, providing (among others) payroll services on behalf of the "client" (the company for whom the employee works), social security contributions and tax payments, and other applicable insurances.

References

ABC News. (2012). *Father relieved daughters returning to Italy*. Australia: ABC News.

AIRINC. (2010). *Diverse expatriate populations—Alternative remuneration packages*. New York: AIR Inc.

AIRINC. (2012). *Giving your managers wings: Flexible mobility policies that work*. New York: AIR Inc.

Anderson, B. (2005). Expatriate selection: Good management or good luck? *International Journal of Human Resource Management, 16* (4), 567–583.

Andreason, A. (2008). Expatriate adjustment of spouses and expatriate managers: An intergrative research review. *International Journal of Management, 25* (2), 382–395.

Andresen, M., Biemann, T., & Pattie, M. (2012). What makes them move abroad? Reviewing and exploring differences between self-initiated and assigned expatriation. *International Journal of Human Resource Management*. 1–16.

AON Hewitt. (2011). *Talent survey: Igniting a high performance culture*. New York: AON Hewitt.

Arp, F. (2012). For success in a cross-cultural environment, choose foreign executives wisely. *Global Business and Organizational Excellence, 31* (6), 40–50.

Arthur, M., & Rousseau, D. (1996). The boundaryless career as a new employment principle. In M. Arthur, & D. Rousseau (Eds.), *The boundaryless career: A new employment principle for a new organizational era* (pp. 3–20). New York: Oxford University Press.

Athey, R. (2008). It's 2008: *Do you know where your talent is? Why acquisition and retention strategies don't work*. London, UK: Deloitte Touche Tohmatsu.

Attridge, M., & Burke, J. (2012). Future trends in EAP. *The Journal of Employee Assistance, 42* (1), 27–31.

Banai, M., & Harry, W. (2004). Boundaryless global careers: The international itinerants. *International Studies of Management and Organization, 34* (3), 96–120.

Bartlett, C., & Ghoshal, S. (2002). *Managing across borders: The transnational solution* (2nd ed.). Boston, MA: Harvard Business School Press.

Beatson, K. (2009). *Divorce—expat style*. UK: Anthony Gold Solicitors.

Becker, B., Huselid, M., & Ulrich, D. (2001). *The HR scorecard: Linking people, strategy, and performance*. Boston: Harvard Business School Press.

Bhaskar-Shrinivas, P., Harrison, D., Shaffer, M., & Luk, D. (2005). Input-based and time-based models of international adjustment. *Academy of Management Journal, 48* (2), 257–281.

Boatman, J., Wellins, R., & Neal, S. (2011). *Women work: The business benefits of closing the gender gap.* Pittsburgh, PA: Development Dimensions International, Inc. (DDI).

Bossard, A., & Peterson, R. (2005). The repatriate experience as seen by American expatriates. *Journal of World Business, 40* (1), 9–28.

Boudreau, J., & Ramstad, P. (2007). *Beyond HR: The new science of human capital.* Boston, MA: Harvard Business School Press.

Brookfield. (2009). *Global relocation trends survey.* Woodridge, IL: Brookfield Global Relocation Services.

Brookfield. (2011). *Global relocation trends survey.* Woodridge, IL: Brookfield Global Relocation Services.

Brookfield. (2012). *Global relocation trends survey.* Woodridge, IL: Brookfield Global Relocation Services.

Brown, R. (2008). Dominant stressors on expatriate couples during international assignments. *International Journal of Human Resource Management, 19* (6), 1018–1034.

Buytendijk, F. (2007). Challenging conventional wisdom related to defining business metrics: a behavioural approach. *Measuring Business Excellence, 11* (1), 20–26.

Caldwell, C. (2005). *China Staff, 11*(4), 14–17.

Cappellen, T., & Janssens, M. (2010). The career reality of global managers: An examination of career triggers. *International Journal of Human Resource Management, 21* (11), 1884–1910.

Carr, S., Inkson, K., & Thorn, K. (2005). From global careers to talent flow: Reinterpreting "brain drain". *Journal of World Business, 40* (4), 386–398.

Cartus. (2006). *Strategic outsourcing: A model for expatriate management.* Wilmington, NC: Cartus.

Cartus. (2009). *Emerging trends in global mobility: Talent management.* Wilmington, NC: Cartus.

Cartus. (2010). *Destination china: An analysis of current and future mobilty trends from the Cartus 2010 China inbound pulse survey.* Wilmington, NC: Cartus.

Cartus. (2012). *Global mobility policy and practices survey: 2012 trends in global relocation.* Wilmington, NC: Cartus.

Cartus, & Primacy. (2010). *Global mobility policy and practices survey.* Wilmington, NC: Cartus.

Cendant. (2004). *Emerging trends in global mobility: Policy and practices survey.* Wilmington, NC: Cendant.

Chambers, E., Foulon, M., Handfield-Jones, H., Hankin, S., & Michaels III, E. (1998). The war for talent. *McKinsey Quarterly,* (3), 44–57.

Cole, N. (2011). Managing global talent: Solving the spousal adjustment problem. *International Journal of Human Resource Management, 22* (7), 1504–1530.

Cole, N. (2012). Expatriate accompanying partners: The males speak. *Asia Pacific Journal of Human Resources, 50* (3), 308–326.

Cole, N., & McNulty, Y. (2011). Why do female expatriates "fit-in" better than males? *Cross Cultural Management: An International Journal, 18* (2), 144–164.

Collings, D., Scullion, H., & Dowling, P. (2009). Global staffing: A review and thematic agenda. *International Journal of Human Resource Management, 20* (6), 1253–1272.

De Cieri, H., & Dowling, P. (2006). Strategic human resource management in multinational enterprises: Developments and directions. In G. Stahl, & I. Björkman (Eds.), *Handbook of research in international human resource management* (pp. 15–35). Cheltenham, UK: Edward Elgar.

Deloitte. (2008). *It's 2008: Do you know where your talent is?* New York, NY: Deloitte Touche Tohmatsu.

Deloitte. (2010). *Smarter moves: Executing and integrating global mobility and talent programs.* New York, NY: Deloitte Touche Tohmatsu.

DeLong, T., & Vijayaraghavan, V. (2003). Let's hear it for B players. *Harvard Business Review, 81* (6), 3–8.

Desmarescaux, F. (2011). *The changing migratory patterns of executives in Asia.* London, UK: Spencer Stuart.

Dickmann, M., & Doherty, N. (2008). Exploring the career capital impact of international assignments within distinct organizational contexts. *British Journal of Management, 19,* 145–161.

Dickmann, M., & Doherty, N. (2010). Exploring organizational and individual career goals, interactions, and outcomes of developmental international assignments. *Thunderbird International Business Review, 52* (4), 313–324.

Dickmann, M., Doherty, N., Mills, T., & Brewster, C. (2008). Why do they go? Individual and corporate perspectives on the factors influencing the decision to accept an international assignment. *International Journal of Human Resource Management, 19* (4), 731–751.

Dickmann, M., & Harris, H. (2005). Developing career capital for global careers: The role of international assignments. *Journal of World Business, 40,* (4), 399–408.

Diez, F., Kothuis, H., & Chua, J. (2012). *Executive compensation in Asia—Best practices in a dynamic environment.* Geneva: Mercer.

Doherty, N., & Dickmann, M. (2009). Exposing the symbolic capital of international assignments. *International Journal of Human Resource Management, 20* (2), 301–320.

Doherty, N., & Dickmann, M. (2012). Measuring the return on investment in international assignments: An action research approach. *International Journal of Human Resource Management, 23* (16), 3434–3454.

Doherty, N., Dickmann, M., & Mills, T. (2011). Exploring the motives of company-backed and self-initiated expatriates. *International Journal of Human Resource Management, 22* (3), 595–611.

Economist Intelligence Unit. (2010). *Up or out: Next moves for the modern expatriate.* London, UK: Economist Intelligence Unit.

Economist Intelligence Unit, & Stepstone Solutions. (2010). *Companies at a crossroads: A talent report.* London, UK: Economist Intelligence Unit.

Ernst & Young. (2010). *Global mobility effectiveness survey.* London: Ernst & Young.

ExpatExpert, & AMJ Campbell International. (2008). *Family matters! Report on the findings of the ExpatExpert/AMJ Campbell international relocation survey.* North Vancouver, BC: http://www.expatexpert.com.

Farrell, D., & Grant, A. (2005). China's looming talent shortage: The emerging global labor market. *McKinsey Quarterly,* (3), 70–72.

Feldman, D., & Ng, T. (2007). Careers: Mobility, embeddedness, and success. *Journal of Management, 33* (3), 350–377.

Fischlmayr, I., & Kollinger, I. (2010). Work-life balance—A neglected issue among Austrian female expatriates. *International Journal of Human Resource Management, 21* (4), 455–487.

Fish, A., & Wood, J. (1997). Managing spouse/partner preparation and adjustment: Developing a meaningful portable life. *Personnel Review, 26* (6), 445–466.

Fitz-enz, J. (2002). *The ROI of human capital.* New York, NY: MacMillan.

Fitz-enz, J., & Davison, B. (2002). *How to measure human resources management* (3rd ed.). New York: MacGraw-Hill.

Gedro, J. (2010). The lavender ceiling atop the global closet: Human resource development and lesbian expatriates. *Human Resource Development Review, 9* (4), 385–404.

Glanz, L., Williams, R., & Hoeksema, L. (2001). Sensemaking in expatriation: A theoretical basis. *Thunderbird International Business Review, 41* (1), 101–119.

GMAC, NFTC, & SHRM Global Forum. (2003–2004). *Global relocation trends survey.* Woodridge, IL.

GMAC, NFTC, & SHRM Global Forum. (2005). *Global relocation trends survey.* Woodridge, IL: GMAC.

Goby, V., Ahmed, Z., Annavarjula, M., Ibrahim, D., & Osman-Gani, A. (2002). Determinants of expatriate success: An empirical study of Singaporean expatriates in The People's Republic of China. *Journal of Transnational Management Development, 7* (4), 73–88.

Granrose, C., & Baccili, P. (2006). Do psychological contracts include boundaryless or protean careers? *Career Development International, 11* (2), 163–182.

Guthrie, J., Ash, R., & Stevens, C. (2003). Are women "better" than men? Personality differences and expatriate selection. *Journal of Managerial Psychology, 18* (3), 229–243.

Guzzo, R., Noonan, K., & Elron, E. (1994). Expatriate managers and the psychological contract. *Journal of Applied Psychology, 79* (4), 617–627.

Harris, H., & Brewster, C. (1999). The coffee-machine system: How international selection really works. *International Journal of Human Resource Management, 10* (3), 488–500.

Harvey, M. (1985). The executive family: An overlooked variable in international assignments. *Columbia Journal of World Business, 20* (2), 84–92.

Harvey, M., & Moeller, M. (2009). Expatriate managers: A historical review. *International Journal of Management Reviews, 11* (3), 275–296.

Harvey, M., & Novicevic, M. (2002). The hyper-competitive global marketplace: The importance of intuition and creativity in expatriate managers. *Journal of World Business, 37* (2), 45–57.

Harvey, M., & Novicevic, M. (2006). The evolution from repatriation of managers in MNEs to "patriation" in global organisations. In G. Stahl, & I. Björkman (Eds.), *Handbook of research in international human resource management* (pp. 323–343). Cheltenham, UK: Edward Elgar.

Harvey, M., Novicevic, M., & Breland, J. (2009). Global dual-career exploration and the role of hope and curiosity during the process. *Journal of Managerial Psychology, 24* (2), 178–197.

Harvey, M., Speier, C., & Novicevic, M. (1999). The role of inpatriation in global staffing. *International Journal of Human Resource Management, 10* (3), 459–476.

Harzing, A.-W. (1995). The persistent myth of high expatriate failure rates. *International Journal of Human Resource Management, 6* (2), 457–474.

Harzing, A.-W. (2001). Of bears, bumble-bees, and spiders: The role of expatriates in controlling foreign subsidiaries. *Journal of World Business, 36* (4), 366–379.

Haslberger, A., & Brewster, C. (2009). Capital gains: Expatriate adjustment and the psychological contract in international careers. *Human Resource Management, 48* (3), 379–397.

Hemmasi, M., Downes, M., & Varner, I. (2010). An empirically-derived multidimensional measure of expatriate success: Reconciling the discord. *International Journal of Human Resource Management, 21* (7), 982–998.

Herod, R. (2009). *Expatriate compensation strategies*. Alexandria, VA: Society for Human Resource Management (SHRM).

Herod, R. (2012). *Benefits, challenges and trends for expatriates and internationally mobile employees*. Geneva: Mercer.

Hippler, T. (2009). Why do they go? Empirical evidence of employees' motives for seeking or accepting relocation. *International Journal of Human Resource Management, 20* (6), 1381–1401.

Ho, V. (2005). Social influence on evaluations of psychological contract fulfillment. *Academy of Management Review, 30* (1), 113–128.

HSBC Bank International. (2010). *The expat explorer survey 2010—Expat economics*. Jersey, Channel Islands: HSBC Bank International.

Hutchings, K., French, E., & Hatcher, T. (2008). Lament of the ignored expatriate: An examination of organisational and social network support for female expatriates in China. *Equal Opportunities International, 27* (4), 372–391.

Hyslop, L. (2012). Expat divorce in Dubai on the rise. *The Telegraph*. UK: The Telegraph.

Inkson, K., & Arthur, M. (2001). How to be a successful career capitalist. *Organizational Dynamics, 30* (1), 48–61.

Inkson, K., Arthur, M., Pringle, J., & Barry, S. (1997). Expatriate assignment versus overseas experience: Contrasting models of international human resource development. *Journal of World business, 32* (4), 351–368.

Inkson, K., & King, Z. (2011). Contested terrain in careers: A psychological contract model. *Human Relations, 64* (1), 37–57.

Inkson, K., & Myers, B. (2003). "The Big OE": Self-directed travel and career development. *Career Development International, 8* (4), 170–181.

Inkson, K., & Thorn, K. (2010). Mobilty and careers. In S. Carr (Ed.), *The psychology of global mobility* (pp. 259–278). New York: Springer Science.

Jansen, J., Tempelaar, M., van den Bosch, F., & Volberda, H. (2009). Structural differentiation and ambidexterity: The mediating role of integration mechanisms. *Organization Science, 20* (4), 797–811.

Jokinen, T., Brewster, C., & Suutari, V. (2008). Career capital during international work experiences: Contrasting self-initiated expatriate experiences and assigned expatriation. *International Journal of Human Resource Management, 19* (6), 979–998.

Kossek, E., Roberts, K., Fisher, S., & Demarr, B. (1998). Career self-management: A quasi-experimental assessment of the effects of a training intervention. *Personnel Psychology, 51* (4), 935–962.

KPMG. (2009). *Tax, demographics, and corporate location survey: A study of the interaction between tax policy and labor migration, and their impact on location decisions*. Geneva: KPMG.

KPMG. (2011). *Global assignment policies and practices survey*. Geneva: KPMG.

Kraimer, M., Shaffer, M., & Bolino, M. (2009). The influence of expatriate and repatriate experiences on career advancement and repatriate retention. *Human Resource Management, 48* (1), 27–47.

Larsen, H. (2004). Global career as dual dependency between the organization and the individual. *Journal of Management Development, 23* (9), 860–869.

Lazarova, M., & Cerdin, J. (2007). Revisiting repatriation concerns: Organizational support versus career and contextual influences. *Journal of International Business Studies, 38* (3), 404–429.

Lazarova, M., & Cerdin, J. (in press). The internationalism career anchor: A validation study. *International Studies of Management and Organization.*

Lazarova, M., Westman, M., & Shaffer, M. (2010). Elucidating the positive side of the work-family interface on international assignments: A model of expatriate work and family performance. *Academy of Management Review, 35* (1), 93–117.

Leung, K., Wang, Z., & Hon, A. H. Y. (2011). Moderating effects on the compensation gap between locals and expatriates in China: A multi-level analysis. *Journal of International Management, 17* (1), 54–67.

Linehan, M., & Scullion, H. (2004). Towards an understanding of the female expatriate experience in Europe. *Human Resource Management Review, 14,* 433–448.

Lowe, K., Downes, M., & Kroeck, K. (1999). The impact of gender and location on the willingness to accept overseas assignments. *International Journal of Human Resource Management, 10* (2), 223–234.

MacNeil, I. (1985). Relational contract: What we do and do not know. *Wisconsin Law Review,* 483–525.

Makela, K., & Suutari, V. (2009). Global careers: A social capital paradox *International Journal of Human Resource Management, 20* (5), 992–1008.

Malewski, M. (2005). *GenXpat: The young professional's guide to making a successful life abroad.* Yarmouth, MN: Intercultural Press.

McNulty, Y. (2012). "Being dumped in to sink or swim": An empirical study of organizational support for the trailing spouse. *Human Resource Development International, 15* (4), 417–434.

McNulty, Y. (2013). Are self-initiated expatriates born or made? Exploring the relationship between SIE orientation and individual ROI. In V. Vaiman, & A. Haslberger (Eds.), *Managing talent of self-initiated expatriates.* UK: Palgrave-Macmillan.

McNulty, Y., De Cieri, H., & Hutchings, K. (2009). Do global firms measure expatriate return on investment? An empirical examination of measures, barriers and variables influencing global staffing practices. *International Journal of Human Resource Management, 20* (6), 1309–1326.

McNulty, Y., De Cieri, H., & Hutchings, K. (2013). Expatriate return on investment in Asia Pacific: An empirical study of individual ROI versus corporate ROI. *Journal of World Business, 48* (2), 209–221.

McNulty, Y., & Tharenou, P. (2004). Expatriate return on investment: A definition and antecedents. *International Studies of Management and Organization, 34* (3), 68–95.

Mercer. (2005–2006). *International assignments survey.* Geneva: Mercer.

Mercer. (2010). *Mercer localization practice survey: China, Hong Kong and Singapore.* Geneva: Mercer.

Mercer. (2011). *Mercer worldwide international assignment polices and practices survey.* Geneva: Mercer.

Mercer. (2012). *2011/2012 Asia executive remuneration snapshot survey*. Geneva: Mercer.

Meyskens, M., von Glinow, M., Werther, W., & Clarke, L. (2009). The paradox of international talent: Alternative forms of international assignments. *International Journal of Human Resource Management, 20* (6), 1439–1450.

Morris, S., Snell, S., & Wright, P. (2006). A resource-based view of international human resources: Toward a framework of integrative and creative capabilities. In G. Stahl, & I. Björkman (Eds.), *Handbook of research in international human resource management* (pp. 433–448). Cheltenham, UK: Edward Elgar.

Morrison, E., & Robinson, S. (1997). When employees feel betrayed: A model of how psychological contract violation develops. *Academy of Management Review, 22* (1), 226–256.

Nahapiet, J., & Ghoshal, S. (1998). Social capital, intellectual capital, and the organizational advantage. *Academy of Management Review, 23* (2), 242–266.

Neijzen, M., & De Bruyker, S. (2010). *Diverse expatriate populations: Alternative remuneration packages*. New York: AIRINC.

O'Donnell, L., & Royal, C. (2010). The business case for human capital metrics. In J. Connell, & S. Teo (Eds.), *Strategic HRM: Contemporary issues in the Asia Pacific region* (pp. 110–138). Prahran, Australia: Tilde University Press.

ORC Worldwide. (2006). *Expatriate selection, management, and repatriation*. London: ORC Worldwide.

ORC Worldwide. (2008a). *Flash survey: Cost savings initiatives*. New York: ORC Worldwide.

ORC Worldwide. (2008b). *Survey on local-plus packages in Hong Kong and Singapore*. New York: ORC Worldwide

ORC Worldwide. (2008c). *Worldwide survey of international assignment policies and practices*. New York: ORC Worldwide.

Osland, J. (2000). The journey inward: Expatriate hero tales and paradoxes. *Human Resource Management, 39* (2/3), 227–238.

Paik, Y., & Vance, C. (2002). Evidence of back-home selection bias against US female expatriates. *Women In Management Review, 17* (2), 68–79.

Parker, P., & Inkson, K. (1999). New forms of career: The challenge to human resource management. *Asia Pacific Journal of Human Resources, 37* (1), 76–85.

Pascoe, R. (2003). *A moveable marriage: Relocating your relationship without breaking it*. North Vancouver, BC: Expatriate Press Limited.

Patterson, J. (1988). Families experiencing stress. *Family Systems Medicine, 6* (2), 202–237.

Patterson, J. (2002). Intergrating family resilience and family stress theory. *Journal of Marriage and the Family, 64* (2), 349–360.

Perlmutter, H. V. (1969). The tortuous evolution of the multinational corporation. *Journal of World Business, 4*, 9–18.

Permits Foundation. (2009). *Employment, work permits, and international mobility*. The Hague, The Netherlands: Permits Foundation.

Permits Foundation. (2012). *International mobility and dual career survey of international employers*. The Hague, The Netherlands: Permits Foundation.

Phillips, L., & Fox, M. (2003). Compensation strategy in transnational corporations. *Management Decision, 41* (5/6), 465–476.

Porter, M. (1987). From competitive advantage to corporate strategy. *Harvard Business Review, 65* (3), 43–59.

PricewaterhouseCoopers. (2006). *Key trends in human capital: A global perspective*. London: PricewaterhouseCoopers.

PricewaterhouseCoopers. (2007). *International assignment perspectives: Critical issues facing the globally mobile workforce*. New York: PricewaterhouseCoopers.

PricewaterhouseCoopers. (2008a). *Confronting corruption: The business case for an effective anti-corruption programme*. New York: PricewaterhouseCoopers.

PricewaterhouseCoopers. (2008b). *Millennials at work—Perspectives from a new generation*. New York: PricewaterhouseCoopers.

PricewaterhouseCoopers. (2010a). *Key trends in human capital: A global perspective*. London: PricewaterhouseCoopers.

PricewaterhouseCoopers. (2010b). *Talent mobility 2020—The next generation of international assignments*. New York: PricewaterhouseCoopers.

PricewaterhouseCoopers, & Cranfield. (2005). *Understanding and avoiding the barriers to international mobility*. London: PricewaterhouseCoopers.

Richardson, J., & McKenna, S. (2003). International experience and academic careers: What do academics have to say? *Personnel Review, 32* (6), 774–795.

Robertson, A., & Abbey, G. (2003). *Managing talented people*. Essex, UK: Momentum/Pearson Education.

Rousseau, D. (1996). Changing the deal while keeping the people. *Academy of Management Executive, 10* (1), 50–59.

Rousseau, D. (2004). Psychological contracts in the workplace: Understanding the ties that motivate. *Academy of Management Executive, 18* (1), 120–127.

Rousseau, D. (2005). *I-deals: Idiosyncratic deals employees bargain for themselves* Armonk, NY: ME Sharpe.

Salimaki, A., & Heneman, R. (2008). Pay for performance for global employees. In L. Gomez-Majia, & S. Werner (Eds.), *Global compensation: Foundations and perspectives* (pp. 158–168). Milton Park, UK: Routledge.

Salt, B. (2008). *The global skills convergence: Issues and ideas for the management of an international workforce*. Switzerland: KPMG.

Schein, E. (1996). Career anchors revisited: Implications for career development in the 21st century. *Academy of Management Executive, 10* (4), 80–88.

Scullion, H., & Collings, D. (2006). *Global staffing*. London: Routledge.

Selmer, J., & Leung, A. (2002). Career management issues of female business expatriates. *Career Development International, 7* (6), 348–358.

Selmer, J., & Leung, A. (2003). Provision and adequacy of corporate support to male expatriate spouses: An exploratory study. *Personnel Review, 32* (1), 9–21.

Shaffer, M., & Harrison, D. (2001). Forgotten partners of international assignments: Development and test of a model of spouse adjustment. *Journal of Applied Psychology, 86* (2), 238–254.

Shaffer, M., Harrison, D., Gregersen, H., Black, J., & Ferzandi, L. (2006). You can take it with you: Individual differences and expatriate effectiveness. *Journal of Applied Psychology, 91* (1), 109–125.

Sims, R., & Schraeder, M. (2005). Expatriate compensation: An exploratory review of salient contextual factors and common practices. *Career Development International, 10* (2), 98–108.

Stahl, G., & Cerdin, J. (2004). Global careers in French and German multinational corporations. *Journal of Management Development, 23* (9), 885–902.

Stahl, G., Chua, C., Caligiuri, P., Cerdin, J., & Taniguchi, M. (2009). Predictors of turnover intentions in learning-driven and demand-driven international assignments: The role of repatriation concerns, satisfaction with company support, and perceived career advancement opportunities. *Human Resource Management, 48* (1), 89–109.

Stahl, G., Miller, E., & Tung, R. (2002). Toward the boundaryless career: A closer look at the expatriate career concept and the perceived implications of an international assignment. *Journal of World Business, 37* (3), 216–227.

Stanley, P. (2009). Local-plus packages for expatriates in Asia: A viable alternative. *International HR Journal, 3* (Fall), 9–11.

Stroh, L. (1995). Predicting turnover among repatriates: Can organizations affect retention rates? *International Journal of Human Resource Management, 6* (2), 443–456.

Sturges, J., Conway, N., Guest, D., & Liefooghe, A. (2005). Managing the career deal: The psychological contract as a framework for understanding career management, organizational commitment, and work behavior. *Journal of Organizational Behavior, 26* (7), 821–838.

Sullivan, S., & Arthur, M. (2006). The evolution of the boundaryless career concept: Examining physical and psychological mobility. *Journal of Vocational Behavior, 69* (1), 19–29.

Süssmuth-Dyckerhoff, C., Wang, J., & Chen, J. (2012). *Women matter: An Asia perspective—Harnessing female talent to raise corporate performance.* Shanghai, PR China: McKinsey & Co.

Suutari, V., & Taka, M. (2004). Career anchors of managers with global careers. *Journal of Management Development, 23* (9), 833–847.

Takeuchi, R. (2010). A critical review of expatriate adjustment research: Progress, emerging trends, and prospects. *Journal of Management, 36,* 1040–1064.

Taylor, S., Beechler, S., & Napier, N. (1996). Toward an integrative model of strategic international human resource management. *Academy of Management Review, 21* (4), 959–985.

Tharenou, P. (2003). The initial development of receptivity to working abroad: Self-initiated international work opportunities in young graduate employees. *Journal of Occupational and Organizational Psychology, 76*, 489–508.

Thite, M., Srinivasan, V., Harvey, M., & Valk, R. (2009). Expatriates of host-country origin: "Coming home to test the waters". *International Journal of Human Resource Management, 20* (2), 269–285.

Thomas, D., & Inkson, K. (2009). *Cultural intelligence: Living and working globally* (2nd ed.). San Francisco, CA: Berrett-Koehler.

Thomas, D., & Lazarova, M. (2006). Expatriate adjustment and performance: A critical review. In G. Stahl, & I. Björkman (Eds.), *Handbook of research in international human resource management* (pp. 247–264). Cheltenham, UK: Edward Elgar.

Thomas, D., Lazarova, M., & Inkson, K. (2005). Global careers: New phenomenon or new perspectives? *Journal of World Business, 40* (4), 340–347.

Thomas, W., & Feldman, D. (2009). Age, work experience, and the psychological contract. *Journal of Organizational Behavior, 30* (8), 1053–1075.

Thorn, K. (2009). The relative importance of motives for international self-initiated mobility. *Career Development International, 14* (5), 441–464.

Tung, R. (2008). Human capital or talent flows: Implications for future directions in research on Asia Pacific. *Asia Pacific Business Review, 14* (4), 469–472.

Tungli, Z., & Peiperl, M. (2009). Expatriate practices in German, Japanese, UK, and US multinational companies: A comparative survey of changes. *Human Resource Management, 48* (1), 153–171.

Vance, C. (2005). The personal quest for building global competence: A taxonomy of self-initiating career path strategies for gaining business experience abroad. *Journal of World Business, 40* (3), 374–385.

Vance, C., & McNulty, Y. (in press). Why and how women and men acquire global career experience: A study of American expatriates in Europe. *International Studies of Management and Organization.*

Von Bertalanffy, L. (1972). The history and status of general systems theory. *Academy of Management Journal, 15* (4), 407–426.

Warneke, D., & Schneider, M. (2011). Expatriate compensation packages: What do employees prefer? *Cross Cultural Management: An International Journal, 18* (2), 236–256.

Yan, A., Zhu, G., & Hall, D. (2002). International assignments for career building: A model of agency relationships and psychological contracts. *Academy of Management Review, 27* (3), 373–391.

Index

OTHER TITLES IN THE HUMAN RESOURCE MANAGEMENT AND ORGANIZATIONAL BEHAVIOR COLLECTION

Jean Phillips and Stan Gully, Rutgers University, Collection Editors

- *Manage Your Career: 10 Keys to Survival and Success When Interviewing and On The Job* by Vijay Sathe
- *Culturally Intelligent Leadership: Leading Through Intercultural Interactions* by Mai Moua
- *Letting People Go: The People-Centered Approach to Firing and Laying Off Employees* by Matt Shlosberg
- *The Five Golden Rules of Negotiation* by Philippe Korda
- *Cross-Cultural Management* by Veronica Velo
- *Conversations About Job Performance: A Communication Perspective on the Appraisal Process* by Michael E. Gordon and Vernon Miller
- *How to Coach Individuals, Teams, and Organizations to Master Transformational Change Surfing Tsunamis* by Stephen K. Hacker
- *Managing Employee Turnover: Dispelling Myths and Fostering Evidence-Based Retention Strategies* by David Allen and Phil Bryant
- *Effective Interviewing and Information Gathering: Proven Tactics to Improve Your Questioning Skills* by Thomas Diamante
- *Essential Concepts of Cross-Cultural Management: Building on What We All Share* by Lawrence Beer
- *Growing Your Business: Making Human Resources Work for You* by Robert Baron
- *Developing Employee Talent to Perform: People Power* by Kim Warren

Announcing the Business Expert Press Digital Library

Concise E-books Business Students Need for Classroom and Research

This book can also be purchased in an e-book collection by your library as
- a one-time purchase,
- that is owned forever,
- allows for simultaneous readers,
- has no restrictions on printing, and
- can be downloaded as PDFs from within the library community.

Our digital library collections are a great solution to beat the rising cost of textbooks. E-books can be loaded into their course management systems or onto student's e-book readers.

The **Business Expert Press** digital libraries are very affordable, with no obligation to buy in future years. For more information, please visit **www.businessexpertpress.com/librarians**. To set up a trial in the United States, please contact **Adam Chesler** at *adam.chesler@ businessexpertpress.com;* for all other regions, contact **Nicole Lee** at *nicole.lee@igroupnet.com.*

www.ingramcontent.com/pod-product-compliance
Lightning Source LLC
Chambersburg PA
CBHW060351200326
41519CB00011BA/2110